THE STARS WHO CREATED KABUKI

THE STARS WHO
CREATED KABUKI

Their Lives, Loves and Legacy

Laurence R. Kominz

KODANSHA INTERNATIONAL
Tokyo • New York • London

Reference numbers for the illustrations provided by The Tsubouchi
Memorial Theatre Museum of Waseda University are as follows: Fig. 17
(100–2346); Fig. 18 (ロ 11–742); Fig. 20 (= 14–13); Figs. 22 and 29 (ロ 5–
1881); Fig. 30 (イ 11–778); Fig. 31 (イ 11–789).

Distributed in the United States by Kodansha America, Inc., 114
Fifth Avenue, New York, N.Y. 10011, and in the United Kingdom
and continental Europe by Kodansha Europe Ltd., 95 Aldwych,
London WC2B 4JF. Published by Kodansha International Ltd., 17-14
Otowa 1-chome, Bunkyo-ku, Tokyo 112, and Kodansha America, Inc.

First edition, 1997
97 98 99 00 9 8 7 6 5 4 3 2 1
ISBN 4-7700-1868-1

Library of Congress CIP data available

CONTENTS

PREFACE

Who was the greatest actor in the history of kabuki? Kabuki does not
have a single god, it has a trinity: Danjūrō, Tōjūrō, and Ayame, who
made their fame at the end of the seventeenth century. They are
kabuki's greatest culture heroes. Ayame brought convincing female
impersonation to kabuki; Danjūrō created the bravura style, with his
martial heroes performing superhuman feats of derring-do; and
Tōjūrō ventured further into "realism" than anyone else ever had on
the Japanese stage, in his portrayals of romantic, vulnerable young
men. While other actors may have wielded more authority for a
longer time than these three did, the only performer to rival them as
creators of the art of kabuki is the sixteenth-century shrine maiden
Okuni, the first kabuki dancer, whose life and career remain shroud-
ed in mystery. It was Danjūrō, Tōjūrō, and Ayame who, a century
after Okuni danced alluringly on the riverbank in Kyoto, moved
kabuki decisively away from the realm of burlesque and vaudeville
and transformed it into one of the world's richest, most exciting theaters. Kabuki is first and foremost an actors' theater, and Danjūrō,
Tōjūrō, and Ayame are remembered most for the innovations they
made as actors, but they were also playwrights, producers, theorists
and teachers, and their creative work in these fields prepared the
ground for their own triumphs onstage and for the legacy those triumphs would create.

No biographies of these actors have ever appeared in English,
and even the studies of them written in Japanese have been schol-

arly exercises, focusing on the nature of their professional work and the impact they had on succeeding generations of performers and on the history of kabuki in general. As I collected and read material documenting the lives and careers of Danjūrō, Tōjūrō, and Ayame, including diaries, anecdotes recorded by friends and colleagues, observations by theater critics, and play texts, I became more and more engrossed in their conflicted personalities, their varied relationships with colleagues and rivals, and their ironic fates. These actors' lives were as exciting and as full of struggle and ominous coincidence as were the plays that they had brought to life on the stage.

In their prime Danjūrō, Tōjūrō, and Ayame were wealthy men who enjoyed the adulation of thousands, men with religious beliefs and sexual orientation that seem strange to us today. This makes them seem exotic, very different from the common man at the turn of the twenty-first century, but there is much in their lives and personalities that draws us to them. The three actors were men who faced barriers imposed by tradition and found paths to success, not by destroying the old, but by forging new creations. Each was a hero to the masses of theatergoers, yet also had to be an effective leader or team player to achieve success in ensemble kabuki productions. Each had a strong sense of professional responsibility, not just to colleagues and students, but to the future of kabuki as a whole, and sought constantly to better the tradition. The old time-honored leveler, the tragic flaw of hubris, was present to a greater or lesser degree in each of them and led them to make mistakes—sometimes dangerous mistakes—yet each man strove to right his errors and move forward. Most notably, none ever allowed himself to stop growing as an artist. Perhaps each man sensed that to stand still was to begin to die.

My inquiry into the lives of Danjūrō, Tōjūrō, and Ayame has been a time-machine journey to a remarkable era. I have been wonderfully entertained, as is only right, for these men were professional entertainers. But their lives contain lessons that transcend the time and distance separating us, and that have nothing to do with their apotheosis as saints of kabuki. I hope that you who journey with me to seventeenth century Japan in *The Stars Who Created Kabuki* will feel the excitement of a young art form bursting with new vitality, and will recognize the universality of the spiritual and personal values that fuel creative artistic endeavor, whatever the land or age.

The life and work of Danjūrō, Tōjūrō, and Ayame has been influential and inspirational throughout the history of kabuki, but never more so than today. Some of the finest actors on the contemporary stage are emulating them, seeking to embody in their own work today the energy, the elán, and the spiritual qualities of their forebears of three hundred years ago. Others are seeking to recapture the authority and commitment to innovation that characterized the careers of the great actors of the turn of the seventeenth century. The links tying kabuki's creators to today's stage are the subject of the concluding chapter of the book.

* * *

The Stars Who Created Kabuki: Their Lives, Loves, and Legacy would have been impossible without the help of many teachers, friends, and colleagues. A Japan Foundation Professional Fellowship allowed me to spend a year at The Tsubouchi Memorial Theatre Museum of Waseda University in 1992–1993, researching the Ichikawa Danjūrō family line and connections between kabuki and popular urban religion. Waseda University professors Torigoe Bunzō and Furuido Hideo gave me encouragement and direction during that year. It was a happy coincidence that in 1992 Takei Kyōzō was teaching a graduate seminar that was reading the diary of Danjūrō I, a class I joined right away.

With the enthusiastic support of Kodansha International Executive Editor Michael Brase, the project was off and running. As work on *The Stars Who Created Kabuki* progressed, my kabuki scholar friends Mark Oshima, Faith Bach, and Katherine Mezur rendered invaluable assistance with proofreading and introductions to actors

whom they know much better than I do. Colleagues in Portland,
Linda Parshall and David Johnson, helped me to redirect my writing
toward nonspecialist readers. Many Japanese scholars and kabuki
actors generously took time from their busy schedules to consult
with me; Gunji Masakatsu, my newfound friend and mentor, and
one of Japan's great storehouses of wisdom on kabuki, provided
invaluable insights into the actors of the past. Hattori Yukio's probing of kabuki's ties to religion and art helped set the foundations of
my own work. Torigoe Bunzō, Director of The Tsubouchi Memorial
Theatre Museum of Waseda University, made available numerous
illustrations from Genroku-period kabuki plays. Contemporary kabuki
greats Ichikawa Danjūrō XII, Nakamura Ganjirō III, Ichikawa
Ennosuke III, and Bandō Tamasaburō all took time out to talk with
me backstage about their career paths and goals. Without Executive
Editor Michael Brase's commitment to *The Stars Who Created
Kabuki*, the project would never have gotten off the ground. At
Kodansha International, Elizabeth Floyd was my editor, and her critical eye and boundless energy were invaluable in bringing the book to
completion.

I am thankful that my wife Toshimi, and children, Leo and
Maya, still show me affection after months of sacrificing family time
to the selfish pleasure of writing on my favorite topic. Toshimi is my
editor for letters to the agents of celebrity kabuki actors, letters in
which the slightest nuance of language can be critical. And kabuki
might never have become my field of research had my father not
taken the family to live in Japan twice in the 1950s and 1960s and
had my mother not taken me to a kabuki performance twenty-nine
years ago. My thanks for their steady support of my career goals at
times when they must have seemed impractical indeed.

1

SETTING THE STAGE
Kabuki Theater in 1680

Danjūrō, Tōjūrō, and Ayame: Kabuki's First Three Superstars

Kabuki was initially a showcase in the three major cities of Japan for the latest fashions in clothing and dance, as well as for romantic dalliance, but it changed radically between 1675 and 1700. Kabuki then emerged as an art form that attracted Japan's most creative writers to serve as its playwrights and critics, and whose audience expanded to include men and women of every class and income level.

Three charismatic actors were especially important in the reshaping of kabuki in the last two decades of the eighteenth century: Ichikawa Danjūrō I (1660–1704), Sakata Tōjūrō (1647–1709), and Yoshizawa Ayame (1673–1729). Ichikawa Danjūrō, working on the Edo (now Tokyo) stage, pioneered the *aragoto*, or "wild style," used to depict martial superheroes and violent gods. In Kyoto and Osaka, Sakata Tōjūrō was acclaimed as the greatest romantic male lead in the history of kabuki and as the creator of realism on the stage. His acting style, which was diametrically opposed to Danjūrō's aragoto, would come to be called *wagoto* ("gentle acting"). From the 1630s, women had been banned from the public stage, and men forced to play their roles. While men had performed in women's garb in kabuki from the beginning of the seventeenth century, Yoshizawa Ayame first turned the playing of women's roles into a serious artistic pursuit, demanding of *onnagata* actors (specialists in the female roles) a lifetime of dedication and training. Ayame and his onnagata followers attracted women fans to kabuki in greater numbers than ever before.

Even after these three great actors had died, critics, playwrights, and performers themselves continued to extol them, creating for kabuki its first icons, men whose stature seemed unmatchable by mere mortals, but who were held up as models for later actors to emulate. Kabuki did not remain static for the next three centuries, however, and later actors proposed theories and invented stage practices that ran counter to the precepts and models established by Danjūrō, Tōjūrō, and Ayame. Still, their status as founders of kabuki's acting traditions has never been called into question.

The work of these three actors was just one facet of an outpouring of artistic and literary energy called "Genroku culture" (the term "Genroku period" designates the years 1688–1704, but the culture of the period is seen as spanning the years from 1680 through 1720). Over these forty years, the urban commoner classes reached an unprecedented level of education, wealth, and class pride (Figure 1). The newly wealthy bourgeoisie patronized the theater, the pleasure districts, and all manner of arts, and talented men appeared in every field of cultural endeavor. The honor roll of Genroku culture heroes includes not only the most creative and most influential artists of the entire Tokugawa period (1600–1868) but of the whole of Japanese history. Among them are Basho, the "saint" of haiku; Saikaku, the master of fiction; Chikamatsu, Japan's premiere playwright; and Moronobu and Kiyonobu, founders of *ukiyo-e* art. Without writers, painters, and illustrators to celebrate their achievements, these three actors could never have become the superstars they were in their own time, or the icons they were for later generations.

Danjūrō, Tōjūrō, and Ayame had dramatically different family backgrounds which set their careers on divergent paths early on. Danjūrō was the son of a merchant who was a popular Edo man-about-town, and whose ancestors had reputedly been samurai vassals of a feudal house destroyed in the warfare of the late sixteenth century. Tōjūrō was the son of an established actor who also sometimes produced kabuki plays. Tōjūrō was trained as an actor from childhood, but had to earn his later stature and wealth for himself on the stage, rather than simply inheriting them from his father. Ayame was the first-born son of poor Osaka commoners. His father died when Ayame was still a toddler, and his mother, unable to support the family, sold her eldest son to the male brothel district in Dotombori. Through good fortune and hard work, Ayame was able to emerge from the exhausting, cutthroat world of male prostitution to become universally acclaimed as the finest actor in all Japan.

None of the three was hailed as a young prodigy at the time of his debut. They were all "late bloomers." Nevertheless, all three were determined to rise to the top of their profession. Each was faced with the challenge of achieving greatness despite a lack of skills and physical traits recognized at the time as requisite for a stellar career in kabuki, such as a beautiful voice, ability in dance, and effeminate good looks. To compensate, each actor created new stage arts at which he could excel, and which so captured the imagination of audiences and critics alike that other great actors suddenly seemed out-of-date and stale. These innovations enlivened kabuki and remain a vital part of it today.

Throughout the centuries after their deaths, Danjūrō, Tōjūrō, and Ayame have been used as models to instruct and inspire future generations of actors. Thus, to understand what kabuki has become today, an understanding of their impact on the development of the theater and later perceptions of them is critical. Despite their iconization, these were real men who experienced great success but also knew hardship and failure—and whose relationships—professional and personal—were often stormy. The stories of their lives continue to fascinate readers today because of the many remarkable twists

Fig. 1 Panoramic view of a Genroku-period theater (the Nakamura-za Theater in Edo) by Hishikawa Moronobu. The artist is clearly as interested in the theater milieu as in the performance itself. A line of actors, dressed to play a wide variety of roles, dances onto the stage (left and center), while barkers and placards (right) draw passersby into the theater. The theater entrance is under the drum tower decorated with the Nakamura-za crest, a ginkgo leaf. Courtesy of Tokyo National Museum.

and turns in their roads to glory. Fate seems to have been particularly capricious in dealing with Danjūrō and Tōjūrō. It bestowed upon the latter a fine voice, together with the will and intelligence to use it in innovative new ways, then crippled that voice with a stroke just nine months after Tōjūrō's crowning onstage achievement. Danjūrō's fall was even more precipitous. At the age of forty-four, at the peak of his powers, he was murdered in the theater by a rival actor, in the most shocking crime in the history of kabuki.

In 1680 the kabuki theater and its social milieu were very different from what they are today. It was a world dominated by beguiling young onnagata who doubled as professional homosexual partners for wealthy connoisseurs of pleasure, a world of rapidly changing fashions in music, dance, clothing, and erotic tastes. Japan's straitlaced governing elite felt very threatened by the lawless, sensual atmosphere of kabuki performances, and by many of the activities that were part and parcel of the theater world. The danger and the allure of kabuki had been intrinsic to the form from its birth at the turn of the seventeenth century. While Danjūrō, Tōjūrō, and Ayame would change the artistic quality and content of kabuki, they knew that the excitement and energy that the shrine maiden Okuni had brought to the stage a century earlier must remain the foundation of all kabuki performance.

The Earliest Days: Okuni Founds the New Art of Women's Kabuki

Kabuki was founded in the last decade of the 1500s by Okuni, a former shrine dancer, who led her all-female troupe to Kyoto, then the capital of Japan, to make her fortune. Her kabuki was a kind of vaudeville or burlesque show consisting of solo and group dances, skits depicting erotic and romantic encounters between patrons and girls in the pleasure district, and sideshow acts. The word "kabuki" derived from "kabuku," which in the late sixteenth century meant "to speak or act in an ostentatious, antisocial, eccentric, or erotic manner."

While dance was the mainstay of early performances, kabuki also included short skits and mimicry. The setting for skits was inevitably the pleasure quarter. Two of the most common motifs were *keisei-kai* ("procuring a courtesan"), in which an amorous man engages and converses with a courtesan, and *furo-agari*, ("leaving the bath"), in which a brothel guest steps out of the bathhouse and converses with the women attendants.[1] Okuni often played and danced male roles, and her whole company dressed in fashions that were the radical chic of their day and made from the most sumptuous fabrics available. Okuni herself often sported items of Portuguese dress, setting these off with a large golden rosary around her neck. Although she later added male performers to her troupe, she and her women dancers remained the prime attraction. Kabuki performers sometimes reenacted the well-known affairs of real-life playboys and courtesans, and the contemporaneity of kabuki's subject matter and style stood in stark contrast to all other performing arts in Japan.

Okuni's kabuki was vigorous, lusty, and full of innuendo. Crowds flocked to her shows; wealthy and powerful patrons arranged command performances. By 1610, kabuki fever was sweeping the country and numerous troupes sprang up to capitalize on the craze. Nearly all the imitators featured performances by prostitutes, who danced by day and paraded from the theaters back to the licensed pleasure districts to entertain more privately at night. Women's kabuki became known as "prostitutes' kabuki"—although there is no evidence that Okuni or her women were prostitutes.

Kabuki was an excellent means to showcase beautiful young women, and performances often gave rise to violent disputes in the theaters among would-be late-night customers. Traveling kabuki troupes ranged from Kumamoto in the south to Kanazawa and Sendai in the north. Whenever kabuki came to town, the excitement of the performances inspired debauchery, drunkenness, and violent behavior among the spectators. People of every stratum of society joined in the revelry. Samurai lords invited the most appealing dancers to private parties, and their wives were equally enthusiastic: attending performances that were thronged with common people, then enjoining their seamstresses to make for them fashions modeled after the ones they saw onstage. All this could not escape the notice of government authorities, who were angered and frightened not only by the threat of violence associated with the performances, but even more by the breakdown of the rigid, legally-binding class structure that occurred whenever kabuki was performed. Kabuki performances were banned in various provinces in the 1610s and 1620s and, finally, throughout the country in 1629.

Boys' Kabuki

Boys' (*wakashu*) kabuki was performed as early as 1617, when the authorities had begun to crack down on women's performances. Attractive young performers, usually aged between fourteen and twenty, made it as lucrative and as sensually appealing as women's kabuki. The content of the shows remained essentially the same, although an influx of disenfranchised *nō* and *kyōgen* actors after the ban on women's kabuki helped to improve the quality of the music and dance.[2] Many skits and dance numbers relied on the boys' erotic appeal, and wealthier theater patrons were able to buy their sexual favors after the show.

In the seventeenth century homosexual prostitution was considered no more immoral than its heterosexual equivalent. Bisexuality had been the norm for hundreds of years in the samurai class, and many Buddhist priests favored male love, considering heterosexual relations sinful. In both these classes the pattern of homosexual liaison called for an older man to take a boy as his partner. Among samurai the typical pairing was the master and his page, while among the clergy, it was the priest and his acolyte.[3] Homosexual love was extolled by many samurai and priests as purer and more selfless than heterosexual bonds.

There is evidence that samurai and priests flocked to wakashu kabuki and engaged the boys as lovers, but their influence did not dominate boys' kabuki or Edo-period male love. Rather it was the urban commoner class that co-opted the practice of homosexual love, just as it had appropriated classical literature and art and refashioned them to its own tastes. Wealthy merchants soon outnumbered samurai and priests as patrons. Innocent, devoted pages and acolytes were replaced in the new "way of male love" by alluringly beautiful but often grasping performer-prostitutes. These professional boys studied the secrets of their trade just as assiduously as did their sisters in the Yoshiwara and Shimabara pleasure districts, and their most profitable skills were not singing and dancing, but techniques for enticing patrons and giving sexual pleasure. On the kabuki stage, the boys played both young men and women, and although they tailored their offstage personae to appeal to specific patrons, their erotic appeal was based mainly on an androgynous, boy-girl composite.

A Ban on Boys' Kabuki Brings a New Homosexual Aesthetic

As enthusiasm for boys' kabuki and for the new "way of male love" increased in the 1630s and 1640s, the same sorts of problems arose at performances and theaters that had taken place at women's kabuki a generation earlier. Between 1642 and 1651 numerous edicts were issued, but they failed to stem violence or to bring the homosexual prostitution associated with kabuki under control. Finally, following several egregious fights at theaters and in the residences of feudal lords, wakashu kabuki was banned nationwide in 1652. However, it took another four years of official prohibitions to end wakashu kabuki for good.

The ban did not, in fact, prevent young men from acting, it just forced them to change their appearance. For their erotic appeal the boy actors had relied heavily on their beautiful, long forelocks, which the authorities ordered cut off. The boys had to shave the top of their heads in adult male fashion, creating the same sort of effect a mustache would have on a man impersonating a woman. The actors were not without their resources, however, and quickly devised scarves and loose caps to cover the ugly patch of exposed scalp, and

eventually began using wigs onstage. Asai Ryōi, a government official attending a performance in 1662, describes the undiminished
erotic appeal of the young actors:

> When these youths, their hair beautifully done up, with
> light makeup, and wearing splendid padded robes, moved
> slowly along the runway, singing songs in delicate voices,
> the spectators in front bounced up and down on their but-
> tocks, those in back reared up, while those in the boxes
> opened their mouths up to their ears, and drooled; unable
> to contain themselves, they shouted, "Look, look! Their
> figures are like incarnations of deities, they are heavenly
> stallions!" And from the sides others called, "Oh, that
> smile! It overflows with sweetness. Good! Good!" and the
> like, and there was shouting and commotion.[4]

Male prostitution continued to thrive, organized by senior
actors, theater managers, and the restaurants (called teahouses
[chaya]) located around the theaters in the three big cities. Since
unlicensed prostitution was illegal, organizers listed all their charges
as actors, and most did appear onstage, if only as extras. Officials
were bribed to overlook this illegal trade in male love.

But changes were beginning to take place onstage and in the boys'
bordellos that would lead to new career possibilities for actors of the
Danjūrō–Tōjūrō–Ayame generation. The wakashu kabuki ban had
forbidden performers to carry short swords offstage, and the elimination
of this masculine accoutrement helped put an end to the samurai ideal
of young homosexual men in the kabuki world. Ukiyo-e art, along with
stories and nonfiction accounts extolling the charms of courtesans,
began to create a powerful new aesthetic of ideal feminine beauty and
accomplishment. The result was the superimposition of feminine
ideals on homosexual romance. In The Great Mirror of Male Love
(Nanshoku Ōkagami), Ihara Saikaku, the leading writer of the 1680s,
wrote the following in the guise of a traditionalist homosexual:

In the old days, boy love was something rough and brawny.
Men swaggered when they spoke. They preferred big,
husky boys, and cuts on their bodies as a sign of male love.
This spirit reached even to boy actors, all of whom bran-
dished swords. It goes without saying that such behavior is
no longer appreciated.

Boys these days are expected to be delicate, nothing
more. In Edo, a boy actor is called "Little Murasaki" or in
Kyoto is given the name "Kaoru," soft-sounding like the
names of courtesans and pleasing to the ear. [Actors]
accentuate their natural beauty by wearing women's red
underskirts, a habit men find very erotic."[5]

In *The Great Mirror of Male Love* the characters and the narrator often compare beautiful actors to women, showing how feminine beauty, generosity, and courtesan-like skills marked the new
kabuki boys as erotic and appealing:

Matsushima Han'ya was already as beautiful as the diving
girls of Matsushima and Ojima islands.[6] Moreover, he was
deeply affectionate and sophisticated at entertaining his
patrons; he excelled in the serving of saké. No other actor
could even approach his love letters in style.

He was, in particular, by birth so skilled in lovemaking
that he could almost kill a man with pleasure. But perhaps
the boy's primary point of attraction was his generous
nature. He never touched those heavy golden objects that
most people craved, and he was completely lacking in vul-
gar greed.[7]

Most performers dedicated the years of their youth to playing
women's roles, and in the 1660s and 1670s young and attractive
onnagata dominated kabuki as wakashu roles declined in number

and importance. In the early 1680s young actors' salaries were low, with Matsushima Han'ya (Figure 2), the onnagata paragon extolled by Saikaku in the passage above, making only 30 *ryō* (equivalent to about U.S. $20,000 now) a year as his top salary.[8] This was not nearly enough to cover actors' expenses, since they were obliged to purchase sumptuous wardrobes for use both onstage and off. Patrons were thus absolutely essential. Onnagata routinely purchased expensive clothing on credit, counting on the support of steady patrons. When these patrons left their boys in the lurch, suicide was sometimes seen as the only alternative.[9] Onnagata had to capitalize on a few short years of youthful beauty to achieve financial security for the rest of their lives. Some tried to build reputations onstage that they could parlay into careers in other acting specialties—male leads, villains, or old women's parts—although such parts were relatively few. Others sought to amass enough money to set themselves up in business. Starting a clothing or cosmetics store was a popular choice. Failure to achieve either goal meant a bleak future, so competition was intense. At the same time, the managers of male prostitution sought to further control their charges by regulating the industry and assigning ranks and prices, even introducing cheaper, non-actor prostitutes. But they never managed to dominate the freewheeling boys of kabuki as their counterparts did the women of the licensed pleasure districts.

The Great Mirror of Male Love presents an idealistic view of male love, depicting onnagata and wakashu actors and their patrons as firmly convinced of the purity of homosexuality. Most of Saikaku's onnagata and wakashu avoid women and regard heterosexual love as impure and degrading. Offstage, boy actors did not emulate women's dress but affected an androgynous style incorporating elements of women's fashion. Their style and flair attracted even women admirers. Although bisexuality was probably more common than homosexual purists of the day cared to admit,[10] in Saikaku's accounts many young men spurn even the most devoted and attractive women, saying with a sigh, "Oh, if only she were a man!"

Fig. 2 Onnagata Matsushima Han'ya (at right) is performing when an admirer leaps up onto the stage and suddenly cuts off his own finger to demonstrate how much he loves Han'ya. Book illustration. From *Nanshoku Ōkagami Kinsei Bungaku Shiryō Ruiju Ihara Saikaku-hen*, Vol. 7. Courtesy of Benseisha.

The irony of the kabuki of the 1680s was that although an authentic, womanly appearance was much admired onstage, many onnagata actually spurned the company of women and thus knew little about them firsthand. Onnagata were attractive, chic and sophisticated onstage and off, and while they mimicked the activities of courtesans and women entertainers in their plays, their imitation remained superficial. Women characters of other walks of life appeared infrequently on the kabuki stage. This became a potential problem because the Genroku-period economic boom was already underway by 1680, and with housewives controlling the finances of urban families, women were going in larger numbers to see kabuki. Beautiful homosexual boys had less appeal for them than for the male audience, and women were likely to be attracted to theaters that could present a variety of convincing women characters onstage. Actors needed to increase their repertory of styles if kabuki was to take full advantage of the disposable wealth suddenly flowing so liberally throughout the merchant districts of the three major cities. By the end of the Genroku period, women customers may have accounted for sixty percent of the gate receipts at kabuki theaters,[11] evidence that important changes had occurred. Tōjūrō and Ayame were the men who instigated these changes.

Moving Toward Drama

In 1680, next door to the principal kabuki theaters in Kyoto (on Shijō, or Fourth Avenue) and Osaka (on Dotombori) there were rival theaters that drew large crowds although their performers lacked erotic good looks. These theaters were puppet theaters, presenting *ningyō jōruri* ("puppet ballad drama," now called *bunraku*). The leader of the puppet performance ensemble was a senior chanter who spoke every character's lines, sang the narration, and prepared the play scripts. In the performance of the play he was accompanied by a shamisen player and a troupe of puppeteers, the latter hidden by a curtain while they manipulated the puppets, one puppeteer to a puppet.

By 1680 puppet plays were long, complex, large-cast historical dramas in five or six acts, with the repertory including adaptations of the great medieval literary classics *The Tale of the Heike* and *The Tale of the Soga Brothers*. Puppet plays also featured numerous spectacular stage effects such as decapitations, flying monsters, and the use of real fire. In the 1660s several fine chanter-playwrights were already working in the puppet theater, and in 1675 a forty-year-old former samurai, Uji Kaganojō (1635–1711), opened a new theater in Kyoto, which was to prove a turning point. Kaganojō applied structural and performance theories from the classical nō drama to puppet theater; he improved and updated singing, musical composition, and musical notation; and he broadened the range of literary sources. Moreover, he attracted great writers to his theater to work as playwrights. Saikaku wrote two plays for him, and Chikamatsu Monzaemon (1653–1725) worked as Kaganojō's apprentice and assistant playwright for several years before embarking on his own illustrious career.

In the 1650s and 1660s the most important lesson to be learned from puppet theater by kabuki producers was that sexy performers were not necessary to turn a profit—it was exciting drama that was attracting crowds to the puppet theater. Until the ban on boys' kabuki, the only dramatic scenes had been brief exchanges of conversation and erotic innuendo, either between men and women or between two men. The most common setting was at parties in the pleasure district, where scenes such as the previously mentioned kei-sei-kai (procuring of courtesans) and furo-agari (leaving the bath) highlighted the changing mores and fashions of that demimonde.

After the ban of boys' kabuki, producers experimented with dances and short plays based on a variety of contemporary and historical material. Erotic appeal came to be seen as just one form of entertainment. Dances and skits relied on humor or spectacle, and some one-act plays began to investigate more complex, nonromantic human relationships. This increase in breadth, and the success of six-act puppet plays, gave kabuki producers the confidence to stage longer works. In 1664, in Osaka, kabuki presented its first two-act play, *The Outlaw's Revenge (Hinin no Katakiuchi)*.[12] It was also the first time a playwright (his name was Yagozaemon) was given credit publicly for writing a kabuki play, and it was in 1664 that the word "theater" (*shibai*) was first applied to kabuki.[13]

The next year Edo's Morita-za theater staged a three-act play entitled *Soga*. The actor Kawarazaki Gonnosuke wrote the script using material often presented with puppets—three episodes from the story of the Soga brothers' vendetta, Japan's archetypal revenge tale dating from the 1200s. The play ended with an exciting fight dance during which the villain was slain, and there is no evidence that amorous dances and scenes were presented. The tearful parting of the Soga brothers from their mother and the energetic martial scenes made *Soga* a hit.[14] This play's strategy for success was based closely on the content, if not the music, of puppet plays. Although dances and short amorous scenes would continue to be staged in kabuki, and beautiful onnagata would remain the undisputed darlings of the kabuki world, long dramas now opened the way for *tachiyaku* actors (specialists in mature male characters), to build solid stage careers and rise to the top of kabuki's acting hierarchy.

East and West: Edo Warriors Versus Kansai Dandies?

As early as the 1200s most Japanese believed that the culture and society of eastern Japan (the Tokyo region, or "Kantō"—meaning "east of the barrier") was very different from the home provinces around Kyoto (the areas surrounding Kyoto were also called "kami-gata," the "upper region"; or "Kansai," "west of the barrier"). The great medieval war epics and ballads that minstrels carried to the far corners of the realm created the archetypes of the "rough eastern warrior" and the "cultured and effete Kyoto courtier." The "truth" of this cultural dichotomy even influenced important political decisions in the medieval era: "wise" shoguns such as Minamoto Yoritomo and Tokugawa Ieyasu built their capitals in the east because history seemed to show that governments located in Kyoto were influenced by the effete ways of the nobility and became victims of their own increasing internal weaknesses.

Japanese historians and theater critics were no less influenced by the power of these archetypes than were political leaders and the populace at large. Danjūrō, the "god of aragoto" in Edo, and Tōjūrō, the master of romantic roles in Kyoto and Osaka, were regarded as characteristic and inevitable products of dominant regional cultures. While Danjūrō and Tōjūrō were still active, critics questioned the actors' ability to succeed outside of their cultural home bases. Danjūrō, who was usually supremely confident of his art, expressed similar misgivings himself.

However, surviving performance records from 1650 to 1700 reveal that in kabuki, at least, the regional stereotypes had already begun to break down in the seventeenth century. The merchant class dominated the theater, and just as it tied Edo to Osaka and Kyoto in a tight commercial network, so it linked the three cities

social role of theatre

artistically. Many of the old regional differences remained, but among the merchants, attitudes toward those differences were changing. In the medieval period regional traits elicited disdain and contempt from outsiders—literary and historical sources tell us that Kyoto courtiers and eastern samurai were often rivals who, when they collaborated, did so more out of necessity than good will. But among the commoner classes in the Edo period, regional differences inspired fascination and often imitation. Kansai audiences enjoyed, and Kansai playwrights imitated, the violent, spectacular puppet plays from Edo (the Kimpira plays),[15] and the Edo Shimabara kyōgen boom of 1658 demonstrates Edoites' fascination with the refined ways of Kyoto's Shimabara courtesans,[16] the new representatives of the traditional "beautiful and graceful Kyoto woman."

The artistic careers of the first generation of great tachiyaku (male lead) actors further demonstrates that the old regional stereotypes did not apply to early kabuki. The first dominant actor in Osaka was Arashi San'emon (1635–1690), and he is credited both with inventing an important new romantic character (the *yatsushi,* or romantic lover in disguise) and developing new techniques for playing swaggering samurai heroes. Tōjūrō's main rival, Yamashita Hanzaemon (1652–1717), made his reputation with *jitsugoto* acting—convincing portrayals of strong, virtuous samurai retainers and strong martial acting. Had Tōjūrō not appeared on the scene, jitsugoto might have become the acting style most typical of Kyoto. At the same time Edo produced its own great actor of gentle, romantic male parts. He was Nakamura Shichisaburō (1662–1708), and at the turn of the eighteenth century he and Danjūrō competed for the title of "the best actor in Edo." From this, it seems clear that Danjūrō, with his "wild style," and Tōjūrō, with his "gentle acting" reestablished regional archetypes for kabuki rather than following in the mold of firmly established models. In other words, they were not products of preexisting practices but created new ones.

A major difference between Edo and Kansai kabuki that strongly influenced the careers of Danjūrō and Tōjūrō was managerial, not artistic. In the Kansai, top actors were designated as play producers (*zamoto*) on a yearly basis. The zamoto was the leading member of a three-man production team that also included the theater owner (*nadai*) and financial backers (*kinshu*). The zamoto chose or ordered plays, influenced the writing, did the casting, led rehearsals, and, most significantly, received a percentage of profits from box office receipts, adding to his already substantial salary. In Edo, the hereditary heads of four licensed families served as theater owners (sometimes lessors) and producers. These men were also called zamoto, and while they usually appeared onstage as actors, rarely were they top actors. While it is apparent that leading actors like Danjūrō could choose plays or even write their own, and while they were able to influence casting decisions and direct rehearsals, the profits from successful plays remained with the producers and their financial backers. Top Edo actors received salaries alone, supplemented by whatever bonuses a producer might choose to bestow. These very different arrangements mirrored regional social and political differences: hereditary, autocratic lines of authority characterized the military government of Edo in contrast to the oligarchic self-rule exercised within the merchant communities of Kyoto and Osaka. It is easy to see why Danjūrō envied his Kansai colleagues, and at least once considered moving there for a prolonged period.

Spreading the Word: Publishing Plays and Theater Reviews

In life, and therefore in history, timing is all. Danjūrō, Tōjūrō, and Ayame appeared on the kabuki scene at just the right moment, a moment when, for the first time, fortunes could be made in acting. Theaters grew in size, ticket prices rose with the growing Genroku economy, and actors' salaries sky-rocketed. By 1690 the best onnagata could support themselves and their families on acting salaries— wealthy patrons were no longer necessary. More importantly, this was a moment when significant artistic innovation was demanded by producers and acclaimed by audiences. Danjūrō, Tōjūrō, and Ayame were not the only actors to sense this; they had no choice but to best their rivals if they wished to rise to the pinnacle of wealth and fame.

Writers, critics, and illustrators in the Genroku period began to document and report on the world of kabuki in voluminous detail. Without their efforts, Danjūrō, Tōjūrō, and Ayame could not have become national celebrities, nor could they have had such a huge impact on the theater of their own and later generations. The print media of the era took numerous forms, but for these three pioneering actors, the most influential were playbooks, actor evaluation books (*hyōbanki*), collections of theater anecdotes and actors' "words of wisdom" (*geidan*), and ukiyo-e wood-block prints.

Illustrated kabuki playbooks (*e-iri kyōgen-bon*) began to be published in the 1680s. They ranged from novelizations of plays to relatively accurate reproductions of stage dialog. The existence of a market for these books shows that as a form of written entertainment, kabuki plays had reached a level of quality comparable to puppet plays. Specific actors were identified in a program at the beginning of each book and by distinctive family crests on their costumes in the illustrations. Less than one-third of all Genroku kabuki plays went into print, but these books give us a good idea of what Danjūrō, Tōjūrō, and Ayame actually did onstage. Many printed playbooks preserve dialog from scenes that were particularly well received, and two-page ukiyo-e illustrations depict the most dramatic and popular moments in Genroku-period kabuki.

Actor evaluation books (*hyōbanki*) date back to 1655. The early ones were modeled after courtesan evaluation books (*yūjo hyōbanki*), and consisted only of brief descriptions of the actors' charms. But by 1687 a universally understood ranking system was brought into use, and by the 1690s long, detailed critiques began to appear, often in the form of heated debates about the merits and demerits of a given actor. Danjūrō's diary indicates that actors in his day took these evaluations and ratings seriously. In fact, they made use of high ratings and good reviews, along with box office success, as ammunition in their yearly salary negotiations with theater producers.

Fig. 3 Danjūrō as Soga Gorō uprooting bamboo in *The Origin of the Soga Warrior* (1697). *Ō-ōban tan'e* print by Torii Kiyomasu, ca. 1697. Courtesy of Tokyo National Museum.

The earliest collections of actors' teachings and anecdotes (*geidan*) document the Genroku period. Geidan are testimony to widespread interest in kabuki actors as celebrities. Since neither Tōjūrō nor Ayame left diaries, several geidan published in a book called *The Actors' Analects (Yakusha Rongo,* or *Yakusha Banashi),* provide our chief insight into the personalities and professional philosophies of these two great figures. Geidan tend to be very reverent in tone, and *The Actors' Analects* makes Tōjūrō and Ayame seem larger than life. These geidan complete the portraits of Tōjūrō and Ayame, but readers should temper the *Analects'* praise of the two actors with more critical material that appeared when they were alive.

Danjūrō was the only one of the three to leave an autobiographical account, his *An Account of My Prayers (Ganmon)*, which covers his life from 1690 to 1696, although it was not meant for publication. In it Danjūrō describes life in the city and in the theater, reveals family and personal problems, sets forth his religious convictions, and states his opinions on professional issues ranging from salary levels to his philosophy of acting. Scholars consider the diary an accurate record of his times, as well as of Danjūrō's opinions and beliefs.

Of the three actors, Danjūrō stands out for his imposing personality, the pervasiveness of his influence, and the dramatic vicissitudes of his life and career. He epitomizes the energy and vitality of kabuki in the Genroku period. Ukiyo-e prints were first published in Edo, so Danjūrō is the only one of the early greats to appear in prints—bold, energetic representations (Figure 3). Danjūrō wrote his own plays, and they attest to his originality as a playwright and his dynamism as an actor. The hyōbanki leave a detailed record of his mercurial career, but more than any other source it is Danjūrō's own words, recorded in his diary, that make him seem as alive today as he was for enthusiastic fans in 1700.

ICHIKAWA DANJŪRŌ I
The Wild God of Edo Kabuki

The Danjūrō Name and Aragoto Acting

Tōjūrō and Ayame are culture heroes in the world of kabuki, but the name Ichikawa Danjūrō is known to virtually every adult Japanese, including those who have never seen a kabuki play.[1] This is partly due to the fact that an actor with this name, Danjūrō XII, is working on the kabuki stage today; his name appears in the media and he recently took a leading role in a long-running historical drama on television. Until the twentieth century, each generation of actors bearing the Danjūrō name dominated kabuki in Edo, receiving the highest salaries and greatest acclaim. To Japanese the name Danjūrō and the Danjūrō aragoto acting style are synonymous with kabuki. Aragoto kabuki features warrior heroes engaged in superhuman feats of derring-do. Faces painted with red stripes—the aragoto sign of a warrior hero—adorn posters, T-shirts, and other souvenir items, and aragoto makeup has been adopted as a talisman of power by rock music bands. Stylized aragoto moves, such as the leaping *tobi roppō* exit, and *mie* head snaps, have been appropriated for commercials and children's television programs. These images and movements are as archetypally kabuki as tutus and pirouettes are ballet.

The plays and the acting styles originated by Danjūrō I and his son constitute the most powerful tradition in kabuki today. Leading actors of male roles in almost every family line have striven to master energetic and heroic aragoto roles. Danjūrō VII (1791–1859), recognizing that his forebears had bequeathed him theatrical masterpieces that would ensure his own supremacy in a highly competitive industry, christened the best of them "The Eighteen Great Plays of Kabuki" (*Kabuki Jūhachiban*). These have been at the core of the Edo and Tokyo kabuki repertory ever since. Almost all were creations of the first Danjūrō and his son.

Instilling Ambition and Religious Fervor: Danjūrō's Formative Years

Ichikawa Danjūrō was a man of driving ambition and boundless energy. From early in his career he aimed to become the most famous and highest-paid actor in Edo, and to achieve this end he resolved to use every weapon in his artistic and spiritual arsenal: imagination, education, hard work, and divine assistance. No actor in the history of kabuki was as devout a religious believer or as active in his worship as Danjūrō. He relied on his gods to give him strength and good fortune; he drew artistic inspiration from the rites and iconography of his sect; and he celebrated his gods onstage to thank them for their blessings and to bestow blessings on his audiences. Martial heroics and spectacle had been a part of the theater since the ban on boys' kabuki, but Danjūrō brought them to center stage and demonstrated that an actor could rise to the pinnacle of glory playing wild warriors and gods.

Ichikawa Danjūrō was born in 1660, the only son of Horikoshi Jūzō, a newcomer to Edo who became a moderately prosperous property agent in the booming capital. According to the writings of Danjūrō II, his grandfather was an intelligent, capable accountant, a popular man-about-town, and an amateur haiku poet who enjoyed following the latest trends in city culture.[2] The Horikoshi family thus belonged to the merchant class. Although merchants were technically lower in status than samurai, farmers, and craftsmen, they took pride in their wealth and in the exciting new culture that they were creating and patronizing.

The Horikoshi family also took pride in its samurai ancestry.[3] The oldest known family ancestor was Horikoshi Jūrōemon Yoshinaga, who, in the mid-sixteenth century, reputedly served the Takeda clan, rulers of the region north of Mt. Fuji. With the destruction of the Takeda clan in 1582, the Horikoshi family moved to an adjoining province and served the Hōjō clan until that group was crushed in the siege of Odawara in 1590. Yoshinaga's son then moved to Narita in Shimosa Province and became a commoner. (Narita is the site of Tokyo's international airport, located in present-day Chiba Prefecture.)

Jūzō likely told stories of his samurai ancestors to his son, the future Danjūrō. From the very beginning of Danjūrō's career, martial heroes were his forte onstage. Likewise, we see from his diary that the samurai provided a model of victorious conquest and loyal service that he sought to apply to his work as an actor:

> The true-blooded samurai strives to achieve victory for his allies and take the enemy castle. The true-blooded actor applies pressure to other theaters and takes pride in bringing victory to the one employing him. For the actor, success is paramount.[4]

When the Horikoshi family moved to Narita, they went to worship at Shinshōji, the main temple in town, as did all the villagers. This was a small Shingon temple founded in the 900s to provide spiritual aid to forces setting out to destroy a powerful imperial usurper. Shingon is one of Buddhism's tantric sects; the Great Sun Buddha (Dainichi Nyorai) is its central figure, but believers also worship a large pantheon of other deities, often depicted on ornate mandalas. Rituals include prayers, offerings, ablutions, various abstinences and

austerities, the recitation and copying of sutras and magical formulae, and services by priests, among which is the dramatic *goma* fire
service. Shingon is the branch of Buddhism most closely tied to
Shugendō, a syncretic Shintō-Buddhist sect whose mountain priests
(*yamabushi*) wandered through the wilds of the country, performing
rituals of power. Until the mid–Edo period, yamabushi were sought
after as healers and magicians by people from all walks of life. The
central deity of Narita's Shinshōji was Fudō, (literally, "the immovable"), the demon-quelling avatar of the Sun Buddha and the most
ferocious-looking of the Shingon pantheon. In all religious images of
Fudō: "One eye glares downwards, the other squints divergently
upwards. His mouth is twisted into a snarl, revealing protruding
fangs. His long hair hangs in a coil over his left shoulder. He stands
not on a lotus or animal mount, as do many Buddhist divinities, but
on an immovable rock. Always he is ringed with fire"⁵ (Figure 4). In
his right hand Fudō holds a straight sword to smite demons, and in
his left he carries a rope to bind demons and to rescue the faithful
and raise them to paradise.

Once in Edo, the Horikoshi family likely worshipped Shingon
deities at their home altar. More likely than not, they visited
Shingon and other temples and shrines in the city, trekking on occasion to Narita to worship at Shinshōji, a seventy-kilometer trip that,
at the time, took two days and one night by foot and by boat. It was
probably as a child in the Horikoshi family that Danjūrō began to
learn of the power of the Buddhas and Shintō gods, and how to
serve them. We know for certain from his *An Account of My Prayers*
that as an adult he relied on the Shingon deities and Shintō gods to
aid him in his family responsibilities and theatrical career. He fully
expected their assistance in return for his devoted ritual service.

The Foundations of Aragoto Kabuki

The Horikoshi family lived in Izumi-chō, very near two of the four
licensed kabuki theaters. Danjūrō II records that his father, as a

Fig. 4 A tenth-century wooden sculpture of the deity Fudō. Courtesy of Tokyo National Museum.

child, had loved kabuki.[6] The producer at the Yamamura-za theater was a friend of Jūzō's, and it was there that Danjūrō was apprenticed at age twelve.[7] No record remains of who his teachers were.

According to Ichikawa family oral history, Danjūrō made his stage debut in 1673 at age fourteen, playing a young warrior hero of the tenth century named Sakata Kintoki at the Nakamura-za. Kintoki had a long history in folklore and in theater, and his exploits had

inspired the wildest and most spectacular puppet plays, which featured the exploits of Kintoki's son Kimpira. The Ichikawa family
records tell us that Danjūrō wore a robe patterned in bold checks for
his debut, painted his face in red and black, carried a large battle-axe,
and danced with hunters and an ogre—all features that would later
be integral to the aragoto style. There is no corroborative evidence
that this initial play was, in fact, performed; the episode may possibly
have been fabricated by Danjūrō's successors to show that the iconic
actor had begun to create aragoto from the time of his very first
stage appearance.

Danjūrō must have appeared onstage regularly in the 1670s, but
few records of his performances survive. However, at some point
between 1680 and 1683 he almost certainly played the warrior Fuwa
Banzaemon in a play called *The Dispute over the Courtesan (Yūjoron)*.
Fuwa, a rough samurai, is one of two rivals for the love of the courtesan Kazuraki; the other, Nagoya, is an urbane, sophisticated rake.
Danjūrō would perform Fuwa numerous times over the course of
his career. In 1685 he played Sakata Kimpira in the play *Kimpira's
Visits to the Sixth Avenue Pleasure District (Kimpira Rokujō Gayoi)*,
and two later commentaries state that this was his first aragoto role.[8]
One source says that the play was a great success, and that from
1685 on, all Edo theaters required one actor to perform in the aragoto
style in order to draw crowds.[9]

In the 1680s Danjūrō laid the foundations for career and family,
but just as scanty records make it hard to document his career at this
time, so the details of one important family event remains obscure—
the date of his marriage and the identity of his wife. The marriage
must have taken place by 1685 or 1686, because he later writes that
for several years he prayed to Fudō that he might have a son.[10] A
daughter came first, but on the eleventh day of the tenth month of
1688 a son was born. The son was named Kuzō, and would become
the second Danjūrō.

In 1688 Danjūrō took a leading role in *The Soga Warriors in Ten
Scenes (Tsuwamono Soga Jūban Tsuzuki)*, a play that had an impres-

sive two-month run and was described as a "smash hit" and as "the
play that made the first Danjūrō."¹¹ Danjūrō played Soga Gorō, the
younger and wilder of the two famous avenging Soga brothers.
Another top Edo actor, Miyazaki Denkichi, played the gentle older
brother, Jūrō, pioneering a tender parting scene with Jūrō's lover
that would remain part of Soga kabuki plays for centuries.¹² For
Danjūrō, Soga Gorō became, like Fuwa Banzaemon, a favorite and
oft-performed character.

On the strength of this play, Danjūrō enjoyed a fabulous debut
in the hyōbanki (actor evaluation books) in the summer of 1688. The
somewhat overblown prose of A Stylish Mirror of Male Actors (Yarō
Yakusha Fūryū Kagami) reads as follows:

> This man called Ichikawa is the number-one sexy lover-
> boy unparalleled in 3000 worlds. He is the most handsome
> actor in Edo and looks fabulous when he comes swagger-
> ing on stage. His voice moves all under Heaven.
>
> There will never again be a performer in Japan or
> abroad who will go as far as he will. Whether he does jitsu-
> goto, villains, or anything else, he does it well. He excels
> most remarkably in learning, and his reputation as a play-
> wright is known to all. He is the founder of flamboyant act-
> ing in this age, and there is no actor his equal in Edo. The
> radiance of his glory shines down from Heaven, and he is
> likely to become the model for actors down through future
> ages.¹³

The last line of this critique was remarkably prophetic, but the assertion of Danjūrō's supremacy in Edo at the time was, as we shall see,
premature.

The reference to Danjūrō's learning and activities as a playwright come as a surprise. Earlier records of his career make no mention of this. We have no way to know how or when he acquired his
education, but by the late 1690s Danjūrō would become one of

Japan's most successful and prolific playwrights. It is not clear which plays or parts of plays he may have written during the 1680s and early 1690s, but we can assume that he wrote some of the plays in which he appeared.

The hyōbanki's brief description of Danjūrō's talents reveals something of the development of his aragoto techniques even as early as the late 1680s. The swaggering entrances (*tanzen*) and straightforward martial acting (jitsugoto) had been invented by Kansai actors and were standard fare on both sides of the barrier. Playing villains was unusual for tachiyaku actors, but Danjūrō was apparently doing so even early in his career, and villain acting would later inspire him to create dangerous, even ferocious, leading roles notable for the "dark side" of their characters. In 1688 Danjūrō was still a handsome young man, just twenty-nine by the traditional reckoning whereby a baby is counted as one year old at birth. He apparently used his good looks to full advantage onstage. Danjūrō was beginning to put his own stamp on kabuki, but in 1688 he was probably just a bit more flamboyant than other actors of martial roles.

Vows Made and Vows Broken: Danjūrō Gets Fired

Although the record is frustratingly thin, 1689 may well have been a bad year for Danjūrō. A 1700 hyōbanki states that at this time audiences rated his acting as inferior to that of a fellow tachiyaku actor at the Ichimura-za.[14] As early as the winter of 1689, Danjūrō had been considering making a major spiritual commitment in return for greater support from the deities he revered, and on the eighth day of the third month in 1690, he presented a list of vows in return for divine assistance in assuring his parents' long life, his ability to support them, the protection of his family from misfortune, and help in his professional career. Danjūrō's list of vows is over a page long. They include giving up alcohol for as long as his parents lived, and three years of abstinence from extramarital sex. He also dedicated himself to three years of unfailing ritual worship of eight deities, including the great Sun Buddha, Fudō, and the Shintō divinities of the sun, moon, and stars. The rituals that Danjūrō vowed to perform included cold water ablutions, thrice-daily prayers, visits every ten days to Ryōtaishi Temple in Ueno, special offerings for specific deities at regular intervals, and a yearly pilgrimage to Shinshōji in Narita.[15]

Why did Danjūrō write down these pledges and prayers? One simple reason was probably the length of the list. It would be dangerous to forget to perform a promised ritual when angry deities had the power to cause calamity; a written record was essential as a memory aid. Another reason was probably Danjūrō's rather pragmatic relationship with his deities—an attitude he shared with many other Edo townsmen. Scholars of religious anthropology reason that social structures largely determine the nature of relationships between worshippers and deities. Commoners flocked to Edo from outlying villages and agricultural areas to become laborers, merchants, and craftsmen, and found themselves there in a very unfamiliar social environment. In the countryside, every aspect of life had fit into a stable hierarchy in which secular and religious concerns were inextricably linked. Country Japanese met and dealt with the same people, day in and year out. In Edo, however, newcomers from rural areas met or saw hundreds of new people every day, and their financial success or ruin could depend on relationships with people they barely knew. Life could be very uncertain in Edo's boom-and-bust economy. Generally speaking, in situations of social or economic instability or competition, people turn to gods for blessings to help them through daily life.[16] Where contractual, and not hereditary, relationships govern social intercourse, believers enter into similarly contractual relationships with their gods. People want demonstrable results in return for their prayers and offerings, and will change gods or sects quite readily in order to get them. Diary entries by Edo-period commoners include petitioners' detailed records of offerings made to new deities, followed by notations of financial failure, and resolutions to shift loyalties to deities worshipped by acquaintances whose gods have done better by them.[17] Danjūrō may well have recorded his prayers and pledges and set a three-year time limit on his vows to make it easier to evaluate his deities' efficacy.

In the eleventh month of 1690 Danjūrō joined the company of the Morita-za. All theaters hired actors on one-year contracts which were negotiated in the spring, and the new theater season began on or about the first day of the eleventh month, two months before the new calendar year. Using the old, lunar calendar, the eleventh month would fall during early-to-mid winter. The first show of each theater season was a gala event called the *kaomise,* or "face show-ing." Kaomise were festive and action-packed, designed to showcase the entire company. Audiences flocked to see their favorite actors in new combinations, and kaomise shows brought glitter and excite-ment to the three big cities of Japan during the coldest, gloomiest season of the year.

Danjūrō's kaomise show at the Morita-za in 1690 apparently went well. All we know about it is that while playing a samurai he did an impersonation of a drunken old lady, and that he made an effec-tive partner to one of kabuki's top onnagata. Surviving records for the performance of plays in 1690 and 1691 in general are scarce, but it seems that Danjūrō had a solid season. His first play of 1692 was a tremendous success. Playing the twelfth-century strong-man Asahina, he wielded a six-foot-long sword, and crowds thronged to the theater.[18] Representatives from Kyoto and Osaka theaters called on him to invite him to the Kansai; the Morita-za producer, in an unprecedented move, raised his salary from 200 to 250 ryō in mid-season, paying him the additional 50 ryo during the run of the Asahina play.

Danjūrō wrote, "My prayers were answered by the power of the deities and today my name is known throughout Japan."[19] He took pride in his pay raise, noting that he was the first Edo actor to make as much as 250 ryō, but he vowed to remain humble despite the accolades. Humility and pride vie with each other in his words:

Look at me. Among all the arts, there is not one I have mastered, that I am better at than anyone else, and I am not naturally skilled in martial arts, nor am I exceedingly clever. It is the deities Sanbōkōjin, Ganzan Taishi, Dainichi, Fudō, Aizen Myōō, and especially Nitten who shine on me. Because the gods protect me, I am called "unrivaled in Japan," "the top actor," "the founder of a new temple of kabuki in the modern age." My name is revered, but this not due to the work of a mere mortal.[20]

But even in early 1692 when his star was rising, there were those who did not revere Danjūrō, nor consider him Edo's top actor. *A Stylish Mirror of Male Actors*, which had lavished so much praise on Danjūrō in 1688, had been published in Edo and reflected the opinion of that city's critics alone, but in 1692 *The Great Mirror of Actors (Yakusha Ōkagami)*, a Kyoto publication, gave him very mixed reviews. It said that Danjūrō was "striving to become one of Edo's best actors," and praised his sword-fighting skills, but criticized his aragoto acting as "ostentatious, childish, pretentious, and affected," and censured his "heavy-handed imitations of old women."[21] His formal speech (*kōjō*) during the Asahina play had been "marred by heavy breathing, tedious, and altogether disappointing."[22] *The Great Mirror of Actors* concluded by giving Danjūrō a ranking of "high" (jō), second to "high-high" at the time,[23] and rated him the third-best actor in Edo. The critics decided not to rank him lower only because of his remarkable midseason pay raise, which for them was proof of his box-office appeal.[24]

The discrepancy between Danjūrō's popular success and his evaluation in *Great Mirror* shows that the tastes of Kansai literati and theater connoisseurs differed from those of Edo commoners, but Kyoto and Osaka theater producers reckoned that audiences in the Kansai would resemble those of Edo, and they attempted to lure Danjūrō west.

Danjūrō's career was flying high in the summer of 1692, but he was soon beset by misfortune. Although he played a famous historical warrior hero in the 1692 Morita-za kaomise play—the sort of role at which he had always excelled—the house remained half-empty. The usual response to a "bomb" in kabuki was much the same as it is on Broadway today. The producer, Bandō Matakurō, quickly closed the play down and had his writers start working on a new one. In his own writing, Danjūrō complained that the producer was unfair for considering the failure solely Danjūrō's fault, and described the way Matakurō's former warmth and friendliness had evaporated. Later Danjūrō would write eloquently that a show's success is not completely dependent upon the leading actor. Play texts are important, he said, and playwrights deserve more recognition, better pay, and a share of the blame too if things go poorly.[25] In any case, the makeshift new kaomise play was just beginning to bring crowds back to the Morita-za when, two days before the start of the new year, Danjūrō fell ill and was forced to leave the stage.

Danjūrō did not appear in the theater for the first play of 1693, and audience numbers plummeted. A new hyōbanki came out in the first month of the year: *One Hundred Poems Comparing the Colors of Theater Past and Present (Kokon Shibai Iro-kurabe Hyakunin Isshu)*. The entry for Danjūrō began with a satirical poem:

> Always overdoing it
> He looks so haughty.
> But with just his usual red-painted face
> He cannot do great things.[26]

The author added that "if Danjuro lives long enough," he might become a great actor in the Kansai style.[27] This is a continuation of the Kansai critics' denigration of the aragoto style, but the hyōbanki also gives some useful, detailed images of Danjūrō onstage, noting his proud bearing and ferocious bulging eyes, and suggests that after he had made his religious vows in 1690 he began to portray the deities he worshipped: "his living Fudō, saints, and wild niō [Deva kings] turn the play into a festive display of religious images."[28] This sort of kabuki clearly appealed to Edo theatergoers, if not to writers in Kyoto.

For the present, Danjūrō was ill and his employer was losing money. His producer begged him to return, and even had a new play written, incorporating a sick character, in hopes of getting the actor back onstage and making some return on his investment. The new play was well received and crowds did begin to return to the theater, but things were not going well on the contract negotiation front. Matakurō spoke openly of cutting back on his salary, and theater management began to encourage Danjūrō to look elsewhere for employment. In his diary Danjūrō wrote at some length about a rumor he'd heard of Matakurō's nephew's plans to fire him and use the 250 ryō thus saved to hire a top onnagata and a middle-ranking tachiyaku who could team up to do "a splendid kaomise even without Danjūrō."[29] This plan was in fact soon adopted, and Danjūrō was told that he would not be hired again at Morita-za. No other Edo theater wanted him either. But at this critical juncture he was saved by Murayama Heiemon's company in Kyoto, which stepped in to offer him employment for the 1693–94 season, and thus prevented his career from coming abruptly to a close.

The period of disappointment and uncertainty Danjūrō suffered in the spring of 1693 inspired some of the most profuse and bitter entries in his diary:

> Nothing is quite as mean-spirited as the ways of producers, financial backers and the leaders of theater. Since theater is a business ruled by profit and loss, it is only natural that the management discards all civility. As long as an actor brings them profits, they're so remarkably warm and friendly—*then* they'll let a person make a living. But if a play should fail and you don't figure into their plans anymore, how strange it is, for suddenly you can feel a fickle autumn wind blowing on you. If I think about it, I'm just a

commodity. And you can't sell something by trying to force it onto a place where there's no market for it …

When my livelihood hung in the balance between Edo, Osaka, and Kyoto, how did I feel, being pulled this way and that, with half-digested rumors flying around about how little or how much I would be paid? I am a man, after all.

They say that human beings fall seven times. We actors fall hard, but eventually we manage to pull ourselves back up again. So long as I am able to work to support my family, they can throw me out, but I won't just disappear. Even if I have to use the Ichikawa name to sell aloes oil, I'll still make more money than most actors do."[30]

Danjūrō's determination to weather misfortune is in the same "never-say-die" tradition that was embodied time and again in the Edo townsmen's rapid recovery from the devastating fires that periodically swept through the city's crowded merchant districts. In his diary Danjūrō proceeded to "count his blessings": healthy parents, a healthy family (including a new son), the esteem of many, and a relatively easy job, or at least one that presented few physical hardships. Danjūrō sought, in his writing at this period, to understand the reason for his humiliation and misfortune. He did not blame the gods for failing him. He was honest, and admitted having broken his vows.

Repentance and Rededication

This year I wasn't up to my usual standards—I was unsuccessful onstage and my acting reviews were poor. My innate power weakened, and the way that people inside and outside the theater viewed me was completely changed from the year before. This is not in the slightest the fault of others, nor does it mean the deities have truly

abandoned me. These things stem entirely from the evils
of my own heart. They result from the fact that I have
conducted myself wrongly.[31]

Danjūrō's wrong conduct consisted of erotic liaisons with three
young actors, including at least one disciple.

Truly the room of religion is as wide as the ocean, but if
your heart leads you astray, there is no way to enter it. If
you let your heart stray, even huge mountains can crum-
ble instantly away. If you let your will weaken, everything
can turn to dust. It is true, after I relaxed my attitude, all
sorts of difficulties arose.[32]

Danjūrō rededicated himself to success in the theater. "If I do
not have the will to strive for future success and fame, and am content to remain as I am now, it will be a terrible waste," he wrote,
adding, "There can be no greater pleasure than getting three hundred or four hundred ryō out of theater producers of Edo."[33] Danjūrō
was going to Kyoto for a time, but the samurai in him wanted
revenge on the theater producers of Edo, who had spurned him. He
was a townsman and an actor; his revenge would be complete only
when those who would now pay him nothing had begun to compete
amongst themselves as to who could hire him and pay him the highest salary in kabuki.

Danjūrō next addressed the problem of how to accomplish his
goals. He must take new vows, and this time not break them:

The two problems are alcohol and sex. First, concerning
alcohol, I resolve, for the good of my parents, to give up
alcohol for as long as they live. I make this strict vow to the
Sambō deities. Next, concerning extramarital sex with
women and young men … to get involved in this is the worst
possible thing. The marriage relationship can be traced all

the way back to the first male and female deities, and the failure to produce heirs is clearly unfilial. This is fundamentally important, since the husband and the wife are the pillars supporting the family, which is the basis for the system of laws governing society. With the exception of my wife, therefore, as long as I continue to care for my parents, I revoke all forms of erotic liaisons with either young men or women, and all other forms of erotic liaisons.[34]

All of Danjūrō's writings about his weaknesses and about "right conduct" indicate that for him extramarital relations with men and women were equally dangerous. To him, these were not sins in the Christian sense, but morally wrong because they were powerful distractions that prevented him from fulfilling his duties to his family. Further, they weakened his work onstage, for which Danjūrō believed that he needed concentration and focus.

On the eighth day of the fourth month (the Buddha's birthday), Danjūrō climbed up onto the roof of the Morita-za theater to communicate directly with the deities of heavenly light. He made his vow of sexual abstinence and pledged himself anew to ritual worship. In return for his devotion and abstinences he enumerated his requests to the gods:

—that he be master of a fine family
—that he be ranked among the top actors in the evaluation books
—that he be considered one of the greatest actors in Osaka and Kyoto, though he knew well that this kind of recognition had never before been granted an actor specializing in his kind of kabuki
—that he be acclaimed as one of the great theater producers of all time

—that he be able to pass on his name to his son, Kuzō

—that he be counted peerless among all actors in Japan.

He concluded with the invocation, "Hail the Buddha! Almighty Sun Deity of the Heavenly Way!"[35]

Danjūrō had prayed for something close to godhood in the world of kabuki. The deities would see fit to help him attain, in just ten years, almost everything he wished for. But Danjūrō had forgotten, or had not chosen, to pray for a long life. The gods would not overlook this omission.

Vindication in Kyoto

Late in the tenth, or early in the eleventh, month Danjūrō set out for Kyoto with his whole family: his wife, three children, sixty-five-year-old father, and fifty-four-year-old mother. They traveled the Tōkaidō Road, probably by palanquin, in a journey of about a week to ten days.

Danjūrō's luck began to turn during the 1693–1694 season in Kyoto. Kyoto kabuki had its own pantheon of star actors, but for this season Osaka theaters had lured away the top three Kyoto tachiyaku, including Tōjūrō and Hanzaemon. Not only would Danjūrō be free to work in a less than highly competitive field, but the Murayama company, operating in the Nakanoshibai ("Central Theater") had landed Mizuki Tatsunosuke (1673–1745), then the top onnagata in Japan, for the season. Barring a calamity, the company was virtually assured a prosperous year.

Danjūrō probably arrived in Kyoto only days before the opening of the kaomise show and had little time to rehearse or become familiar with his new colleagues. The play did not include an aragoto part, so Danjūrō played a low-ranking samurai and performed in a more straightforward acting style (jitsugoto). He was given two fight scenes and one scene in which he disguised himself as a drunken old woman. The actor reviews credited him with doing a competent job in the play and he apparently worked well with Tatsunosuke,[36] but it was not a particularly memorable Kyoto debut.

The first play performed at the theater in 1694 was a different story altogether. Danjūrō played two roles, an ox-driver in a short, romantic play that followed the main feature, and the warrior super-hero Asahina for most of the day in the historical drama *The Power and the Glory of the Genji Warrior (Genji Musha Homare no Seiryoku)*. Asahina was the role that had brought Danjūrō fame and fortune two years earlier. As Asahina, Danjūrō was able to demonstrate Edo aragoto to the curious and expectant Kyoto crowds—he wore a full suit of armor, wielded a six-foot sword, dispatched hordes of foes, and singlehandedly smashed his way through a castle gate.

Kyotoites' expectations of the play were so high that the crowd on the opening day was far bigger than the theater could handle; fans broke down the theater door and stormed into the hall, clamoring to see Danjūrō. The actors were not yet ready to begin, so the producer had minor actors do group dancing to entertain the gate-crashers. This merely angered the spectators, who demanded to see Danjūrō. Murayama Heiemon gave in and Danjūrō strode onto the stage, immediately silencing the crowd with his huge voice. He gave a long, impressive formal speech, but due to the ongoing confusion and violence outside the theater the producer decided to delay the start of the run until the next day. The audience was allowed to do a hand-clapping ceremony to wish Danjūrō good luck just before the hall was cleared.[37] The incident served as great publicity, and the play became a smash success. The theater was sold out from the fifth day of the run, and people flocked from as far away as Osaka to see Danjūrō. The management is said to have jammed two thousand spectators into the theater each day,[38] although this figure is likely exaggerated, since it was more than twice the building's normal capacity. *The Power and the Glory of the Genji Warrior* ran for forty days, which in 1694 was a very substantial run.

Danjūrō did not write about daily life in Kyoto, so we do not know if he took time to go with family or friends to enjoy the beautiful gardens and temples of the old capital. He did take lessons in *haikai* poetry, studying under a master named Tsuchimoto Saimaro. Danjūrō took the pen name Saigyū ("Talented Ox"); the "sai" (meaning "talent") was taken, as is customary, from his teacher's name, and the "gyū" ("ox") was derived from his ox-driver's role. Kyoto was still Japan's literary capital at the time, and Danjūrō likely took the opportunity to acquire nō plays, contemporary plays, and other literary works that he could use as raw materials for his playwriting. Danjūrō's output as a playwright accelerated after his year in Kyoto and it is clear from his new plays that Chikamatsu was one source of inspiration. However, 1694 is a "mystery year" for Chikamatsu. We do not know if he was in Osaka or Kyoto that year, though in the 1692–1693 season he had worked as staff playwright for the Mandayū-za, which was either across the street or around the corner from the Central Theater.[39] There is nothing in the historical record to indicate that these two great men of the theater ever actually met.

In the second Murayama-za play of 1694,[40] *Seigen at Kiyomizu (Kiyomizu Seigen),* Danjūrō played Seigen, a lecherous priest who, in his self-destructive obsession for the beautiful Princess Sakura (played by Tatsunosuke), attempts to kill her, only to die at her hand instead. Seigen then becomes a ghost determined to haunt the princess for the rest of her life. *Seigen at Kiyomizu* featured spectacular and macabre special effects. The fatally wounded Seigen fell into a hole, and then, thanks to a hidden trap-door and lift mechanism, rose mysteriously up again. His face turned from red to blue (Danjūrō did quick makeup changes) to mark his transformation from a man into a vengeful ghost. Later in the play, Danjūrō appeared as Fudō to save both Sakura and Seigen from their suffering, and his "violent Fudō dance astounded Kyoto audiences."[41] Danjūrō treated the Kyoto audience to an acting style and characters they had never seen before—a lustful and murderous aragoto hero and a major deity come to life on the kabuki stage.

For Danjūrō's third play of 1694, Heiemon had his playwrights link the play's story to an upcoming festival event, a *kaichō,* or special temporary display of secret religious statuary. Connections between religious and theatrical events dated back hundreds of years, but only recently had theaters started to try to increase gate receipts by scheduling and writing plays so as to take advantage of the public's fondness for festival events. Temples sponsoring festivals and kaichō also benefited from plays written about them. These were a form of free publicity that increased the turnout at festival events, bringing more income to the temples.

The Murayama-za play coincided with a kaichō that featured a display of Buddhist statuary brought all the way to Kyoto from Zenkōji Temple in the Japan Alps. In the play, the Buddha of Zenkōji resurrects a slain hero who then becomes a devoted Zenkōji priest and restores the land to legitimate rule. Danjūrō did not play the hero, but instead took the role of the major villain. This character is an immortal old man who beheads himself in the first act and is reborn as the evil Prince Kintama ("Kintama" means "golden jewels" or "golden testicles"). Prince Kintama exiles his father, the emperor, and usurps the throne before being defeated by the forces of righteousness, aided by the accumulated spiritual power of Zenkōji.[42] Danjūrō's Seigen, in the previous play, had been more evil than heroic, and Prince Testicles was an out-and-out villain. This was a remarkable turn of events: Danjūrō's villains were packing the Kyoto theater.

In the ninth month of 1694 Danjūrō's wife learned that she was pregnant. Danjūrō already knew that he was returning to Edo for the next season, and the family thought it best that his wife return at once to Edo. Danjūrō sent his whole family back to Edo on the seventeenth day of the ninth month, slightly over a month before he was scheduled to depart. Right after his family left, Danjūrō went to Kyoto's most popular temple, Kiyomizu-dera, to pray for their safe return to Edo. Kiyomizu-dera is built high on the eastern hills overlooking the old capital and is just the sort of place in which Danjūrō would have felt comfortable communing with the divine. He prayed to the main deity of the temple, Kannon, the bodhisattva of mercy, and not to the deities of his own Shingon sect. This demonstrates the practicality of Danjūrō's approach to worship. Kannon was clearly a powerful deity in the city of Kyoto, and efficacy was one of the most important criteria in selecting a deity to entreat. Danjūrō prayed to Kannon directly, and paid for priests to read sutras and do a fire service on his behalf. He prayed that his family would be safe and healthy, that he himself would not be "allowed to go astray, that he would have a successful kaomise show at the Yamamura-za, that he would regain the love of the Edo audiences, and that any theater that employed him would enjoy boundless prosperity."[43] He promised further abstinences and ritual devotions so that these wishes would be granted: he would refrain from having sexual relations even with his wife for three years and would stop using salt altogether. He would regularly worship the full moon and perform daily cold water ablutions.[44] This was to be Danjūrō's last recorded major petition to Buddhist deities.

Few of Danjūrō's poems survive, but it was during his family's absence from Kyoto that he wrote one of his best haiku:

(Written in the tenth month when a cricket crawled into my futon)

Is it a foster child clinging to me?
The cricket in my bedding.[45]

The poem suggests a gentle family man separated from his young children. For centuries it has been a typical arrangement in Japanese families for little children to sleep in the same bed with their parents. The sympathy with which Danjūrō addresses a humble insect, and the suggestion of deep feelings of affection toward his own children form a sharp contrast to the public image of the ambitious and haughty superstar who depicted ferocious deities, lecherous villains, and rambunctious samurai heroes.

Danjūrō's last Kyoto role was not that of a villain. Instead he played the famous historical samurai Kumagae, the archetypal Eastern warrior of *The Tale of the Heike* who kills a young foe,

Atsumori, in battle, but is so saddened by the event that he leaves his family and his military calling to become a priest. Kumagae devoted the rest of his years to serving the Buddha and to saving souls, including that of Atsumori. Danjūrō gave his Kumagae an aragoto twist—he did a leaping tobi roppō entrance on his way to visit a Buddhist saint, and he killed Atsumori's evil male lover by hurling a huge temple bell at him—but Danjūrō also acquitted himself well in gentler, more emotional scenes, such as those showing the parting from his wife and child, and his prayers for Atsumori's salvation.[46]

Tōjūrō had been in Osaka for the 1693–1694 season. Osaka is just twenty-five miles from Kyoto—in those days, as now, a day trip—but there is no clear record of Danjūrō's ever going to Osaka to see kabuki there, nor any record of Tōjūrō's ever returning to Kyoto to watch Danjūrō perform. We know that Danjūrō had followed Tōjūrō's career and was impressed not only with his ratings in the hyōbanki but with his salary. One unconfirmed account survives which refers to a meeting between Danjūrō and Tōjūrō at Tōjūrō's house in Kyoto a few days before Danjūrō returned to Edo. It claims that Tōjūrō was ill and at first refused to see the visitor, only relenting when informed by his servants of how angry Danjūrō was at this snub. All that we know for certain is that after Danjūrō returned to Edo he reputedly often said that Tōjūrō was such a great actor that there was no point in any Edo actor's performing in Kyoto as long as Tōjūrō was alive.[47] Danjūrō's chief Edo rival, the wagoto actor Nakamura Shichisaburō, did not heed this advice. He went to Kyoto four years later and bested Tōjūrō for half a season with a play that catapulted Shichisaburō to the top of the ratings. Danjūrō was wrong. Tōjūrō was mortal.

Although Danjūrō had been a huge box-office draw in Kyoto in 1694, his critical reception was mixed. One critic pooh-poohed his popular success, saying Danjūrō had done well only because Kyoto's top three actors were in Osaka that year, but by and large the hyōbanki praised Danjūrō for his popular appeal. The 1695 edition of *The Great Mirror of Actors* rated Danjūrō as a top ("high-high") villain actor, but noted that his acting style was rather hybrid: "thirty percent male lead (tachiyaku) and seventy percent villain. Just when you think he's playing a villain, he'll do hero routines, and just when you think he's playing a hero, he'll change into an excellent ("high-high") villain. He is roundly praised for this variety."[48] The same hyōbanki described his appearance and style as follows:

> He looks solid and imposing coming through the curtain and entering along the bridgeway. There is breadth to all of his performance, and he handles his onstage speeches with skill. His physical abilities suit male roles well. In addition, his work is by no means confined to the portrayal of villains. His jitsugoto, ghosts, lamentations, love scenes, his work in disguise, and his dancing are always done with an excellent sense of timing. It would be perfectly correct to regard him as a tachiyaku actor, although this year we have evaluated him as a villain actor.[49]

The 1694 hyōbanki *Actors' Lightning (Yakusha Ikazuchi)* wrote that Danjūrō makes it "seem that Buddhas and bodhisattvas have come to life for a brief period, before your very eyes," but also ruefully noted that "the words he speaks are hard to hear, like wind blowing cherry blossoms off an old tree."[50] The entry on Danjūrō concluded by calling him "the patron deity of the four [Edo] theaters and a famous product of Edo."[51] In 1695 most Kansai critics tended to prefer Hanzaemon and Tōjūrō's more subdued acting, while recognizing that Danjūrō did embody the spirit of Edo, even if some producers there were loath to work with him.

Surviving Fires, Illness, and Bad Plays

In his autobiographical writings prior to 1695 Danjūrō focused on his religious vows and prayers and on the issues that led him to make spiritual commitments, but in 1695 and 1696 he wrote about many events onstage and off, and recorded his philosophical and professional opinions. This record is of vital importance as a source of data about Genroku-period kabuki, but is even more interesting as a window into the heart and mind of Danjūrō, the actor and the man.

Danjūrō's notes on his performances during this period describe success after success. His salary for the 1694–1695 season at the Yamamura-za was 300 ryō (about $200,000). Producers would not pay salaries like that if they did not expect to make a good return on their top actors, and according to Danjūrō's diary the Yamamura-za producer told him that his first kaomise show after his return from Kyoto had been a remarkable success: the producer "had not seen the theater this full in thirty years."[52] Edoites turned out in force to welcome their hero home. Danjūrō played a familiar character, Kimpira, the swashbuckling young samurai, but no record survives of the story or the action of the play.

Danjūrō's first play of 1695 was even more successful—so much so that Yamamura Kazaemon, the producer, had makeshift work done to increase the seating capacity of the theater in order to accommodate the throngs who came to see Danjūrō.[53] The play, *Kazuraki and Kokiden (Kazuraki Kokiden),* opened two days into the new year, and Danjūrō wrote that it was a fine play and would probably enjoy a long run. But nature intervened: early in the second month, fire burned much of Edo south and west of the shogun's palace. The four kabuki theaters were spared, and shows were canceled for only one day. But next, prolonged heavy winter rains discouraged fans from braving the weather long enough to get to the theater. Natural disasters thus cut short what had seemed certain to be a long-running play.[54]

For the rest of 1695 the Yamamura-za put on a series of six short-run plays, several of which Danjūrō describes as very successful.[55] He often comments on the quality of the scripts, suggesting that most were by playwrights other than himself, and he always attributes poorly received shows to bad scriptwriting. The Yamamura-za summer play was a very popular version of the Seigen and Princess Sakura story, with a concluding scene that featured Fudō come to life, played of course by Danjūrō. During the course of its run the Yamamura-za had permanent work done expanding the size of the theater.

The kaomise season of 1695 was a hectic one because of box-office failures at the Morita-za. The Morita-za and the Yamamura-za were natural rivals since both were located in Kobiki-chō (now Higashi Ginza, near where the Kabuki-za theater stands today). The other two Edo theaters were further north and east. Because of two box-office failures during its kaomise season, the Morita-za was forced to change shows twice in one month, and Yamamura Kazaemon felt pressured to make a hasty change of plays himself just to stay competitive.[56] Then disaster struck. Danjūrō wrote:

> When we were in the midst of rehearsals for the New Year's show, on the night of the twenty-sixth, fire broke out in Sukiyabashi (now Ginza 5-chōme). It quickly became a conflagration and crossed the river, and the houses in Kobiki-chō, the theaters, and Tsukiji outside the temple's main hall were all in flames by seven o'clock in the morning.
>
> Even now, when I recall the danger of that night, it tears at my heart.
>
> From eight o'clock that night until dawn on the twenty-seventh, the spreading flames burned ferociously. It was terrible. Sadly, when the fire finally subsided, all that was left was a charred wasteland … There was no place to walk. Storehouses had burnt down, fire had entered cellar storerooms, and wherever you went there were people whose fortunes had been wiped out. Quite a few people died of burns, and there were many who were injured, or who barely managed to escape with their lives, stark naked, just as they were when the fire reached them.
>
> But soon people were putting up temporary bamboo

fences around the houses they were rebuilding one alongside the next, and the city once again grew lively.[57]

According to this same text, one of the two theaters in Kobiki-
chō, the Yamamura-za, started presenting plays on the twenty-sev-
enth day of the first month. The Morita-za started doing shows on
the twenty-fourth day of the second month.

Danjūrō's vivid description of the 1695 "flower of Edo" clearly
owes a great deal to Kamo no Chōmei's classical description of the
calamities that struck the old capital in the 1180s, but this is only
what we would expect of a man of Danjūrō's education. The
resilience and resourcefulness shown by the residents of Edo in the
aftermath of the fire rings true to the spirit of the city and sets this
account apart from any earlier models. It is apparent that the spirit
of rivalry between theaters extended even to a competition to see
which could rebuild first and get back to business. Danjūrō must
have been pleased to beat out his old nemesis, the Morita-za, in this
competition. But it was ironic that the Yamamura-za burned down
just half a year after completing a major expansion project.

In 1695 Edo playwrights had not yet begun regular publication
of plays, so we have no detailed records about the characters
Danjūrō played, nor do we know exactly which plays he wrote.
Nevertheless, it is clear from his diary that Danjūrō was doing some
work writing and adapting plays for the stage, and that he was very
concerned with the writer-actor relationship and its effect on the
success of a performance. Danjūrō wrote that play texts were important and that writers deserved much higher salaries. Actor-writers
like himself were well paid, but only because of their acting.
Playwright specialists started at 15 ryō a year (about $10,000), and
most made only double that at the peak of their careers. The top playwright in Edo made just 65 ryō a year.[58] Danjūrō wrote that quality
playwriting and acting were both essential, "like the two wheels on a
cart" or like samurai who, in order to succeed, needed equal levels of
skill in the military and literary arts.[59] Good plays could enjoy a

degree of success even when poorly acted, and a fine acting performance could draw audiences despite a bad script, but Danjūrō wrote that giving a fine play to a skilled actor was like "giving an iron bar to a demon."[60] By this he meant something like "arming a man who is already dangerous."

Danjūrō also wrote about the nature of the actor's art. Not surprisingly, he spoke of losing himself completely in his characters:

> I don't know about other actors but when I go onstage and play a role I don't feel my body to be my own. It is transformed into a stage character and consumed by the performance. When I am exerting all my strength I wouldn't even notice if my flesh were pierced.[61]

Danjūrō describes his acting as something like the "fighting frenzy" of a warrior in battle.[62] He does not give details on just how he prepared for roles, but judging from the evaluations of the hyōbanki, it would appear that his energy and conviction gave his exaggerated superheroes and deities a life and reality of their own onstage.

In the third play of 1696 Danjūrō played a character who would become a great favorite of his descendants, the evil, vindictive priest Narukami who uses his magical powers to bring drought to the realm. The beautiful Lady Taema is sent to seduce him, thus destroying his powers and restoring rain and life. In the concluding act of the 1696 version, Danjūrō also took the role of the Chinese demon-quelling deity Shōki. Danjūrō was elated with the success of his Narukami role and wrote that an actor needed two big hits like this every season in order to sustain a 300–400 ryō salary.[63] Danjūrō thought that the play would run into midsummer, but an "old illness" flared up, forcing him again to leave the stage.[64] Attendance dropped off and the producer closed the play and began a new one. Danjūrō sat out the new play and went to a spa to take curative waters. On the eighth day of the sixth month, he fainted at the spa, and rumors soon flew around Edo that he was dead.[65] The Yama-mura-za now had no choice but to put Danjūrō back onstage, despite his sickness, to quell the rumors. They added a new scene to the play in which Danjūrō sat still and told the story of a visit to hell. The play, *The Chronicle on Oguri's Sleeve (Oguri Sode Nikki)*, could well have been written by Danjūrō, because it featured a typical deus-ex-machina appearance by Fudō in the last act. But Danjūrō was too weak to play the Fudō role. The Yamamura-za producer took the part instead.

Danjūrō Writes on Fate, Faith, Ambition, and Family

In his autobiographical writings Danjūrō pondered the meaning of his life and dealt directly with the moral and spiritual contradictions confronting him. Like all educated Japanese of the premodern era, Danjūrō was very conscious of the transitory nature of human existence. In 1696 he described in detail the accidental death of the two-year-old daughter of an actor friend, a tragedy that occurred at about the same time a sixty-six-year-old colleague passed away. Because the girl was the same age as his own daughter Miyo (the child conceived in Kyoto), and the old man just a little younger than his father, these deaths heightened Danjūrō's sense of the uncertainty of human life.[66] But they did not inspire him to prepare for the Buddhist afterlife. Earlier in the diary he had written, "I have lived thirty-seven years, but I may die tomorrow," and "The way of death is beyond comprehension."[67] He knew that many men believed life and death to be in the hands of some uncontrollable fate, but he was convinced that his own life had been strongly influenced by the blessings of powerful deities, and when he pondered the deaths of the old actor and his friend's little girl, then observed his own healthy family, he concluded that his good fortune was "all thanks to the gods and Buddhas. I must express my gratitude with fervor, again and again, to Dainichi, Kannon, Senju, Enmei, Atago, Kōjin, and Fudō."[68] Danjūrō's faith in his gods was too strong for him to accept the concept of random fate. He counted on the deities he worshipped to aid him in his life on earth, and probably expected that they would serve him when his turn came to die. But in the mid-1690s he was still young and strong, and his concerns were firmly centered on his professional and family life.

Danjūrō recognized that excessive concern with worldly wealth and glory would be likely to turn the gods against him. In a self-critical moment in 1693, when things were going badly for him, he wrote:

> I am intent on my desire for money and fame, and all I want to do is to be better than others, grabbing fame and fortune for myself. I don't think there has ever been a greedier actor than me.[69]

Danjūrō took filial and family obligations very seriously. Confucian moral law held these duties to be paramount, and Danjūrō could justify to himself his drive to attain wealth and glory provided that the fruits of his efforts were used to benefit his parents and children. He often ended his prayers for success with statements that he sought wealth and glory not for his personal gain, but for the sake of his family. And whereas individual men were sure to die, families could go on forever. Perhaps the traditional Japanese obsession with preserving the family line is an attempt at achieving some form of immortality. Danjūrō again turned to the samurai as a model for his own ambition:

> For an actor, success is paramount. People may call this overly ambitious, but that is the way that cowards think. The samurai strives to perform brave deeds and to take spoils on the battlefield, and in return receives rewards of wealth and land for his valor. These riches then become his own and can be passed on to his children. The actor strives for success on the stage because he wants the same

rewards. But wanting too much is as bad as not wanting enough. One must not strive solely for worldly success.[70]

For Danjūrō, support from the deities was critical, but actions like ritual worship and abstinence, or refraining from excessive greed would not by themselves guarantee the gods' support. "If you strive but do not achieve your goals, then that is the working of fate, but you must have made every possible effort. If you do not complete your lessons and train diligently, the deities are sure to withhold their support."[71] The work ethic of the merchant class in Edo-period Japan has perhaps never been more cogently stated than in this last sentence, and it is remarkably similar to the Protestant work ethic that was developing half a world away at the same time in history.

Danjūrō made his last entry in *An Account of My Prayers* on the Buddha's birthday in 1696 (the eighth day of the fourth month). He recognized that nearly all the prayers he had made on the Morita-za roof and at Kiyomizu Temple had been granted:

> My work onstage has been made worthy of merit, and my rise to success has been complete. No theater where I work fails to enjoy prosperity.
>
> I have been blessed in all things with divine favor. I am most thankful that my family remains healthy.[72]
>
> There have been difficulties, but my endeavors were granted good fortune, and the hyōbanki called me an actor without peer in Japan. At the Yamamura-za I work for a salary of 320 ryō, and I have made my name known in the world.[73]

He concluded with a last prayer:

> I will remain steadfast in my belief, so that clouds of sin and retribution will not settle over me. I will keep my parents near me while they live, be sincere in my devotion to

them, and remember my duties every day. I pray fervently
that life and death shall come in their natural order, and
that this and my other prayers shall be realized. All I can
do is leave everything to the will of the deities and to fate.
I speak in reverence, "Hail the Almighty Buddha!"[74]

Danjūrō had finally prayed for "death in its natural order," but this
was the one prayer that fate did not see fit to grant the god of Edo
kabuki.

A Family Triumph: The Origin of the Soga Warrior

The year 1697 marked a major turning point in Danjūrō's life and
career. He made a final copy of his diary that year, and then apparently ceased his autobiographical writing, perhaps because he was
too busy. Between 1697 and 1703 he was onstage constantly and
published twelve long plays. He probably wrote quite a few more.
Finally one Edo firm, Kaifuya of Sakai-chō, was ready to do what the
more advanced Kyoto publishers had been doing for some years—
publish popular kabuki plays targeting the reading public.[75] Danjūrō
was the first major Edo playwright to have his work made available
in bookstores, which meant that he had to revise and edit the hand-
written play scripts he prepared for use in the theater to suit the different requirements of general readers.

Danjūrō's two sons were growing up and he was busy training
them and helping to shape their careers. As Danjūrō matured his
fame grew, as did the number of his young professional disciples. It
was his responsibility to teach them the acting trade and guide them
on their career paths. Finally, after 1697, Danjūrō's religious life
ceased being a purely private, family affair. He became a publicly
recognized lay religious figure.

All these new directions in Danjūrō's life and career were embodied in The Origin of the Soga Warrior (Tsuwamono Kongen
Soga), Danjūrō's greatest triumph until that point, which played in

the Nakamura-za during the fifth and sixth months of 1697. *The Origin of the Soga Warrior* was more than just a play; it was a family celebration and regional event that cemented Danjūrō's hold on Edo kabuki and on the hearts of Edoites. Danjūrō wrote the play. It was the second one he published in book form and the second one certain to have been written by him. Danjūrō's oldest son, Kuzō, made his stage debut in *The Origin of the Soga Warrior.* Because Danjūrō regarded the boy as "Fudō's gift," Kuzō would play Fudō, in a work intended to demonstrate Fudō's power and glory. Danjūrō surely believed that Fudō would see to it that this particular play would be a resounding success. Danjūrō also gave an important part to his leading disciple, Ichikawa Dannojō, and the play launched Dannojō's adult career. Edo's other leading aragoto actor, Nakamura Denkurō (1662–1713), played Asahina, but Denkurō was clearly subordinate to Danjūrō. Denkurō had been developing his own comic aragoto style and Danjūrō had played supporting roles in Denkurō vehicles prior to the Kyoto trip, but in *The Soga Warrior,* Danjūrō's Soga Gorō was far and away the dominant role, and Danjūrō's aragoto, with its supernatural qualities and overtones of evil, would emerge as the dominant aragoto line.

The Origin of the Soga Warrior is a four-act play with the most important action coming in Act Two. For this act, Danjūrō rewrote the familiar story of Soga Gorō's first meeting with Kudō Suketsune, the warlord who had murdered Gorō's father when Gorō was a little boy. All versions of the Soga tradition—whether in prose or drama— agree that Gorō's mother had sent him to Hakone Temple to train to become a priest, and that Gorō first encountered his blood enemy when Suketsune visited the temple with his entourage. In Danjūrō's play, setting and context both follow the tradition (Figure 5), but he completely reworked the encounter itself. In *The Origin of the Soga Warrior,* Gorō, young and weak though he is, resolves on the spot to avenge his father, and attacks Suketsune twice, whereupon he is pinned to the floor and rendered helpless. Only the intervention of the temple abbot, Gorō's patron, saves the boy.

Fig. 5 In *The Origin of the Soga Warrior*, Soga Gorō (Danjūrō, at left) bows in greeting to his blood enemy Kudō Suketsune. Gorō wears a robe decorated with the Ichikawa family *mimasu* (three rice-measure crest) with its three concentric squares. Kudō holds two swords. The Hakone abbot (left panel, in white robes) and Hōjō Tokimasa (right panel, above) look on. Book illustration dating to 1697 attributed to Torii Kiyonobu. Courtesy of Tokyo Geijutsu Daigaku.

Humiliated by this failure, Gorō turns to Fudō. In traditional versions of the Soga story Gorō's divine assistance comes from Hakone Gongen, the main deity of the temple, but in Danjūrō's play Gorō prays to Fudō that he be transformed into the most powerful warrior in Japan so that he may avenge his father's murder.[76] Fudō, still invisible to the audience, responds by transforming the boy before the spectators' eyes into a ferocious, bright red, muscle-bound superhero (see figure 3), and prescribes a series of wild rituals to complete the

Fig. 6   Danjūrō's son Kuzō, top left, as a little yamabushi who dances for the Hakone abbot and the Soga retainer Dōsaburō. In the right panel, Danjūrō uproots bamboo in his role as Soga Gorō. This panel is littered with fragments of hoe blades and also shows a stupa that Gorō will demolish after he has finished pulling up the bamboo. Attributed to Torii Kiyomasu and Torii Kiyonobu. Courtesy of Tokyo Geijutsu Daigaku.

genesis of the Soga warrior. These rituals are parodies of actual austerities performed by yamabushi (mountain priests): Gorō had to smash hoes, uproot living bamboo, and demolish stupas (Figure 6).

When his transformation is complete, Gorō becomes a powerful, violent creature who terrifies even the family retainer Dōsaburō (played by Dannojō) and the abbot of the temple. All the characters exit, and a little yamabushi appears. This was Kuzō's first appearance onstage. After Kuzō performed a solo travel dance (*michiyuki*)

Fig. 7   Asahina (Nakamura Denkurō, left) challenges Gorō (Danjūrō, right) but their fight is stopped by the deity Fudō (Danjūrō's son Kuzō) in *The Origin of the Soga Warrior.* Courtesy of Tokyo Geijutsu Daigaku.

and had a comic dialog with Dōsaburō as a prelude to his first encounter with his father onstage. Danjūrō's Gorō then reenters the scene, glares at the little yamabushi, and attempts to kill him. But the yamabushi disappears magically and instantly.

Gorō charges down to the temple's sacred lustration river where he easily dispatches four warriors. Asahina enters and throws a horse into the river, at which point he and Gorō—the two strongest warriors of twelfth-century Japan—challenge one another and begin to fight. At that moment Fudō, also played by Kuzō, appears out of nowhere to put a stop to the fight (Figure 7). The two wild warriors bow in reverence. Fudō orders them to refrain from fighting. They are blood relatives, and Asahina is to aid Gorō in his righteous quest for revenge. Act Two concludes:

NARRATOR: Both men express profuse thanks. They bow in worship to this manifestation of Fudō which has appeared before them in real life. Stouthearted and full of joy, each returns to his home; Gorō to Soga and Asahina to Kamakura.[77]

The Origin of the Soga Warrior was one of the greatest successes of Danjūrō's career. People flocked from Narita to see the play. During its two-month run, many members of the audience responded to the power of the Fudō they saw onstage as they might to a religious ritual or a display of impressive statuary in a temple. They threw coins and other offerings onto the stage and offered spontaneous prayers to Fudō. Descriptions of The Origin of the Soga Warrior production are the first mention ever made of this kind of audience response to the portrayal of a deity on the kabuki stage. When the play closed, Danjūrō led a pilgrimage of worshippers to Shinshōji in Narita. There he gave generous gifts of thanks for his theatrical success.[78] After The Origin of the Soga Warrior, Danjūrō began using the yago (house name) "Narita-ya," a public acknowledgment of the importance of his religious beliefs,[79] and his descendants have used it ever since. The Origin of the Soga Warrior marks Danjūrō's conscious decision to make his private worship of Fudō and other deities public.

The Origin of the Soga Warrior confirmed Danjūrō's status as Edo's premiere martial actor. His aragoto rival had this time taken a subordinate, supporting role. Danjūrō's superiority was symbolically demonstrated in the fourth act when, as Gorō, he bests Asahina (Denkurō) in the famous armor-pulling tug-of-war at a banquet held by Asahina's father, Wada Yoshimori (Figure 8). Gorō's gentle elder brother Jūrō was played by wagoto specialist Murayama Shirōjirō, and this role too was clearly subordinate to that of Soga Gorō.

Fig. 8 *The Origin of the Soga Warrior.* Gorō (Danjūrō, left panel, upper right) defeats Asahina (Nakamura Denkurō) in the "armor-pulling tug-of-war" scene (left). At right, the warlord Wada Yoshimori, Gorō's elder brother Jurō, and the Soga brothers' lovers, the courtesans Tora and Shōshō, look on. Courtesy of Tokyo Geijutsu Daigaku.

For Danjūrō, art, family, career, and worship were fused in the process of bringing *The Origin of the Soga Warrior* to the stage. The play displayed the power and virtue of a deity, but it also had a religious context in Danjūrō's personal life. He considered the play to be an offering of thanks to Fudō for granting him a son, and although Danjūrō fashioned the play to showcase his own skills he gave his son plenty of opportunity to demonstrate his talent and charm: a michiyuki travel dance, an ad-libbed dialog with Dannojō playing the family retainer Dōsaburō, a face-off with his father, and a Fudō dance at the climax of Act Two. If current kabuki audience response to child actors is any indication, then it is easy to imagine how nine-year-old Kuzō likely stole the scene whenever he was onstage. In fact, performance records show that the audience loved the scene when Kuzō, as Fudō, emerged from a rock cave, as well as the verbal interchanges and glaring contests (nirami-ai) between father and son.[80] The published version of the play suggests that Kuzō was given few lines of text, but this does not mean that his was an insignificant role. Illustrations in playbooks showcase the most important, popular scenes and characters, so the fact that Kuzō is featured in two of the six illustrations is strong evidence of his importance to the play.

The Origin of the Soga Warrior was much more than a play about Soga Gorō and Fudō. It was a public expression of faith in and gratitude to a deity by a man of wealth and fame. In its presentation of Kuzō, the play was also a celebration of the Ichikawa family's bright future. When audience members watched Kuzō perform they saw multiple layers of meaning in what occurred onstage. While they enjoyed the interaction between Gorō and Fudō, many regarded the onstage Fudō as in fact invested with divine power. Audience members also carefully watched and evaluated any new child performer. They must have compared Kuzō with his father, and with other young actors, wondering if this boy would become Edo's next big star. Kuzō's ad-libbed lines more than likely contained a number of references to his own background as Danjūrō's son, as well as expressions of gratitude to his teachers and audience.

With The Origin of the Soga Warrior, Danjūrō took a significant step toward the creation of a very loyal group of fans and patrons, people on whom he could count to support his descendants. He did this by inviting the audience to share in his family celebrations (Kuzō's debut and Dannojō's coming-of-age) and in his family religion. With this play, Danjūrō began to extend his family group, the most essential and supportive social group in Japanese society, to include audience members and professional associates. He would make this an integral part of his career strategy for the rest of his life. From the Genroku period until today, kabuki actors have used ritualized family events such as name-taking ceremonies (*shūmei*) and formal expressions of gratitude to the audience during onstage speeches (kōjō)—to enable fans to feel connected to the actors they idolize.

Bringing Superheroes to Life Onstage

Danjūrō built his fame and fortune on aragoto acting. Aragoto acting and roles are still an important feature of today's kabuki, testimony to Danjūrō's lasting impact through the generations, but the costuming, makeup, and specific physical movements we see in today's aragoto roles, as well as the rhythms of performance and musical accompaniment, are all somewhat different from their counterparts at the turn of the eighteenth century. What did Danjūrō really look like, and just what was he doing onstage that so excited Edo audiences in the late 1690s? In the absence of film or video records we cannot know for certain, but surviving written and pictorial records do give us a vivid impression of Danjūrō's aragoto art.

Exaggerated, bold, and violent action was at the core of aragoto acting. According to hyōbanki entries in the years 1698 to 1701, aragoto routines included "drinking saké from huge cups, smashing gates, tearing tigers to shreds, ripping off enemy heads, picking up huge boulders, trampling wild bears to death, pulling huge trees up from the roots and swinging them about, throwing people around like stones, and running here and there like one possessed."[81] These descriptions show that by 1700, Danjūrō's aragoto had gone far beyond the routine heroics of the jitsugoto style, which at its most extreme featured a single warrior hero defeating dozens of enemies in sword fights.

Act Two of *The Origin of the Soga Warrior* demonstrates how Danjūrō integrated mayhem and (sometimes comically) exaggerated feats of strength into effective dramatic scenes that were central to plot development. We enter Act Two just after Gorō's humiliation at the hands of Kudō Suketsune and his subsequent prayers to Fudō:

GORŌ: I was so upset that in my heart of hearts I prayed to Fudō. I asked him to grant me bravery and strength, to make me a demon or a god so that I can avenge my father. At first I thought my face was changing color only because of the smoke from the holy fire, but if it's really turning red, this means my prayers are being answered. This is wonderful!

NARRATOR: Gorō runs out of the temple and down a mountain path. The abbot and Dōsaburō shout:

ABBOT & DŌSABURŌ: Did you hear him? Did you see how red his face is?

NARRATOR: Now they see Gorō coming back, and what an incredible sight he is. A ferocious warrior charging up the steps!

[Danjūrō performs an aragoto dance to the accompaniment of the following narration.]

NARRATOR: His wild training is fearful to behold. During the first seven days he rips apart new hoes. During the second seven days he tears living bamboo up by the roots.

[An interlude follows which features the abbot doing a comic routine and Gorō ripping up bamboo by the roots.]

NARRATOR: During the third seven days he smashes stupas. The abbot and Dōsaburō are terrified and order everyone to take refuge inside the temple. Presently the priest Tsūrikibō appears.

[Ichikawa Kuzō, Danjūrō's son, enters and performs a travel dance.]

YAMABUSHI: I come begging alms.
NARRATOR: Dōsaburō ventures out to greet him.
DŌSABURŌ: Where do you come from, little priest?

[The yamabushi and Dōsaburō engage in an ad-libbed comic dialog.]

NARRATOR: Gorō spies them.

GORŌ: You look like a clever priest. How would you like me to grab you and kill you?

NARRATOR: As Gorō pronounces these words, the yamabushi suddenly disappears.

DŌSABURŌ: That was witchcraft! We've got to do something! We've got to stop the evil spirit!

NARRATOR: He rushes off to the Sagami River to perform daylight lustration rituals.

[At the river, four warriors perform a dance representing a fight over a horse. Then Asahina enters, leading a horse named Black Fan K'uai[82] to the river, where it stops to drink. Next, Gorō enters.]

GORŌ: You upstart lout! You're polluting the lustration site! I'll take you on and give you a big surprise.

NARRATOR: Gorō splashes into the river, panicking Black Fan K'uai.

ASAHINA: Who are you? You look like a kid. Where do you come from?

GORŌ: I come from the land of Brahma!

ASAHINA: You look tough enough, for a kid. Okay, let's fight!

NARRATOR: They fight furiously, back and forth. Then the yamabushi suddenly reappears.

YAMABUSHI (IN FACT FUDŌ): Both of you! Stop fighting and listen to me! In response to Gorō's prayers to Fudō, from this moment until the time that Gorō meets his blood enemy, he shall be granted strength greater than that of the breakers on the shore. But Soga and Miura are the same family and must not fight. I am, in fact, Fudō Myōō. Behold my true appearance!

[Ichikawa Kuzō performs a Fudō dance.][83]

In this scene, aragoto acting is used to depict Gorō's transformation into a ferocious warrior. Danjūrō's wild movements were accompanied by other special effects that also showed supernatural powers at work: the weird transformation of Gorō's skin color, the yamabushi's magical transformation into Fudō, and Fudō's sudden appearance and disappearance.

Many of the elements in this scene were basic to Danjūrō's aragoto style, but the tool most fundamental and essential to this actor's craft was in fact his own body. Ukiyo-e artists were not yet doing portraits of actors, so we do not know just what Danjūrō looked like, but he was described as being of medium stature, with a strong but sometimes gravelly voice. He was "strong and robust, with thick calves."[84]

Dancing, stamping, and glaring were common to all aragoto roles, and specific mimetic acts, such as uprooting massive stalks of bamboo or "tearing tigers to shreds" were often performed incorporating these three ground elements. Danjūrō's dance was often described as *hataraki,* the term used to categorize the most vigorous and mimetic sort of dance in nō theater. In nō plays, hataraki dance is used to depict violent activity by warriors, demons, and wild gods. In the short excerpt above from *The Origin of the Soga Warrior,* the stage directions use the word "dance" four times,[85] suggesting how important dance was to Danjūrō's stage art.

Vigorous stamping is used in all hataraki dances, and Danjūrō's stamping was renowned throughout Edo: "When he stamps his feet it makes loud crashing noises and the pottery shops within a half-mile radius suffer terribly."[86] Glaring and challenges were essential preliminaries to martial combat. In the scene related above, Gorō and the little yamabushi engage in a glaring match just before the yamabushi disappears,[87] and Asahina and Gorō would surely have glared and scowled at each other before their fight. Glaring was accompanied by defiant physical postures. The dramatic kabuki poses that feature rolling and jerking the head, then settling into a ferocious glare, are now called *mie,* although the term does not seem to have been current in Danjūrō's day.

The 1700 hyōbanki *Yakusha Dankōzuku (A Lively Discussion on Actors)* wrote of Danjūrō, "There is visual appeal in everything he does," and it is not surprising that Danjūrō inspired more works of art than any other actor in his day. Book illustrations and prints preserve a crucial visual record of his aragoto acting. We do not know for sure how true-to-life these representations are. They were no doubt idealized to some extent, but the poses of certain human figures, such as the powerful and defiant postures of Gorō and Asahina (see figure 7) seem so close to today's mie postures that it is safe to assume that book illustrations and prints do represent action onstage and not just free illustrations conceived by artists. This interpretation is supported by the actors' crests that decorate the costumes in book illustrations, calling attention to the figures' identities as performers rather than characters.

Early hyōbanki describe how Danjūrō colored his face and body red for heroic aragoto roles, and this is confirmed by colored *tan'e* prints such as the one seen in figure 3.[88] The bulging muscles and "power sinews" that are trademarks of aragoto kabuki illustrations by Torii Kiyomasu present a dilemma:[89] did Danjūrō paint them on, were they meant to represent Danjūrō's actual physique, or did Kiyomasu add them to his illustrations to idealize Danjūrō's superheroes on the page? We have no way to know. Illustrations confirm hyōbanki accounts of Danjūrō's use of bulging eyes to demonstrate emotional intensity (Figure 9). Danjūrō never used striped face makeup to represent aragoto superheroes. Striped *suji kuma* makeup was his son's invention, and from the time of Danjūrō II, solid red coloration was used to represent villains, not heroes.

Danjūrō's sources of inspiration for aragoto acting have been hotly debated by theater scholars in Japan for the last three-quarters of a century. Some contend that Danjūrō's aragoto paralleled, and can be said to represent, the adoption by the merchant class of samurai traits as a means of expressing a sense of class pride and accomplishment, and at the same time of defying the ruling class in the heart of the samurai capital. This sociopolitical *raison d'etre* for

Fig. 9 Danjūrō as the priest Narukami (right panel, lower left) in *Gempei Narukami Ki* stares intently at a beautiful aristocratic woman who is washing clothes in a river (at lower left). In hopes of bringing drought to the land, Narukami has imprisoned the rain-bringing dragons in a cave (right panel, bottom). Book illustration attributed to Torii Kiyonobu. 1698. Courtesy of Tokyo Geijutsu Daigaku.

aragoto bravado is attractive to social scientists, but examination of Danjūrō I's plays and diary, and of others' commentary on his plays lends little credence to the "defiance of the samurai" thesis. In his diary Danjūrō brought samurai social and moral values to bear on his own situation, and seems to identify with, rather than oppose, the samurai class. Heroic and villainous samurai alike appear in Danjūrō's plays, but his writing is not marked by the same spirit of townsman-versus-samurai class conflict that appeared later in some of his son's plays. One important source of evidence that does link Danjūrō I

with the "defiance" thesis is the following colorful account, supposedly written by Danjūrō himself:

> When invited to a daimyō's residence, after saké was served,
> I was asked to demonstrate aragoto. Therefore, to the
> chanting of the nō play *Kagekiyo,* I stripped to my under-
> clothes and violently smashed the *shōji* and *fusuma* (slid-
> ing doors) with my feet. Whereupon the patrons asked,
> "What are you doing?"
>
> When I replied, "This is aragoto," the daimyō was
> delighted and rewarded me generously. Even in front of
> daimyō you must never be afraid, or it won't be aragoto.[90]

The only problem with this account is that it was written in 1772,
almost seventy years after Danjūrō's death and there are no contemporary accounts, or even records from the generation after his death
to corroborate the daimyō mansion visit. In 1772 Edo townsmen had
developed a rich culture that did consciously compete with the elite
world of the samurai.[91] Kagekiyo was Danjūrō IV's signature role,
and the dramatic banquet-wrecking episode is more likely an expression of his era and personality than a description of any actual event
involving Danjūrō I.

Legends and accounts of samurai heroism and exaggerated *kimpira jōruri* versions of warrior exploits were certainly sources of inspiration for Danjūrō's aragoto, but the main font of aragoto movements,
costumes, and characters were the images and rituals of his tantric
Buddhist sect. Danjūrō took multiple roles in each of his plays, and
in over half of them he either enacted a deity in its revealed form or
a man who, like Soga Gorō in *The Origin of the Soga Warrior,* was
possessed of divine powers.

Numerous hyōbanki entries cite the portrayal of fierce deities
like Fudō as central to Danjūrō's aragoto art. As we see them depicted
in Torii Kiyomasu's illustrations, Danjūrō's postures of defiance and
power are clearly related to the contorted poses that sculptors used

Fig. 10 Wooden sculptures of a Buddhist guardian *niō* (Deva king) from the Kamakura period (thirteenth century). *Niō* statues are usually placed at temple gates, with one on either side of the main path of entry to the temple. Courtesy of Kōfukuji.

in carving images of Buddhist guardian deities (Figure 10). When Danjūrō portrayed actual deities he clearly took pains to look as authentic as possible, wearing a huge bristling beard and Chinese robes and boots for Shōki (Figure 11) and a curly wig and Indian robes for Fudō (Figure 12). The bulging muscles and straining sinews in the illustrations of Gorō and Asahina in *The Origin of the Soga Warrior* could almost be direct copies of these features of Buddhist statuary. For his choreography, Danjūrō took inspiration from yamabushi *aramai* (vigorous ritual dances full of stamping), and imitated the powerful droning litanies of yamabushi and Shingon priests in his stage monologs known as *tsurane*. The glare was as important a weapon for Fudō as were his sword and rope—in tantric Buddhist belief his glare was said to have the power to exorcise demons. Danjūrō undertook a week of austerities at Shinshōji before opening his 1703 play *The Avatars of the Narita Temple Fudō (Naritasan*

Fig. 11 Danjūrō as the Chinese demon-quelling deity Shōki in *Sankai Nagoya*. Book illustration attributed to Torii Kiyonobu and Torii Kiyomasu. 1697. Courtesy of Tokyo Geijutsu Daigaku.

Fig. 12 Danjūrō and his son Kuzō (bottom right and left) as twin Fudōs in *The Avatars of the Narita Temple Fudō* (bottom). Book illustration attributed to Torii Kiyonbu and Torii Kiyomasu. 1703. Courtesy of Tokyo Geijutsu Daigaku.

Funjin Fudō), and at the end of that week said that Fudō had appeared to him and bestowed upon him the god's own ferocious glare to use onstage. Danjūrō taught the glare to his son, and it has since been passed down from one generation to the next.

Aragoto acting would evolve continuously over the next three centuries, but religious belief always remained part of the art. Danjūrō was convinced that the gods he worshipped had powers far exceeding those of mortal men, and could provide real men like himself the strength to perform remarkable feats. Again and again hyōbanki describe Danjūrō's acting with phrases like, "It was like seeing Fudō [or another deity] come alive before my very eyes." Danjūrō brought his religious convictions to the stage, and made the remarkable and the supernatural real for his audiences.

Creating Immortal Heroes

When Genroku-period hyōbanki evaluated kabuki actors, they focused on two things: acting styles and roles. Over the course of his career Danjūrō developed a repertory of great roles, some of which he performed repeatedly and others which, while less often revived, still marked pinnacles of artistic achievement. Danjūrō's descendants would choose their personal favorites from among them, and many of Danjūrō I's best roles are among the most popular performed in aragoto kabuki today. Because Danjūrō could control, and in fact often wrote the material he presented, examining his great roles sheds light on his personality, his sense of his own strengths as an actor, and his appreciation of the sorts of heroes and scenes which his audiences would be likely to enjoy.

The one character that Danjūrō played most often was Fuwa Banzaemon. In 1702, *Yakusha Nichō Shamisen (The Actors' Two Shamisens)* noted that Danjūrō had played Fuwa in twelve of the twenty different plays featuring Fuwa that had been presented in Edo to that date.[92] The legendary Fuwa had supposedly lived at about the turn of the previous century, making him one of the most contemporary of Danjūrō's historical heroes. He was also one of the most romantic of Danjūrō's swashbuckling heroes, invariably engaged in a love triangle with his wagoto rival, Nagoya Sanzaemon, and a beautiful woman, often the courtesan Kazuraki. Leading actors of gentle male characters teamed with Danjūrō to perform Fuwa plays, including Nakamura Shichisaburō in the early years and Murayama Shirōjirō later on (Figure 13). The marked contrast between the personalities of Fuwa and Nagoya, and these characters' competition and confrontations, were the major appeal of these plays. Today little remains of pre-kabuki Fuwa legends, but as a playwright Danjūrō created all sorts of original adventures for his favorite hero.

Danjūrō reputedly played Soga Gorō as early as 1675. Though this hero is young, energetic, and virtuous, his character is given depth thanks to his vexed relationship with his mother, his ties of affection to the Hakone abbot and to the courtesan Shōshō, and most of all his knowledge that death awaits him as soon as he succeeds in his quest for revenge. In the Soga plays, the rough hero–gentle hero contrast took the form of collaboration between Gorō and his older brother Jūrō in the plot to kill their father's murderer. Danjūrō played Gorō nearly as frequently as he did Fuwa, but his son would play Gorō over fifty times. Several Soga plays represented milestones in Danjūrō's career: in 1688, *The Soga Warriors in Ten Scenes* was described as the "beginning of the first Danjūrō," and in 1697, *The Origin of the Soga Warrior* marked another new beginning for Danjūrō I and his son. In 1700, Danjūrō's Gorō role in *The Hermit Tekkai in Great Japan (Dai Nippon Tekkai Sennin)* was so powerful that it earned him his first critical acclaim as "the best in Edo."[93]

The power-hungry, lecherous priest Narukami was Danjūrō's favorite dark aragoto hero. The story of Narukami was based on an old legend originating in India about an evil priest who uses his magical powers to cause a drought, after being thwarted in his attempt to seize control of the kingdom. But a beautiful woman saves the land

Fig. 13   Danjūrō as Fuwa Banzaemon (left panel, center) confronts Murayama
Shirōjirō as Nagoya Sanza (right panel, hand to hat) in *Sankai Nagoya*. Book
illustration attributed to Torii Kiyonobu and Torii Kiyomasu. 1697. Courtesy of
Tokyo Geijutsu Daigaku.

from famine by seducing him and thus destroying his powers. The
story was known in Japan because of the nō play *The One-Horned
Hermit (Ikkaku Sennin)*. Danjūrō first played the role in 1684,[94] and
likely played it several more times even before the years 1696, 1698,
and 1703, when conclusive evidence shows him doing Narukami
scenes. This was an easily adaptable scene, and Danjūrō worked it
into plays with different heroes and heroines (Figure 14; see also figure 9). Its appeal included a reversal of the usual male-female roles in
a seduction (here, she plies *him* with alcohol), the comic appeal
inherent in a powerful sorcerer's terribly inept behavior in a roman-

18 plays

Fig. 14 Danjūrō's Ōtomo Kuronushi, here seen as the priest Narukami (upper right) gazing in rapture at Ono no Komachi in *The Avatars of the Narita Temple Fudō*. Book illustration attributed to Torii Kiyonobu and Torii Kiyomasu. 1703. Courtesy of Tokyo Geijutsu Daigaku.

tic encounter, and, of course, the satisfaction of seeing a haughty, evil character defeated. Danjūrō's Narukami plays never end with the lady's triumph. The fallen sorcerer always seeks revenge on her, and a deity intervenes in the last act to rescue or redeem the major characters of the play. Danjūrō II's *Narukami, Fudō and the Cherries of the Northern Hills (Narukami Fudō Kitayamazakura)*, performed in 1742 in Osaka, was one of the biggest hits of his career, and the current version of Narukami is by far the most popular Danjūrō I play on today's kabuki stage.

By the mid-1700s an aragoto scene known as "Wait a Moment!" (*Shibaraku*) had become the definitive ritual aragoto routine of the Ichikawa family, performed faithfully every year at kaomise shows by Danjūrōs II, III, IV, V, and VI. Like the Narukami story, "Wait a Moment!" could be adapted to fit many heroes and stories. Danjūrō

I performed his first "Wait a Moment!" scene in 1697, while playing Fuwa Banzaemon. Fuwa shouted, "Wait a moment!" from offstage, in order to prevent a villain from removing a votive tablet from the wall of the Kitano Shrine, then came onstage and got into a long argument with the villain. This shout from offstage came to signify the scene. The actor's immense costume, his formal address to the audience from the hanamichi runway, and the hero's rescue of innocent victims of an evil courtier were all added to the "Wait a Moment!" routine by Danjūrō II. Danjūrō I performed the scene two or three times after 1697, but it never took on the same importance for him that it did for his descendants.

Danjūrō's longest-running performance of a single character was as Benkei in *The Meeting of the Lover Stars in Twelve Scenes (Hoshiai Jūnidan)* which continued "raking in the spectators" for five months beginning early in 1702.[95] No text survives for this play so we can only speculate on its content, but Benkei was the wild and brawny retainer of the gentle, doomed general Yoshitsune. Together they were perhaps the most beloved pair of historical heroes in Japan. This Benkei role earned for Danjūrō the sobriquet of "a one-in-a-thousand actor,"[96] and Danjūrō took advantage of the Benkei craze he had created in the city of Edo by playing "twin Benkeis" with his son Kuzō in the summer of that same year. Danjūrō VII claimed that Danjūrō I's Benkei inspired his creation of the play *The Subscription List (Kanjinchō)* in 1840, now the most popular aragoto play in kabuki.

Between 1697 and 1704 Danjūrō acted in twenty-six plays. In at least sixteen, he played deities or heroes empowered or resurrected by specific deities. He played Fudō more than any other single god or Buddha; between 1694 and 1697 he played Fudō once a year.[97] We know of seven certain Fudō roles that the actor took on over the course of his career, and he probably played Fudō more often than the surviving records can confirm. Danjūrō's gods were wild gods, and until his last Fudō role in 1703 he used scenes of hataraki dance and violent combat with villains to bring his deities to life onstage.

Danjūrō, along with his son who played a twin Fudō, probably remained motionless in this his last Fudō role. "Fudō" literally means the "immovable one," and this Fudō very much resembled a statue in a temple (see figure 12). When Fudō is performed today he almost always remains motionless, whether sitting or standing.

Danjūrō's Playwrighting

We know that Danjūrō was doing at least some work writing plays as early as the mid-1680s, but the twelve illustrated playbooks (e-iri kyōgen-bon) published from 1697 to 1703 are the only texts that remain as testimony to his career as a playwright. These playbooks only approximate what audiences would have heard in the theaters,[98] but plays' plots, acts, scenes, and characters' identities were true to the stage productions on which Danjūrō based his books, and many lines of dialog in the playbooks do read as if they had been first intended for use onstage.

Why did Danjūrō write plays when relatively few other actors did? His primary motive sprang from his well-documented desire to become Edo's premiere actor. In a bid to give himself every possible advantage onstage, he sought to "arm himself with an iron staff" by using fine plays that would display his particular talents. There is no evidence that Danjūrō ever wrote a play in which he did not appear, and he himself took the most important role in every one of his surviving plays.

In the Genroku period, theaters hired playwrights on staff, as they hired actors. When a theater contracted Danjūrō it hired both an actor and a playwright. Once he had achieved fame as an actor, Danjūrō likely made the freedom to write his own plays a condition of employment. We know that he wrote twelve of the last twenty-six plays in which he appeared, but we have no idea who wrote the other fourteen. It is conceivable that he had a hand in all of them. When he was working at the Morita-za, Danjūrō published playbooks under his own name alone, through Shōhonya Shobei of Kobiki-chō, a publisher located near the theater. Kaifuya of Sakai-chō published playbooks deriving from Nakamura-za productions, and these were designated as having been coauthored by Akashi Seizaburō, then staff playwright at the Nakamura-za. The Morita-za and Nakamura-za plays are so alike that scholars consider the coauthored plays to be the product of Danjūrō's creative efforts. Seizaburō likely worked as his assistant and received some financial remuneration for coauthored playbooks.

The wide range of the subject matter handled in Danjūrō's plays attests to the breadth of his knowledge. By 1697 he knew virtually the entire repertory of nō drama and medieval *kōwaka* ballad dramas, all the great medieval historical legends of Japan, moralistic adventure tales *(sekkyō)*, classical Heian-period literature, a selection of Chinese histories and tales, and most of what had been published in contemporary Edo and Kansai kabuki and jōruri. Danjūrō was a consummate "tinkerer," and all this material was grist for his mill as a playwright.

In the decade before the turn of eighteenth century, playwriting was more advanced in the Kansai than in Edo, and Danjūrō learned a great deal about the playwright's craft during his stay in Kyoto.[99] He observed Kansai playwrights beginning to create seasonal traditions in themes and settings for plays, although he never created a strong seasonal character in his own work.[100] He began to emulate Chikamatsu's appropriation for the puppet theater of elements from nō plays, skillfully reworking these same elements as exciting kabuki performances and texts. Most importantly, Danjūrō learned how effective "succession dispute" *(oie sōdō)* stories were for creating frameworks for multi-act, multifaceted kabuki extravaganzas. The action in these stories revolved around rebellions or succession disputes within aristocratic clans. Even though Danjūrō wrote himself into his plays as the main character (or main two characters) of each play, Genroku-period kabuki custom required that about thirty actors be given roles important enough to showcase their talents. In each of his plays Danjūrō had to create all manner of scenes: amorous encounters and betrayals; demonstrations of samurai fidelity, disloyalty, and combat; partings between beloved family members; murders and suicides; and the workings of the gods and Buddhas. Succession dispute stories moved their characters from one setting to another—from country estates to big-city pleasure districts and mountain temples—as virtuous characters fell in and out of love, tracked down traitors, and marshaled steadfast allies, always to emerge vindicated and victorious at the end, often thanks to the help of the supernatural. Whereas Kansai playwrights like Chika-matsu chose to depict more contemporary provincial barons and their families, Danjūrō put an Edo stamp on the succession dispute genre by setting most of his plays in the distant past and by raising the stakes of conflicts to the national or imperial level.

Danjūrō's kabuki plays are long melodramas with convoluted plots punctuated by aragoto combat and scenes of high emotion. To find dramaturgical building-blocks for his plays he often turned to nō drama, an art form completely different from Genroku kabuki. The best nō plays address the serious task of "baring a human soul"[101] using poetry, song, and dance, but Danjūrō lightheartedly appropri-ated the characters and basic situations of nō plays, removed the poetry, music, and solemnity, added new characters and plot compli-cations, introduced spectacular stage effects, and tied his new nō-inspired scenes to others like them, creating long multi-act plays, usually with a succession dispute for a main plot.

His 1703 *The Avatars of the Narita Temple Fudō (Naritasan Funjin Fudō)* is an excellent example of a "nō collage" play. Danjūrō created a story of lust, ambition, betrayal, self-destruction, and redemption by tying together plots and characters from six nō plays.[102] The characters who unified the different threads of the play were two ninth-century poets—the evil courtier Ōtomo Kuronushi and Ono no Komachi, reputedly the most beautiful woman in the history of Japan. One of the original nō plays retells a legend in which Kuronushi, driven by jealousy of Komachi's poetic talents, plots to discredit her at a poetry contest, but in his kabuki play Danjūrō posits that Kuronushi was also obsessed with sexual desire for the beautiful poetess, thereby giving new dimension to the Komachi-Kuronushi relationship. Danjūrō worked Komachi's other famous love affairs into his play, and in Act Three he reversed the identities of pursuer and pursued when he had Kuronushi become the evil priest Narukami, with Komachi as the seductress (see figure 14). Danjūrō closed the play with a scene unconnected to any nō drama, in which twin Fudōs at Narita Temple intervene to save the soul of the dead Kuronushi and restore sanity to Komachi, who has been wandering the wilds of Japan raving mad (see figure 12).

Although Danjūrō rewrote his plays to be published and read, the strength of his illustrated playbooks is theatrical, while their weakness is literary. This is as true of Chikamatsu's illustrated kabuki books as of Danjūrō's, so it is more likely a feature of the genre than a personal characteristic. Neither the narration nor the dialog in these plays creates a sense of individual character behind the specific types that actors were trained to play. The task of creating individual character, if it was to be achieved at all, was left to individual actors to accomplish using their voices, bodies, and imaginations. In his best plays, Danjūrō creates a sense of milieu, using, for example, up-to-date slang expressions of the pleasure district and the fashions and behavior of its denizens to create a sense of "being there."[103] Nevertheless, his evocation of mood and atmosphere never rivaled Chikamatsu's best work.

Where Danjūrō excelled as a playwright was in his plots and dramatic scenes. Traditional sources provided him with well-known leading characters and "historical worlds," but he then fashioned original plots and peopled his stories with large casts of new and original characters. In the terminology of his day this method was called "inventing shukō," where shukō refers to the alteration of traditional plots or the creation of original subplots set in the historical worlds with which audiences were already familiar. One technique was to mix and match characters from different eras and stories to create intriguing new encounters between old, favorite characters. Occasionally Danjūrō took lofty and solemn works from the classical past and poked fun at them mercilessly by populating them with ostensibly historical characters who in fact thought and acted like contemporary Edoites.

The purpose of most of Danjūrō's shukō was to facilitate *miseba*, or scenes in which actors could display their particular talents to good effect. He was especially good at writing his own miseba, but as the excerpt above from *The Origin of the Soga Warrior* shows, he also gave other actors excellent material. The Gorō-Asahina tug-of-war in *The Origin of the Soga Warrior* had been a major success for both Danjūrō and Denkurō, and inspired Danjūrō and other writers to experiment with all sorts of variations on the tug-of-war theme. Danjūrō loved spectacular stage effects, and his most exuberant version of the tug-of-war shukō was that in *A Courtesan's Ōshōkun* (*Keisei Ōshōkun*; 1701), where a virtuous samurai and his wife team up to outwrestle an elephant that a villain has set on them in the hopes that it will trample them to death. Of course, like all commercial writers and producers, Danjūrō unabashedly "borrowed" stage business and shukō invented by other writers if he thought this would make his plays successful.

What distinguished Danjūrō from other playwrights was the degree to which he incorporated his religious convictions into many of his plays. Chikamatsu too wrote any number of plays which made reference to kaichō events in the Kansai; in some, the deity honored at a kaichō intervenes to rescue the hero or heroine, but in others there is only one scene—often a festive dance—set at a kaichō that was to be open to the public throughout the run of the play. But whereas Chikamatsu—and, we assume, his producers as well—were entirely pragmatic and content to profit from the kaichō of various sects, Danjūrō wrote parts only for deities whom he actually worshipped, and he did not limit his onstage demonstrations of the virtue and efficacy of his gods to plays whose scheduling coincided with kaichō events. In one Danjūrō play after another, gods appeared to rescue or empower the heroes.

The Actor as Religious Leader

Danjūrō's first recorded public religious activity was leading a group pilgrimage to Shinshōji Temple in Narita after *The Origin of the Soga Warrior* had closed in 1697, but two years earlier the saving power of his onstage Fudō had apparently been inspirational: "All at once many Edoites set out on a pilgrimage to Narita Temple to entrust their destinies to Fudō."[104] Visitors from out of town increased, and by the end of the century it was clear that the existing facilities of Narita Temple were too small to serve the increasing number of worshippers. While audiences responded positively to Danjūrō's onstage deities, the sophisticated Kansai critics were not so easily won over. In *A Fistful of Actors (Yarō Nigiri Kobushi)* one author wrote in a sarcastic vein:

> He has tied together all his arts with Fudō's rope, and dispels poverty, illness, and calamity, purifying all with his demon-quelling sword. One has to say he is a rare and efficacious actor and we must be ever thankful for his long monologs, which serve as protective talismans from his friends in the critics' ranks.[105]

In a more down-to-earth style the same hyōbanki noted, "He has been gaining a lot of acclaim among the masses for playing gods, but wise men don't like his presumption."[106] Danjūrō's religious beliefs probably *were* like personal talismans that inured him to the critics. His deities had helped him survive too many vicissitudes of chance and fortune for the biting words of a few intellectuals to change what he did onstage, and cynical references to his religious kabuki disappear from the hyōbanki after his triumph in *The Origin of the Soga Warrior.*

The Origin of the Soga Warrior had a powerful effect on the imaginations of actors, playwrights, producers, and kabuki fans. The Soga Gorō–Fudō connection was so firmly established by Danjūrō that it soon entered the Soga world to stay. Numerous plays, even those that did not employ actors from the Ichikawa family, were written to include Gorō-Fudō scenes,[107] and after the year 1697, Edo-period fiction, as well as religious and secular paintings, include scenes of Gorō worshipping Fudō, or of Fudō coming to Gorō's aid.

No records survive from between 1697 and 1703 to indicate whether Danjūrō continued to lead public pilgrimages or any other form of public worship, but he did keep putting his deities onstage for all Edoites to see. It is clear that in Danjūrō's holistic world, his theatrical celebration of the gods was a form of worship and thanksgiving for the blessings bestowed upon him. He sent a powerful two-tiered proselytizing message to his audiences: first, he showed deities onstage rescuing and empowering great heroes of Japan's historical and legendary past, and second, as a "celebrity believer," he demonstrated the gods' efficacy by example, simply by being rich, famous, and eminently successful. British anthropologist Mary Douglas has shown that in societies marked by intense social and economic competition and in which religious believers enter into contractual relationships with their deities, people idolize and follow "great men" who, through their own power and that of their gods, are able to amass wealth and stature.[108] By 1700 Danjūrō was fabulously wealthy, with a salary approaching 1,000 ryō—he was living proof that Fudō "delivered the goods."

In 1700 a new and energetic abbot, Shōhan I, came to Shinshōji Temple from the Kansai. He began to add new buildings to the temple soon after his arrival, and a new main hall was completed by the third month of 1701. That same month, Danjūrō opened a play at the Nakamura-za in which he played a character who was an apparition of Fudō. The timing was hardly coincidental. One twentieth-century Shinshōji historian believes that there was a secret but very close relationship between Shōhan and Danjūrō.[109] This relationship was strongly suggested by the events surrounding Danjūrō's first and last kaichō play. Kaichō in Edo generally ran for two months at two or three Edo temples that were in the business of sponsoring kaichō for out-of-town temples. These festive events raised large sums of money for the sponsoring temples, and could also be effective prose-lytizing tools. By 1700 there was a two-year waiting list for the provincial temples that wished to use Edo kaichō sites. Shōhan scheduled the first-ever Shinshōji kaichō in Edo for the spring of 1703, and Danjūrō scheduled a major Fudō play—*The Avatars of the Fudō of Narita Temple*—to coincide with it. Danjūrō's son Kuzō played Kūkai, the founding saint of Japan's Shingon sect, and in the concluding scene Danjūrō and Kuzō played two Fudō statues that come to life to restore sanity to the mad heroine Ono no Komachi and redeem the tortured spirit of the play's dark hero. Many in the audience threw offerings onto the stage and directed their own prayers to Fudō during this scene. The text of the concluding scene contains narration derived directly from Shingon theology, material that the Shinshōji historian believes no kabuki actor could have had at his command. He suggests that Danjūrō and Shōhan worked in close collaboration on the kaichō–kabuki play project, and that Shōhan himself wrote these lines of the play for Danjūrō.[110] During the kaichō, when Danjūrō's stage duties permitted, he spent time at the kaichō site, working as a *torimochi*, or a kind of lay assistant who greeted worshippers and provided various forms of assistance to the temple authorities. Danjūrō's presence at the kaichō would certainly have increased attendance at the temple event. One surviving diary by an Edo commoner shows that teamwork by celebrities and tem-ples did have the desired effect—the diarist wrote that he was going to take up worship of Fudō precisely because Danjūrō recommended it and because he had seen Danjūrō at the Shinshōji kaichō.[111]

Succeeding generations of Danjūrōs worked to maintain this close link to Shinshōji, to the mutual benefit of their family and the temple. In 1821 Danjūrō VII made the single largest family contribu-tion to the temple, a building to display votive plaques, that cost 1000 ryō to build. Votive plaques, called *ema*, were painted by lead-ing ukiyo-e artists, and ema halls became the first public art galleries in Japan. Just a few years after this generous donation the temple

Fig. 15 The gate to Narita Temple. (Narita-san is the nickname by which the temple Shinshōji is commonly referred.) Photograph by the author.

was able to return the favor by providing Danjūrō VII with sanctuary for one year after he had been banished from Edo for violation of sumptuary laws. The Edo samurai government ranked kabuki actors just above the pariah class and it was clearly galling to the leadership elite that lowlife characters like the Danjūrōs not only lived lives of wealth and luxury but also acted as religious leaders and were heroes to so many citizens. But the dim view of kabuki actors by the authorities never seemed to trouble the temple at all. Over the years Shinshōji continued to grow, and it is now one of the three biggest temples in the Tokyo area (Figure 15). It had over half a million visitors on New Year's Day in 1993, the third largest number in the region. Statues and memorial markers to several Danjūrōs can be found on the temple grounds (although an arsonist burned down the Danjūrō VII hall in 1965), and the temple museum holdings include beautiful ukiyo-e votive plaques depicting Danjūrō VII, Danjūrō VIII, and other kabuki actors onstage.

Rivalry with Shichisaburō and a New Tenderness Onstage

In a 1696 entry in his diary Danjūrō wrote that fellow actor Naka-mura Shichisaburō was "upholding the prestige of his house, and is an actor with the same stature as a theater producer."[112] Shichisaburō was not only related to Nakamura Kanzaburō, the producer for the Nakamura-za, which was Edo's oldest and most prestigious theater, but was himself bringing honor to Edo kabuki's elite theater family. This is the highest praise bestowed on another actor to be found anywhere in Danjūrō's diary. Danjūrō continued this entry, writing that he too intended to give banner service to his theater and his family and to strive for success, as Shichisaburō was doing. This diary entry was a statement of respect for the man whom he must have sensed would become his main rival in Edo, and a personal commitment to compete with him.

Shichisaburō was two years younger than Danjūrō and had been working for years at developing his young lover roles. He had played Nagoya to Danjūrō's Fuwa in *The Dispute over the Courtesan*, which was Danjūrō's first Fuwa Banzaemon play, and the two made an excellent wild hero–gentle hero team. 1696 was the last year that they worked together onstage, and in the fall of 1697 Shichisaburō went to Kyoto where he competed fiercely with Tōjūrō in the 1697–1698 season. After a dismal first two plays in Kyoto, Shichi-saburō wrote and starred in *The Courtesan and the Peak of Asama (Keisei Asama ga Take)*. The play ran for half a year, solidly outdraw-ing Tōjūrō's Mandayū-za shows. *The Peak of Asama* became the most influential and widely emulated play of the Genroku period, and Shichisaburō's success in Kyoto lifted him to the level of Tōjūrō in the estimation of the Kansai literati who wrote the hyōbanki. Shichisaburō's Kyoto triumph had far surpassed Danjūrō's because Shichisaburō had beaten the great Tōjūrō at his own game, using the acting style critics respected most, while competing directly with the local hero. With his return to Edo, Shichisaburō jumped to the top of the actor ratings, where he stayed until Danjūrō managed to oust him briefly in 1701. After that point they fought nip and tuck for the distinction of "best in Edo." Danjūrō usually outdrew his rival and he did command the higher salary, but hyōbanki critics preferred Shichisaburō's acting style and the characters he played. Shichisaburō was by all accounts a fine actor.

Shichisaburō's success in the hyōbanki forced Danjūrō to recognize the importance of mastery of a diverse repertory of acting skills. Danjūrō had begun his career playing both martial heroes and amorous young men, but in the middle of his career had narrowed his focus to perfecting the aragoto style. He sometimes played scenes in other styles, but until 1700 the hyōbanki were nearly always critical of his work in these scenes. After Shichisaburō returned from Kyoto in 1699, the hyōbanki justified rating him higher than Danjūrō on the basis of Shichisaburō's wider range of skills and Danjūrō's weakness in subtler scenes that required displays of tenderness. Shichisaburō never attempted to emulate Danjūrō's aragoto, but he did play every other sort of masculine hero and perform in every other style. Danjūrō was a competitive man, and not about to concede supremacy to Shichisaburō in all the male role types other than aragoto. Beginning late in 1699, he began to devote serious attention to broadening his skills as an actor, and the hyōbanki indicate that he was successful in his efforts.

Danjūrō wrote into his plays roles that would require him to do the sorts of scenes at which Tōjūrō and Shichisaburō excelled. In his 1699 kaomise play, Danjūrō's aragoto hero disguised himself as a scrap metal merchant and pretended to be a commoner, and in his 1701 kaomise, his Fuwa Banzaemon did a serious, realistic scene in which he had to dress Kazuraki's near-fatal stab wounds.[113] Danjūrō's most difficult challenge lay in the arts that in a few decades would be grouped together and called wagoto: expressions of love, lovers' quarrels, lovers in disguise, and grief over lost loves or family members. In the tradition of Tōjūrō, an actor had to strive to be either convincing enough to elicit empathy or even tears, or witty enough to make people laugh at a character's predicament. Hyōbanki entries from 1701 and later years suggest that Danjūrō had begun to do well as a "realistic" actor. In 1701 *A Huge Freighter Filled with Actors (Yakusha Mangokubune)* rated Danjūrō ahead of Shichisaburō, partly because his face displayed more conviction in love scenes.*[114] The same hyōbanki recognized the challenges that Danjūrō needed to overcome when he sought to portray emotions effectively while playing his traditional historical aragoto heroes:

> Danjūrō got himself in trouble in *Kimpira's Visits to the Sixth Avenue Pleasure District (Kimpira Rokujō Gayoi)*. This was the first time that someone tried having a rough warrior like Kimpira go to Sixth Avenue to procure a courtesan. It would be inappropriate for a warrior to swagger into a brothel and shout out his self-introduction, but a weak-kneed greeting would not be pleasant to watch either. Too strong-willed a character prominently displayed would have seemed wild, and would not be right for a love scene. But playing it very gently would also fail, since this would not seem to suggest a hot-blooded young warrior.
>
> No matter what approach he used, the scene was bound to be difficult.[115]

Danjūrō continued to struggle with the challenge of fusing the martial fighter and the erotic paragon, and it would be another twelve years before a successful character of this kind would emerge to pack the kabuki theaters—with Danjūrō II's romantic swashbuckling version of the hero Sukeroku.

In 1703 Danjūrō I received lavish praise for an utterly convincing depiction of a groveling, low-ranking samurai bent by sorrow and despair,[116] and by 1704 the hyōbanki were giving Danjūrō his due as a "realistic" actor capable of arousing empathy:

> When he pulled off his tabi socks and threw them at his wife and ran around weeping, his voice, his movements,

and the expression in his eyes were just perfect. This scene showed real physical preparation. Not to mention the intensity of his expression when he looked up at Kashiwagi no Emon.

He lost consciousness, and when he regained it his facial expression of joy at simply being alive seemed so real that it must have come from his heart. His suicide in the finale was excellent, and tore at the spectators' hearts.

In sections where he played the lead, the performance was excellent in every instance, but this is only what we would expect of this master, unparalleled in ages present or past.[117]

This praise is couched in the same terms that critics often used to describe Tōjūrō and, with these triumphs in realistic and emotional scenes, Danjūrō was well on his way to becoming the unchallenged master of Edo kabuki.

Murder in the Theater

In the glory years between 1697 and 1704 Danjūrō suffered a family tragedy, the sudden death in 1700, after an illness, of his eleven-year-old second son Senya. The boy had made his stage debut in 1698 playing a samurai child and was working onstage at the Morita-za when he died. No record of the family's grief survives. Throughout those same years Danjūrō's first son Kuzō was gathering acclaim as a promising young actor and a tribute to the excellence of his father's training.

Genroku-period hyōbanki focused almost all their attention on evaluation of actors' work onstage. Only in later decades would gossip about the actors' private lives become equally important to theater critics and the public. Nevertheless, critics did occasionally attempt to evaluate actors as men, and throughout Danjūrō's career, opinions fluctuated wildly on the subject of his own character. He was clearly a very complex man, as the following 1703 hyōbanki entry hints.

> He is not just a talented performer, but is loved and respected by the public. However, some say that with his masculine style he struts about and brags too much. They say they would like him to be as gentle as Shichisaburō, but this is absolutely foolish. He has the face of Aizen and the eyes of Fudō, which means that he crushes villains and mercifully leads the multitudes to salvation. It is safe to assume that gentleness resides in him.[118]

Pride, ambition, hauteur, devotion to his gods, and solicitude toward his family were all parts of his personality, but Danjūrō himself recognized another, potentially dangerous, component of his character: his anger. In 1696 he wrote, "While I am working, if things should anger me, I will talk them over with the company producer ... If I plan to live to a ripe old age I had better not lose my temper."[119]

With all his experience as an aragoto actor, Danjūrō was probably capable of being very frightening indeed when he lost his temper, but we really have no idea if it was a rage, an insult, or some other sort of problem altogether that led to his untimely death. On the nineteenth day of the second month in 1704, the Ichimura-za company was eight days into the second play of the year and Danjūrō was playing two roles—a Kurama Temple priest and Yoshitune's loyal retainer Sato Tsuginobu. That day, there in the theater, he was stabbed to death by fellow actor Ikushima Hanroku (?–1704). Hanroku was apprehended the same day and died a few months later during an interrogation. Hanroku received a guilty verdict posthumously, but the details of the crime and of Hanroku's motives remain a mystery today. Numerous contradictory accounts survive from right after the murder. One description of the crime says that Hanroku hid himself in the folds of the stage curtain and stabbed Danjūrō with a metal sword when Danjūrō came offstage dressed in his priest's garb and armed with only a wooden stage sword.[120] The most dramatic contemporary explanation of Hanroku's motive runs as follows: Hanroku's son Zenjirō was taking acting lessons from Danjūrō at the time, and Danjūrō criticized Hanroku for excessive debauchery with young actors in front of Zenjirō and the other young actors. This public criticism so angered Hanroku that he murdered Danjūrō.[121] This sounds true to form for Danjūrō, but there are other motives that are equally plausible and equally unconfirmable.[122]

No matter what the motive for the crime, when Danjūrō died in 1704 it was as if thousands of Edoites had lost a family elder. The last hyōbanki to evaluate Danjūrō was *Three Saké Cups for Millionaires (Daijin Mitsu Sakazuki)*, probably by Ejima Kiseki (1667–1736), Kyoto's leading fiction writer and an active supporter of Tōjūrō. Kiseki's last sentence on Danjūrō reads: "For a long time I have known that all men must take this road, but for this to happen now … The deities we rely on should be impervious to harm. From now on, whenever I pray to the Narita Fudō, it will be Danjūrō that I see."[123] In the same hyōbanki the characters for Ikushima Hanroku were cut from the woodblock, leaving as a last statement only his mediocre rating, eighteenth of the twenty-two tachiyaku working in Edo.[124] It is significant that Ejima, a sophisticated Kyoto intellectual, chose for his final testament words that affirmed Danjūrō's association with Fudō and, in gracious tribute to Edoites' belief in that special relationship, suggested that he himself had become a worshipper of the Narita Fudō.

Triumphs and Tragedies of the Danjūrō Line

After a month of mourning and a pilgrimage to the temple in Narita, twenty-four-year-old Ichikawa Kuzō declared himself Danjūrō II and resumed his acting career. Danjūrō II (1688–1758) was blessed with his father's ambition and drive, and came into his own as a major actor within a decade of his father's death. He had experimented for

several years with playing gentle, amorous men in addition to aragoto roles, and in 1713 he played his first Sukeroku, a character combining the romantic appeal of the Tōjūrō/Shichisaburō–style
wagoto hero and the martial skills and bravado of his father's aragoto
heroes (Figure 16).[125] Sukeroku would remain a perennial favorite on
the Edo stage, but Danjūrō II also made important innovations in
costuming and makeup for "pure" aragoto roles. His most notable
invention was suji kuma, or striped makeup (Figure 17). This was so
popular that it replaced the solid red coloring his father had favored,
and suji kuma (also called *kumadori*)[126] became the best-recognized
signifier of kabuki.

Danjūrō II assured the popularity of Ichikawa-style aragoto acting by linking his stage art to emerging seasonal rituals in Edo
kabuki. He established the "Wait a Moment!" scene as a regular feature of his kaomise programs, increasing the spectacle and weight of
the scene with spectacular costuming, makeup, and accoutrements.
In 1709 all the kabuki theaters in Edo staged plays on the theme of
the Soga brothers' revenge as their first of the new year, and attendance was so good that they continued this custom and it became a
yearly ritual, surviving until the turn of the twentieth century.
Regardless of which theater had hired Danjūrō II in a given year, in
that first play (*haru kyōgen*) he always took the part of Soga Gorō,
the wilder of the two brothers. Danjūrō II played Gorō over fifty
times, more often than any other single character. Perhaps his best
Gorō role is in a play called *The Arrow Sharpener* (*Ya no Ne*; 1729;
see Figure 17),[127] in which Gorō celebrates the New Year holiday
with many of the same rituals that Edo townsmen observed in the
1720s. Danjūrō II's appeal was such that by the mid-eighteenth century the people of Edo could hardly imagine a kaomise without
"Wait a Moment!" or a New Year without a rambunctious Gorō in
Soga kabuki.

Edo kabuki invented a prestigious position of authority for its
top tachiyaku actors, the *zagashira*, or "company leader." At each
theater the zagashira received the highest tachiyaku salary (the top

Fig. 16 Danjūrō II as Sukeroku in 1749. *Hosoban urushi-e* by Okumura Masanobu. Courtesy of Tokyo National Museum.

onnagata often made as much or more) and he joined with the theater producer in making hiring and casting decisions and in supervising the work of the staff playwrights. The role of the zagashira was similar to that of the zamoto (play producer) in the Kansai, with the important distinction that the zagashira did not share in a theater's

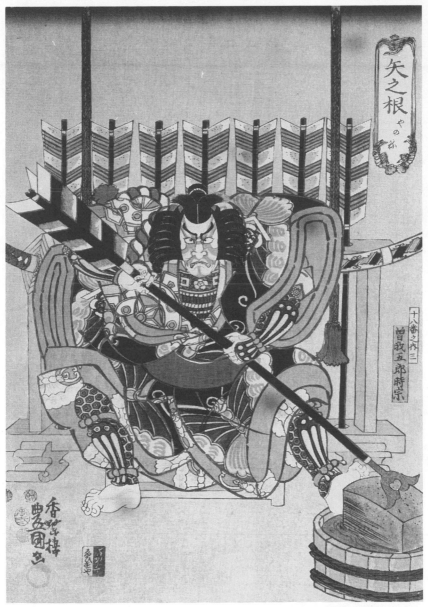

Fig. 17 Danjūrō VII as Soga Gorō in *Ya no Ne*. This 1852 *nishiki-e* by Utagawa Toyokuni III is an excellent example of *suji kuma* makeup. Courtesy of The Theatre Museum of Waseda University.

profits. The zagashira position ensured its holder the freedom to work with chosen colleagues and to have playwrights adapt scripts to suit his own strengths as an actor. Danjūrō II and his successors would dominate Edo kabuki by holding zagashira posts throughout their careers, and by training large numbers of young actors, the most talented of whom would also go on to become zagashira.

Danjūrō II was the great eminence of Edo kabuki for almost half a century, but his family's future was precarious because he had only daughters and no legitimate sons. He adopted the promising son of a disciple as his successor, and in 1735 passed his name on to the four-teen-year-old boy. Danjūrō II then used his father's childhood name, Ebizō, for the remainder of his career. His greatest triumph came during the single year he spent away from Edo: in Osaka in 1742 he was paid the unprecedented salary of 2,000 ryō for one season's work. But just at the moment of this triumph, his chosen successor, Danjūrō III (1721–1742) succumbed to an illness. Fate continued, in the coming generations, to be capricious in its dealings with the Ichikawa family. Right through the 1960s the glory, wealth, and fame of the Danjūrōs have too often been cut short by untimely deaths. Danjūrō V lost both his sons, including twenty-one-year-old Danjūrō VI, to ill-ness, Danjūrō VIII committed suicide at age thirty-two, and Danjūrō XI died just three years after succeeding to the Danjūrō name.

Danjūrōs I and II left their descendants a legacy of popular roles and a dynamic acting style that they hoped would assure their fam-ily's prosperity. Beginning with Danjūrō II, the Ichikawa family jeal-ously guarded its exclusive right to perform the best aragoto plays, scenes, and roles, including Narukami, "Wait a Moment!", *The Arrow Sharpener,* and *Sukeroku.* Danjūrō IV (1711–1778), who may have been the illegitimate son of Danjūrō II, got his start playing vil-lains, and later turned back to the dark heroes that Danjūrō I had done so well. He added *Kagekiyo's Jailbreak (Rōyaburi Kagekiyo)* to the list of "patented" Ichikawa family plays.

By the 1760s kabuki audiences favored actors who could skill-fully play various different kinds of parts in a single play. These versatile and virtuoso actors were called *kaneru yakusha* (multitalented actors) and Danjūrō V (1741–1806) was a brilliant example. During his career he played more different roles than had any previous Danjūrō, and he was the first since Danjūrō I to play a woman character while using the Danjūrō name. Danjūrō V made "Wait a Moment!" his signature aragoto role, but he did not perform the other family classics very often, and he relaxed the Ichikawa monopoly on aragoto plays, confident that he could compete on his own merits with other leading men, in any sort of tachiyaku role.*128 Danjūrō V dominated the Edo stage from the late 1770s through the 1790s and he was also a poet of repute who surrounded himself with a coterie of poets, novelists, and artists—men who became staunch supporters of Danjūrō's aragoto kabuki and the Ichikawa family heritage.

During the early 1800s many talented tachiyaku appeared on the Edo stage, threatening to outshine the young Danjūrō VII (1791–1859) and bring to an end a century of Danjūrō dominance. The literary elite who had been close friends of Danjūrō V's advised the new Danjūrō to return to family traditions, and wrote kabuki's first histories and biographies, in which they celebrated the Danjūrōs' aragoto legacy as kabuki's grandest tradition. Onstage the legacy took the form of the newly-designated "Eighteen Great Plays" (1832), all aragoto classics performed originally by the first two Danjūrōs. Danjūrō VII was by then Edo's leading actor, and he made a great contribution to kabuki in 1840 when he presented kabuki's first *mat-* *subammemono*, a dance drama based on and staged much like the nō. This was *The Subscription List (Kanjinchō)*, now the most popular aragoto play of all. Danjūrō VII's brilliant Edo career was cut short in 1842 when the government banished him from the city for infraction of sumptuary laws. He had lived very extravagantly offstage, and his stage productions were more lavish than anything yet seen in kabuki. The government was particularly angry that he used onstage real samurai weapons and armor that had been donated to or lent him by wealthy warrior families. The banishment lasted ten years, but it did not faze the great actor. Danjūrō VII had always enjoyed traveling and he spent most of the decade in Osaka, where audiences loved him.

The exile of Danjūrō VII also gave his son, Danjūrō VIII (1829–1854) the opportunity to blossom outside his father's shadow. The slender, delicate Danjūrō VIII avoided his family's usual aragoto roles, preferring to play gentle, amorous heroes, and he quickly became the most beloved actor in Edo. His career was cut short in 1854 by his unexplained suicide in Osaka.

Dedication to the Fudō of Narita Temple linked the lives and careers of the men of the Ichikawa line. All served as publicists and proselytizers, performing in plays that testified to the efficacy of the worship of Fudō and other tantric deities. All served the temple in the public eye at kaichō events and donated money and works of art to the temple. Many led pilgrimages to Narita, and some influenced their fellow actors to become Shingon believers and patrons of Shinshōji. In times of crisis, various Danjūrōs turned to the temple, or to Fudō, for succor, and the record shows that it was often provided.

Danjūrō IX (1838–1903) was the fifth son of Danjūrō VII, and he dominated the kabuki world in the Meiji period (1868–1912), when Japan emerged from its self-imposed isolation and began its drive to modernize and to refashion itself into an economic and military power. Danjūrō IX brought kabuki into the modern era by introducing historical accuracy into plays and by campaigning to make the theater a truly national, classical theater that would gain the support of the ruling elite—the same group that had opposed kabuki for three hundred years, beginning when Okuni first danced on the riverbank in Kyoto.

The turn of the twentieth century was a difficult time for the art. Kabuki actor activists were challenging the long-standing internal hierarchies that were based in feudal values, and they were constantly winning greater freedom and power. Kabuki was losing audiences in the competition with film and more modern dramatic forms. At this juncture an up-and-coming entertainment corporation from Kyoto called Shōchiku emerged on the scene and, by buying up large theaters across Japan, gained control of kabuki productions (Shōchiku is now known primarily as one of Japan's largest filmmaking corporations, but it also produces almost all kabuki performances). Shōchiku enjoined leading actors like Danjūrō IX to reassert their authority over the rank-and-file actors and to shorten the length of kabuki shows and arrange programs so that the most dramatic scenes from a variety of classical plays could be shown. Thanks to the alliance with Shōchiku, by the early twentieth century Danjūrō IX's goal of turning kabuki into Japan's national, classical theater had largely been achieved.

The irony of Danjūrō IX's success is that while he solidified kabuki and helped it become a durable classical art, his failure to produce an heir brought an end to the two centuries of domination of Edo and Tokyo kabuki by the Ichikawa family. For more than half a century, between 1903 and 1962, kabuki flourished without a Danjūrō. In the postwar period, Tokyo theater fans began to feel this absence keenly, and the line was restored, but Danjūrō XI (1909–1965) used his prestigious name for only three years before his death, and his son is now just one of many top kabuki stars. The Danjūrōs' dominance of Tokyo kabuki ended in the twentieth century, but the family's artistic legacy continues to thrive. Aragoto acting still thrills audiences, no matter who the actor performing it may be. And the name Ichikawa Danjūrō still signifies kabuki superheroes to the Japanese.

3

SAKATA TŌJŪRŌ
Kabuki's First True Actor

A Thinking Man's Hero and a "Heartthrob" for the Ladies

Two remarkable acts performed by a writer and a lovelorn widow in memory of Sakata Tōjūrō (1647–1709) illustrate what an enigma was this signature actor of Genroku-period Kansai. His most influential supporter, Ejima Kiseki, the leading fiction writer and kabuki critic in Japan, wrote a book-length tribute to Tōjūrō within months of the actor's death. This was the first full-length elegy for a kabuki actor ever written. Ejima had admired Tōjūrō's acting for its intelligence, its realism, and its subtlety, but in his book, *The Character of a Stylish Actor (Kankatsu Yakusha no Katagi)*, Ejima also wrote that "the women and children of Osaka and Kyoto wept when Tōjūrō passed away."[1] Ejima was proud that multitudes of fans—and not just the coterie of kabuki critics who had waxed poetic over him—loved Tōjūrō.

For women spectators, Tōjūrō was kabuki's first "romantic heart-throb." He attracted women to the theater in record numbers, and if the hyōbanki are to be trusted, waves of amorous desire flowed from the ladies' seats to the stage whenever Tōjūrō was at work. *The Character of a Stylish Actor* tells of Tōjūrō's most devoted woman fan, a well-to-do young widow in Kyoto who had been an avid follower of his work.[2] She met him personally just once, and afterward commissioned a sculptor to make a doll in his likeness, which she installed in the Buddhist altar in her home during the day and slept with every night for eight years, until Tōjūrō died. After Tōjūrō's death she went public with her obsession, carrying her doll with her on trips to Ryōanji Temple and attracting flocks of women there to witness the effects of an unrequited love that had driven a fellow admirer to the verge of insanity.[3]

Tōjūrō's appeal to such disparate audiences as Kyoto's male cultural elite and lovelorn middle-class women attests to the breadth of his art. But it must also be noted that Ejima's sense of loss and the outpouring of grief from his colleagues and fans may have been intensified by admirers' awareness that Tōjūrō had left no successor behind to mourn his passing. Acclaimed as one of the great actors and zamoto (play producers) of his era, Tōjūrō never built a family line that could carry his art into the future. This was an anomaly in Genroku kabuki, but there are also signs that this was the way Tōjūrō had wanted it to be.

A Long Apprenticeship: Studying in the Wings

Tōjūrō was the only one of the three pioneering Genroku-period actors who was born to a life in the theater. His father was a tachiyaku actor, skilled and respected enough to have worked as a zamoto in Kyoto.[4] Tōjūrō was born in 1647, eight years before the national ban on boys' kabuki, and he began his apprenticeship during the confusing transition to a new form of kabuki. Children preparing for work on the kabuki stage began (as they still do today) by training in dance and music. Tōjūrō's first teacher of record was a musician, a virtuoso nō shoulder-drum (*ko-tsuzumi*) player named Honeya Shozaemon. It is not surprising that a young actor in the

making would study the shoulder-drum, since learning this instru-
ment helps to improve one's sense of rhythm and timing, which is
indispensible to the dance. In the 1650s and 1660s, dance was the
most important skill that kabuki actors could bring to the stage.
Shozaemon evidently taught Tōjūrō more about performance than
just drum playing: *The Actors' Analects* states that Tōjūrō remained
close to Shozaemon for many years, and suggests that Shozaemon
taught his young charge to be strict with himself about the difference between performing in order to win acclaim and performing
with real integrity.[5] Tōjūrō learned from this teacher's example that
"a great man's art resides in doing what he thinks is right, without
any concern for whether the audience likes it or not."[6] Tōjūrō's sense
of dignity and his insistence that kabuki actors take their work seriously may have derived in part from his early exposure to nō drama
through this teacher.

   History records only one kabuki actor's having served as a mentor to Tōjūrō. This was Sugi Kuhe (fl. ca. 1670–1680), who had formerly specialized in young women's roles and then gone on to found
the speciality in the roles of old women known as *kashagata*.[7] Kuhe's
advice to the twenty-year-old Tōjūrō is one of *The Actors' Analects'*
most famous passages:

> Since I am a kashagata, I have worked hard at imitating
> women. You are a tachiyaku, so you must imitate men.
> When one observes present-day tachiyaku actors, few
> really seem like men. They were never onnagata, so there
> is no reason at all for their lack of masculinity. You must
> work as hard as you can at imitating men![8]

Kuhe is said to have delivered these words of wisdom in 1665, when
wakashu and onnagata roles dominated kabuki. Tachiyaku were
working in kabuki, but were strongly influenced by wakashu, whose
androgynous fashions, carefully crafted youthfulness, and erotic
appeal were directed more toward men than women. When Kuhe

suggested working hard at imitating men, he was in effect advising Tōjūrō to create a male lead with heterosexual appeal.

Kabuki's first great tachiyaku was Arashi San'emon I (1635–1690) of Osaka, who dominated the Kansai stage in the 1670s and did pioneering work in both romantic acting and the creation of strong, martial heroes. There is no evidence to suggest that as a young man Tōjūrō ever studied under San'emon. Tōjūrō worked for a long time as a minor actor; he would not get his first "big break" until he was thirty-two years old. During his lean years, Tōjūrō survived on a salary of about 35 ryō a year, and would have been hard put to purchase all the costumes he needed for his work onstage. Tōjūrō apparently supplemented his income by dancing at wealthy merchants' parties.[9]

Hyōbanki make no reference to Tōjūrō until 1675, when he was twenty-eight. He was working then in San'emon's company at the Miyako Mandayū Theater in Kyoto, and his style was described as "one step ahead" and "masculine, like an older brother."[10] It would seem Tōjūrō had taken Kuhe's advice to heart, and had endeavored during the previous ten years to create a convincing masculine style.[11]

In 1676 Tōjūrō was at a different theater in Kyoto, where he played one of a duo of romantic young samurai in a rudimentary succession dispute play. Yamashita Hanzaemon played the other male lead, and the two men were described as "glittering young actors."[12] It is likely that Tōjūrō met Chikamatsu Monzaemon during these years in Kyoto. Chikamatsu's first work in theater was as an apprentice playwright at the Miyako Mandayū-za in 1677. At the time playwrights also served as set designers, and Chikamatsu created a special stage effect in which wisteria flowers were transformed into a huge serpent. It was so spectacular that it had audiences shouting Chikamatsu's name.[13] Chikamatsu and Tōjūrō were still just starting their careers, but a few decades later they would team up to dominate kabuki in the Kansai.

A Hit Play and a One-Style Actor

Tōjūrō returned to Osaka late in 1677. Six days into the new year, the most popular and sought-after courtesan of Osaka's Shinmachi pleasure district died following an illness, while she was at the height of her beauty and charm. The unexpected death of Yūgiri of the Ōgiya brothel had an impact on Osaka akin to the impact of Marilyn Monroe's death in the United States. Less than a month later, Tōjūrō was onstage as Yūgiri's fictional lover, Fujiya Izaemon, in *Yūgiri's Last New Year (Yūgiri Nagori no Shōgatsu)*, and this was the play that set the actor on the path to fortune and fame. Tōjūrō played the same role in the same play four times that year, with additional runs that began in the sixth, tenth, and twelfth months of 1678. Tōjūrō's zamoto, Kaneko Rokuemon (dates uncertain), made so much money from the gate receipts that in an onstage speech he announced his plan to take a one-year vacation from theater work the following season, and noted that if he wished to, he could afford to take three full years off. It was typical of an Osakan not to feel any constraint about letting the world know just how successful his business ventures had been.

Yūgiri's Last New Year had an immediate impact on all the Kansai theaters. Traveling theater troupes were staging their own versions of the play by the autumn of 1678, and a rival Osaka kabuki theater did a memorial Yūgiri play in the first month of 1679. Yūgiri and Izaemon appeared regularly on the kabuki stage for the next three decades, but no one capitalized on Yūgiri plays as heavily as did Tōjūrō, who played Izaemon in eighteen different plays over the course of his career.[14]

We know frustratingly little about *Yūgiri's Last New Year*, including who wrote it, what was contained in the text, or even which theater presented it. The zamoto surely had a strong say in selecting the play's theme and in casting the work, and the strategy of "cashing in on" the tragic death of a celebrity proved a stroke of genius. Thirty-five years later Chikamatsu used the main scene of the play virtually intact in a puppet play that memorialized the pair of fictional lovers, so we do know something of the action of the play that launched Tōjūrō's career.[15]

Fujiya Izaemon begins the play as Yūgiri's customer, but the two fall deeply in love, with a love that goes far beyond what is proper or safe for either of them as patron and courtesan. She bears Izaemon a child. He squanders so much of his parents' money that he is disowned. He then wanders about under the cold winter skies, dressed only in a paper kimono.

Although he is deeply in debt and too poor to afford trips to the pleasure district, he remains ever the generous, spendthrift millionaire's son.

On New Year's Eve he longs for Yūgiri and wanders about the Shinmachi pleasure district. The master of the expensive Yoshidaya teahouse generously allows him inside. Yūgiri has been ill with worry since Izaemon's split from his family. But she has finally recovered somewhat, and happens to be at the Yoshidaya that evening. The master tells Izaemon that he will bring the two together, and tells Izaemon to wait in an empty room.

Izaemon is so happy he cannot sit still. He cannot wait to see Yūgiri, and peeps into the adjacent room, where she is entertaining a samurai guest. Suddenly Izaemon is overcome with jealousy. He becomes angry and full of self-pity, wondering why he ever lavished so much money on and ruined himself for such a woman.

When at last Yūgiri arrives, he heaps abuse on her, and the two engage in a lovers' quarrel.[16]

This exchange would have had special poignancy for audiences in 1678, whose memories of the actual Yūgiri were still fresh, and who knew that just a week after the bitter New Year's quarrel Yūgiri would be dead.

This scene was part of the keisei-kai ("procuring a courtesan") kabuki tradition pioneered by the female founder of the art, Okuni, who had taken the role of the male customer. It is evident that the celebrity status of the characters depicted onstage was part of the appeal of keisei-kai from the very beginning of kabuki. Keisei-kai scenes could incorporate various interactions between characters and a range of acting styles. In *Yūgiri's Last New Year*, Tōjūrō showed his skill in at least two thespian arts: "the lovers' quarrel" (*kuzetsugoto*) at the end of the scene described above, and the "lamentations" (*ureigoto*) that took place later in the play.

A disowned, formerly wealthy young spendthrift forced to travel incognito was a stock character known as a *yatsushi*, or romantic lover in disguise (Figure 18). San'emon I invented the yatsushi role, but Tōjūrō later became its acknowledged master. Yatsushi scenes soon became essential to Tōjūrō's portrayal of young lovers. They enabled him to show the depth of a character's feelings for a courtesan by demonstrating his willingness to suffer for love. Forcing a for-

Fig. 18 An illustration showing Tōjūrō in one of his yatsushi (disguised lover) roles. His conical hat partially conceals his face as he steals furtively into the pleasure district to meet his beloved. From the hyōbanki *Ogakuzu* (1699). Courtesy of The Theatre Museum of Waseda University.

merly wealthy, confident playboy to undergo the hardships of poverty was also an important ploy in gaining empathy from spectators,
most of whom were not themselves particularly wealthy. And alter-
ing the main character's appearance made it easy for playwrights
and actors to create scenes in which mistaken identity led to humorous or dangerous turns of event.

Tōjūrō took the role of Izaemon again in 1680 in *The Third
Anniversary of Yūgiri's Death (Yūgiri Sankaiki)*, but there was still
plenty of competition among tachiyaku in the Kansai, and Tōjūrō
had yet to break into the top ranks on a permanent basis. In 1682 he
was the second-ranked actor at Osaka's Kado-za ("Corner Theater"),
just behind Yamashita Hanzaemon. But by 1686 Tōjūrō was receiving the best roles at the Iwamoto-za in Kyoto, and one short hyōbanki entry pronounced him "a hit in martial acting and peerless in
his yatsushi roles."[17] This was the first and last time that Tōjūrō
would be praised for his depiction of fierce warrior heroes.

In 1687 *The Great Stage Mirror of Male Lead Actors (Yarō
Tachiyaku Butai Kagami)* introduced the actor rating system that would
be used for the next two centuries. This gave the top rating of *jō-jō-
kichi* ("high-high good fortune") to just two tachiyaku actors in Japan,
including San'emon I in Osaka. Tōjūrō was rated, like most actors, as
chū ("middle").[18] The hyōbanki's detailed praise of Tōjūrō seems to
belie his "middle" ranking, but the author wrote that "so much
acclaim is being lavished on Yamashita these days that it puts even
Tōjūrō in his shadow."[19] *The Great Stage Mirror* pronounced Tōjūrō
"skilled in all sorts of acting," but his only work to receive detailed
analysis were his keisei-kai and yatsushi acting; in these he was declared
the equal of San'emon.[20] Crowds enjoyed the "realistic" suffering of
Tōjūrō's young lovers in disguise, and the hyōbanki author wrote that
"he is polished in all his arts—when his timing is right, his plays seem to
take on a life of their own."[21] On the other hand, although Tōjūrō was a
very "literate man who could write plays if he chose to," he was given to
overly long monologs packed with abstruse allusions.[22] It seems that
he was not always using his education to best effect onstage.

It did not matter that Tōjūrō's expertise was narrow in scope. Because romance still lay at the heart of kabuki's appeal, his best roles were sure to be favorites with audiences. By the late 1680s, Tōjūrō was getting the lead roles he needed to advance his career, and he commanded a salary commensurate with that of a top tachiyaku, probably around 200 ryō a year. He played a variety of roles from 1688 to 1691, including poor, unemployed samurai, a doctor, the historical samurai Soga Jūrō, and of course, wealthy modern young men such as Yūgiri's Izaemon.[23] Tōjūrō's star was rising, partly because he had learned to add humor to the pathos of his disowned young lovers. By 1692 *The Great Mirror of Actors (Yakusha Ōkagami)* had called him one of the best comic actors in the Kansai and said that "he is the sort of actor who can sit at the dining table and make people laugh without even picking up his chopsticks."[24]

Tōjūrō was finally popular enough for people to begin to take interest in his offstage personality, and it is in 1691 that we find the first record of an enduring character trait: love of extravagance. Tōjūrō was working at the Kado-za in Osaka but he had his drinking water shipped in barrels from Kyoto; he also had his rice inspected grain by grain before it was boiled. When he learned that people were beginning to talk about his capriciousness and extravagance, Tōjūrō objected, arguing that because the theater paid him well for his services, his health was of the utmost importance. Were a stone in his rice to damage a tooth, or impure water to make him ill, he would be unable to fulfill his obligations.[25] If we accept Tōjūrō's explanation, this anecdote attests to a character trait that was in fact more relevant to Tōjūrō's professional career than was his extravagance—a nearly obsessive attention to the minutest details.

In 1692 Tōjūrō received the second-highest actor rating of *jō-jō* ("high-high")[26] and became generally known, with Hanzaemon, as "one of two wheels on the cart of Kansai kabuki." *The Great Mirror of Actors* focused on his strengths in comic acting and keisei-kai: "He is at his best in exchanges with courtesans, combining his affection with tears of frustration at their infidelity. His sadness and charm come from the very depths of his heart."[27] One of the most critical hyōbanki ever to be published, *The Fully Colored Great Mirror of Actors (Yakusha Ōkagami Gassai),* also appeared in 1692. It focused on actors' weaknesses and bad habits, revealing details that actors might well have preferred to overlook. Of Tōjūrō, this record noted, "He sometimes sucks on his fingers when he speaks, and [in warrior roles] he has a bad habit of grabbing his sword with his left hand and swaggering about."[28] That Tōjūrō's samurai were weak and unconvincing had been noted for some time, but this hyōbanki attacked even his yatsushi acting: "In yatsushi scenes Tōjūrō doesn't pause long enough during dialogs, and fellow actors have said it can be difficult to work with him."[29] *The Fully Colored Great Mirror* grudgingly admitted that "in Yūgiri plays he does strangely well," but concluded that "in this floating world nothing is ever as we would wish it. All year long we wait for him to seek out the soul of the departed Yūgiri."[30] This critical hyōbanki did have some praise for Tōjūrō as a man, if not as an actor: "His style is dignified but light. He feigns carelessness with his appearance, or perhaps really dislikes ostentation. Wealthy men should be like this."[31] By 1692 Tōjūrō seems to have established his personal style of deportment: tastefully restrained elegance.

Tōjūrō Leads an All-Star Cast in Chikamatsu's First Kabuki Play

Yamashita Hanzaemon rose to the top of Kansai kabuki more quickly than did Tōjūrō. Hanzaemon was seven years younger than Tōjūrō but had always been rated above him in the hyōbanki, and by 1689 Hanzaemon was working as a theater producer (zamoto). A zamoto's primary responsibility was to ensure that the theater enjoyed a successful, profitable season. Hanzaemon recognized that a variety of plays and leading actors was likely to draw the largest audiences, so he followed in the tradition of the great zamoto before him and scheduled plays that would display the top actors in his company to best advantage. In 1693 Hanzaemon was the zamoto at the

Mandayū-za in Kyoto, where he had assembled a brilliant young cast: himself, Tōjūrō, comic actor Kaneko Kichizaemon (d. 1728), and a bevy of attractive onnagata including Kirinami Senju (dates uncertain) and nineteen year-old Yoshizawa Ayame. Chikamatsu was on the team in what was likely his first year as a senior staff playwright for kabuki, and Kaneko Kichizaemon collaborated with him on scripts for the Mandayū-za.

One of the ironies of Hanzaemon's career is that in the plays that represented his greatest successes as a zamoto, other tachiyaku always took the leading role.[32] In the third month of 1693, Tōjūrō starred in Chikamatsu's first surviving kabuki play, *The Festive Display of Statuary at the Temple of Maya, Mother of the Buddha (Butsumo Mayasan Kaichō).*[33] Hanzaemon took a supporting role, and all the glory went to Tōjūrō. Chikamatsu and Kaneko followed the popular practice of linking their play to a kaichō held concurrently, in this case at the Mayadera near Osaka. Best known of that temple's statuary was a seven-faced Kannon which, according to legend, the Buddha himself had commissioned to be carved in the likeness of his mother. A play by the very same title opened in the spring at Osaka's Iwai Hanshirō-za, and ran for an unheard-of one hundred and fifty days. There are differences in the texts of the two plays, and no author is cited for the Osaka version, but Chikamatsu may well have written both. If so, his first kabuki play was a remarkable success in two cities at once.

The Temple of Maya is a complex succession dispute story in three acts that uses the Mayadera Kannon deity and the temple kaichō as a frame to begin and end the play, and weaves the deity and the temple through the story. In this work, a provincial lord's family is threatened with ruin by the machinations of evil relatives and by the fact that Kamon, heir to the family fortune, has been away for seventeen years. Kamon originally set out on a religious mission to China, but when the action of the play begins he is living in the Osaka pleasure district, squandering his life and his family's money on love affairs with courtesans. The first scene of the play is

testimony to the allure of the Genroku-period courtesan. Kamon's
wife pays a large sum to hire a leading courtesan from whom she
hopes to learn the ways of romantic love, in order to keep her husband from straying again after he returns home. In the sort of coincidence typical of Genroku kabuki plays, the courtesan whom she
hires is none other than one of her husband's "true loves."

In *The Temple of Maya*, Kamon enjoys the love and devotion of
no less than three beautiful and virtuous women: his wife and two
courtesans. His complex affairs with them afforded Tōjūrō opportunity to engage in a variety of amorous and argumentative exchanges
and encounters. The story is fanciful and utterly implausible, but it
is evident that Tōjūrō was already beginning to experiment with
"realistic" kabuki. One scene in Act Two stands out for its verisimilitude; it involves a very down-to-earth negotiation between Kamon
and a brothel owner over the terms of the ransom of Kamon's current love. Histrionics and high emotion are the norm for Tōjūrō's
character in this play, and no other section approaches the quotidian
quality of the discussion of the courtesan's fee, but this single scene
is evidence that Tōjūrō was beginning to experiment with theatrical
realism.

Whereas in Danjūrō's plays, Fudō and other deities were the
deus ex machinae that appeared at the end of plays to rescue the
heroes, in Tōjūrō's *The Temple of Maya*, a wealthy clothing merchant from Kamon's domain appears at the end of Act Two; this
man buys both of Kamon's courtesan loves out of the pleasure district and presents them to Kamon. The narration tells us, "That's
how millionaires operate these days."[34] It seems that we are to pre-
sume that Kamon will bring the two former courtesans into his
household, and that he and his three ladies will live happily ever
after. But the play does not end here.

In Act Three all the heroes and heroines proceed to the Temple
of Maya to give thanks for the saving of the courtesans and the rescue of Kamon's domain, and to install the son of Kamon (by the
courtesan Ikoku) as an acolyte of the temple. But the few remaining

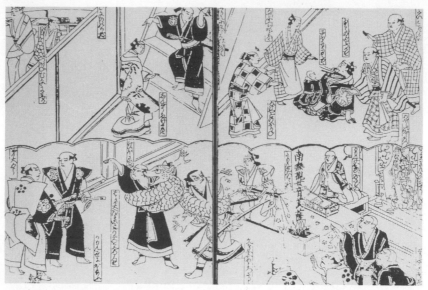

Fig. 19   Scenes from *The Festive Display of Statuary at the Temple of Maya*.
At upper right, the courtesan Ikoku commits suicide while her son clings to her.
Her friend Kofuji (Yoshizawa Ayame) stands watch over the child. Ikoku's lover
and the father of her children, hurries downstairs to save her. Below, the villains
are squeezed by a divine serpent. Kamon (Tōjūrō), who is Ikoku's lover, can be
seen in black at lower left. Kamon's son has been ordained into the priesthood
(lower right, center). At far right of the bottom panel is a statue of Kannon
carved in the likeness of Maya, mother of the Buddha. Book illustration, artist
unknown, 1693. Courtesy of Tokyo Geijutsu Daigaku.

villains appear too, and behead the boy, only to see his head float
into the air and return, unharmed, to his shoulders. As the villains
stand agape, astonished by this miracle, a giant serpent descends
from the clouds and coils around them, squeezing them until they
are close to death (Figure 19). The serpent releases the villains, who
are then bound, summarily tried and convicted, and sentenced to
commit suicide. A Buddhist service and festival conclude the play.
All the heroines don the robes of heavenly angels and perform court
dances (*bugaku*) to celebrate the power and virtue of the Mayadera
Kannon. Chikamatsu combined spectacular stage effects and sumptuous onnagata dancing for Act Three, action which did nothing to
further the plot of the play but which demonstrates how tightly

kabuki remained tied to its origins as variety theater. Exciting "finales" were still essential.

In the context of Chikamatsu and Tōjūrō's entire careers, *The Temple of Maya* is not a masterpiece. It is important, though, because it is the first surviving kabuki text by Chikamatsu, and it provides the first detailed evidence of what Tōjūrō actually did onstage. The text contains basic features of Chikamatsu's dramaturgy that would change little during the ten years he wrote for Tōjūrō. *The Temple of Maya* was a very successful play; all that would be necessary in the future was refinement.

The 1693 season went well for the Mandayū-za company, but 1694 is a mystery year. Danjūrō was enjoying his successful season in Kyoto, but Tōjūrō was in Osaka, and no records survive to tell us what he did there. We do not know if Chikamatsu was in Kyoto or Osaka, and there is no record of the plays written that year. In the first month of 1695, however, Tōjūrō was back in Kyoto, at the Haya-kumo-za. The zamoto was Yamatoya Jimbei (1650–1704), a leading tachiyaku of the day; Chikamatsu and Kaneko were staff play-wrights; and Tōjūrō played opposite Jimbei's nephew, the onnagata prodigy Mizuki Tatsunosuke. Tatsunosuke was a virtuoso dancer, and Tōjūrō was moving away from dance in his own work, so they made an interestingly odd couple onstage. Tōjūrō would work very infrequently with Ayame from this point on. Hanzaemon and Tōjūrō had parted ways, and sometime in the mid-1690s Ayame married Hanzaemon's sister-in-law. After the marriage Ayame almost always worked in Hanzaemon's troupe.

Tōjūrō acted in 1695 in four Chikamatsu-Kaneko plays, three of which survive as illustrated kabuki books by Chikamatsu. In the summer play, Tōjūrō enacted Soga Jūrō in *The Soga Infatuation with Courtesans (Soga Tayū Zome)*, with Tatsunosuke playing Jū-rō's lover, Tora. This play was another milestone for Tōjūrō and Chika-matsu. It was the first time Tōjūrō enacted a famous historical character in a play by Chikamatsu, and the actor's first performance in a historical drama about which we know anything in detail. Playing historical characters enabled Tōjūrō to add weight and import to his acting, if only because his characters' amorous peccadillos had an impact on affairs of national and historical significance. Writing for Tōjūrō under Jimbei's direction forced Chikamatsu to make breaks with the inherited literary tradition that he had not needed to make when writing for the puppet theater in the 1680s.[35] Kabuki gave him the confidence to experiment with traditional literary sources in an almost cavalier way, and this led, eventually, to some masterpieces of theatrical writing.

From the 1200s through the year 1695 the Soga vendetta had always been presented as a tragedy, no matter its literary form: oral recitation, written tale, or play. Then, in *The Soga Infatuation with Courtesans*, Chikamatsu and Kaneko rewrote the story as a melodrama with a happy ending, and converted the heroic warrior brothers into amorous rakes so incompetent as samurai that they could not conceivably complete their vendetta without the aid of their lovers, a pair of valiant and resourceful courtesans. The prime motivation for this overhaul of the medieval classic was the need to create scenes to suit Tōjūrō's skills, as well as those of Tatsunosuke and the other onnagata. While Soga Jūrō's love for just one woman, Tora, is essential to his virtuous character in all traditional versions of the story, Chikamatsu and Kaneko gave him a second courtesan mistress, Kamegiku. This change made it possible to incorporate all the stage business on which Tōjūrō thrived: lovers' quarrels, hollow professions of true love, empty promises, teeth-gnashing over the plight of the women one loves, and lamentations over lost love.

Disguises and cases of mistaken identity abound in the play. Jūrō, Tora, Gorō, and his lover Shōshō all begin the play in disguise, as yatsushi. The women disguise themselves as men (meaning that male actors were playing women disguised as men) and the Soga brothers disguise themselves as these "men's" servants. The scene most remarkable for its confusion of identity takes place when lovers Jūrō and Tora are compelled to enact a comic *kyōgen* play about a cheating husband while both are in disguise and unaware of each other's true identities. It is only during the presentation of the play-within-a-play that the two finally recognize each other. They then continue to act out the farce, mixing into the play-within-a-play comments made directly from one character to the other about their own love affair.[36]

In its five-hundred-year history as Japan's archetypal heroic revenge story, the vendetta of the Soga brothers had never been as rudely treated as it was by Chikamatsu and Tōjūrō in this play. It and others like it represented the culmination of a trend spanning several decades, in which playwrights and performers developed new romanticized and contemporized treatments of Japan's past, placing great medieval heroes into new stories in which their love affairs were far more important than their acts of martial heroism. These plays always included scenes set in the contemporary pleasure district, and which in no way reflected the historical age in which the plays' heroes lived. For the balance of the Genroku period, the only plays about Japan's past to be seen on the popular stage were hybrids of Edo-period and pre–Edo-period culture, values, and settings.[37]

A Winning Combination: The Tōjūrō–Chikamatsu–Kaneko Production Team

In the fall of 1695, Tōjūrō assumed the position of zamoto at Kyoto's Miyako Mandayū-za. He was forty-eight years old when at last he reached the most prestigious, and potentially the most remunerative, position that an actor could achieve in the Kansai. He would continue to serve as the Mandayū-za's zamoto for the next five seasons. Chikamatsu and Kaneko Kichizaemon (also known as Kaneko Ikkō) were his staff playwrights the entire time that he was at the Mandayū-za. Tōjūrō was in a position to command the finest dramatic writing team in Japan to do his bidding, and it is clear that both playwrights found it a joy to work with Tōjūrō, not least because he recognized and valued their rare talents.[38] Scholars have

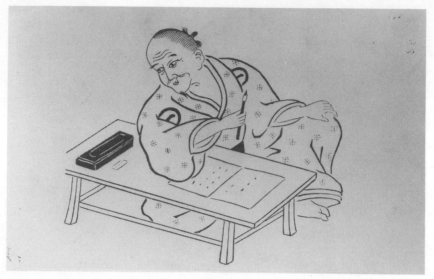

Fig. 20 Portrait of Chikamatsu Monzaemon from *Souvenirs from Naniwa [Osaka] (Naniwa Miyage)*. Courtesy of The Theatre Museum of Waseda University.

written that Tōjūrō would have been a run-of-the-mill tachiyaku without Chikamatsu, and there is much truth in this assertion (see figure 20 for a portrait of Chikamatsu).

Tōjūrō's Mandayū-za plays come down to us in the form of illustrated kabuki books (e-iri kyōgen bon) signed by Chikamatsu alone, but we know that Chikamatsu and Kaneko were collaborating staff playwrights at the theater. Chikamatsu's sole authorship of the only surviving plays had long convinced historians that he was the senior, more responsible playwright, but entries in Kaneko's recently discovered 1698 diary indicate that plays previously thought to be solely the work of Chikamatsu were in fact collaborations, on which Kaneko often did the larger share of, and indeed the most creative work. Nevertheless, none of the published plays make any reference to Kaneko as author. Why was this the case? One likely explanation is that because Kaneko Kichizaemon worked as a comic (*dōke*) actor (for many years he was rated *jō-jō-kichi*, or the best in his specialty),

he was much busier than Chikamatsu. Chikamatsu had more free
time to do the editing and rewriting necessary to prepare handwrit-
ten stage scripts into books for publication. Thanks to his apprenticeship as a playwright for the puppet theater, Chikamatsu had
developed relationships with Kyoto publishers which he continued
to nurture throughout his career as a kabuki book author. It is also
very possible that Kaneko allowed Chikamatsu to take sole credit for
published versions of their collaborative work because Chikamatsu
needed the income more.[39] As we have seen, Danjūrō's diary makes
clear the terrible discrepancy between actors' and playwrights' salaries.

The relationship between Chikamatsu and Kaneko appears to
have been one of approximate equals, but Tōjūrō was clearly superior to both. Tōjūrō occasionally provided the initial concept for a
play, but more often he allowed playwrights to use their own resources, and then guided and edited their work. Tojuro reserved the
right to make final and definitive changes to the text before the first
general rehearsal.[40] Tōjūrō made sure that in any play in which he
was to star, all the characters and scenes helped display his own talents to maximum advantage, but Kaneko wrote that Tōjūrō was a
zamoto who also tried to ensure that every actor in his company
looked good. He strove for effective ensemble kabuki in his work
onstage, in rehearsals, and in his supervision of playwrights.

The fine plays that Chikamatsu and Kaneko provided Tōjūrō
enabled the actor to bring two innovations to the stage: kabuki's first
realism, and humor based on situations rather than on antics and
buffoonery. In backstage conversations recorded by Kaneko, Tōjūrō
says again and again that actors do not need to "ham it up"; if they
remain true to a play's text they will be much more effective.
"Nowadays, actors playing a serious (jitsugoto) part are always slap-
ping their scabbards at each other, sticking their noses in each
other's faces, and confronting each other with sword-drawing postures; this is hardly the sort of thing a real samurai would do. When
writing speeches the same considerations must be borne in mind.
Can this sort of thing actually be called serious acting?"[41]

Chikamatsu's kabuki texts do also include exaggerated confrontations between samurai, because these were essential scenes for other
actors, but when Tōjūrō wanted verisimilitude in his drama, Chikamatsu was able to provide it, and these more realistic scenes inspired
Tōjūrō to say, "If you want to be praised, the best thing to do is forget about the audience and perform as if the events onstage were
real."[42]

Tōjūrō maintained that "it is realism that is comic," and even
Hanzaemon admitted that "there is no actor like Tōjūrō for saying
something serious and making people laugh at it."[43] The scholarship
that pays tribute to Chikamatsu tends to overlook one important
aspect of his kabuki playwriting—he was the finest comic writer of
his day. He was a master of irony and wit, and his comic monologs
provided Tōjūrō some of the biggest successes of his career (see
pages 165–169 for examples). Using elaborate scenes of mistaken
identity and misunderstanding, Chikamatsu was able to infuse amusing double meanings into superficially straightforward dialogs. Dōke
actors relied on buffoonery, but Chikamatsu created situations in his
plays that were so inherently amusing that the "straighter" Tōjūrō
played them, the funnier they seemed. Some of the best examples of
this can be seen in *The Courtesan on the Buddha Plain* (*Keisei
Hotoke no Hara*; 1699). In Act Two, Tōjūrō's character, Bunzō,
sneaks into the mansion of his former lover, the courtesan Ōshū,
who has been ransomed by a wealthy samurai and is now that man's
wife. The night is pitch-dark, and Bunzō hides in the garden near a
stone washbasin. One of Ōshū's maids enters, intending to use the
basin, but she is unable to make out just where it is. She pours water
on Bunzō, then rests offerings of saké and rice cakes on his head
(Figure 21). If Bunzō is to remain unseen, he must suffer these indig-
nities as quietly as possible, and audiences found Tōjūrō's silent,
restrained reactions to his situation much more amusing than the
outrageous antics of dōke actors to which they were accustomed.
Humorous situations could also be given an erotic twist, as we see in
a later scene in which Bunzō is forced to disguise himself as a

Fig. 21 *The Courtesan on the Buddha Plain.* A maid-servant has mistaken the location of the stone wash-basin in the dark and has inadvertently placed an offertory altar on Bunzō's (Tōjūrō's) shoulders. Bunzō drinks saké from it as he hides outside the veranda of his long-lost lover Ōshū (upper right). At lower left, he escapes his enemies by fleeing onto the roof. Book illustration, artist unknown, 1699. Courtesy of Osaka Prefectural Nakanoshima Library.

kotatsu in a pleasure district establishment. A kotatsu is a low table covered with a quilt, with protected, live coals underneath to warm the legs of the person using it. To effect his disguise, Bunzō gets down on all fours and covers himself with a kotatsu quilt. The situation simply begs for young women to approach and stick their legs under the quilt, with silly and suggestive exchanges to follow their inevitable surprise.⁴⁴

Tōjūrō formulated the first thematic requirements for seasonal presentations in kabuki, relying on two shows in particular to bring him success each year: a courtesan play as the second work of the year (called the *ni no kawari* play) and a Soga play during the *obon* festival season in summer. The former always featured a fictional young heir to a contemporary samurai family who became embroiled in a succession dispute complicated by love affairs with courtesans, and the latter always depicted the fictionalized romantic escapades of the Soga brothers, with Tōjūrō playing Jūrō, the older, more amorously-inclined brother. Tōjūrō also had Chikamatsu and Kaneko set plays in Heian Japan (800 to 1100 A.D.) and the world of *The Tale of Genji* with some frequency, but the actor made his reputation mainly by playing contemporary young men. Chikamatsu would only demonstrate his complete range of knowledge and skill as a writer after he had left kabuki and gone to work as a full-time author of puppet plays. Nevertheless, during the crucial decade from 1693 through 1703, when Tōjūrō established his supremacy in Kansai kabuki, Chikamatsu was, to use Danjūrō's metaphor, "giving an iron bar to a demon."

Competing Against Yamashita Hanzaemon

Tōjūrō's appointment as zamoto of the Mandayū-za in 1695 established him as the main rival to the man who was then the toast of Kyoto, Yamashita Hanzaemon. As an actor, Hanzaemon's strength was in playing samurai in the jitsugoto style. He had begun his theatrical training in nō drama, and was able to apply the weighty stage presence of the nō to his samurai characters.[45] One critic wrote, "When he comes onstage he exhibits such dignity and calm that even country viewers attending the theater for the first time know enough to point at him and say 'that's the main actor in today's play' before he even begins to act."[46] He was excellent in fight scenes. Humor was essential to kabuki in the 1690s, but Hanzaemon's approach was more direct than Tōjūrō's. Hanzaemon often "broke character" and joked onstage about the situation of the play or other contemporary topics. His rough-and-ready wit endeared him to male spectators of the less sophisticated sort, whose numbers were large enough to ensure him a powerful following. In the mid-1690s Hanzaemon was at the peak of his popularity, and in 1694 and 1695 he played himself onstage in two different plays.[47] Tōjūrō was too

dedicated to the actor's calling—that is, to becoming, in a convincing fashion, someone he was not—ever to portray himself.
Hanzaemon's art was based on his consciousness of kabuki audiences' adulation of their favorite actors, and his plays often exploited
conscious conflation of the personae of actors and stage characters.
Hanzaemon expressed his gratitude to his Kyoto supporters when,
in 1705, he changed his name to Kyōemon, using the character "kyō"
from Kyoto as part of his new stage name. Hanzaemon could alter-
nately impress audiences with his dead-on impressions of feudal
lords, or send them into uproarius laughter at impeccably timed,
impromptu off-color jokes.[48]

From the 1690s until long after Hanzaemon and Tōjūrō had
both died, critics and historians loved to contrast the two rivals, as
actors and as theater producers. In 1692, the author of *The Great
Mirror of Actors* noted that their styles were totally different:
"Someone in a position to know once said that Tōjūrō's martial acting looked twenty percent inferior to Yamashita's. 'Tōjūrō just does-
n't look right somehow carrying two swords.' This comment was
then refuted by someone else: 'But as a courtesan's customer, Tōjūrō beats Yamashita by twenty percent, so they're even.'"[49] The hyōbanki tended to evaluate the two actors as equally skilled opposites
from the early 1690s through the spring of 1699, when Tōjūrō's fabulously successful *The Courtesan on the Buddha Plain* put him at the
top of Kansai kabuki to stay.

From the time of his first, ground-breaking hyōbanki, *The Actors' Vocal Shamisen (Yakusha Kuchijamisen)* in 1699, through the
publication of his elegaic book in 1709, Ejima Kiseki remained a
devoted Tōjūrō supporter. He expressed the differences between Tōjūrō and Hanzaemon with metaphorical language: "Tōjūrō's art is
like fresh Asakusa *nori* seaweed: light, with a mild flavor. Hanzaemon's is like dumplings grilled on cedar coals. Everyone says they
like them, and they're fine for filling up on, but if you eat too many,
they seem a little heavy. True aficionados of the theater prefer
Tōjūrō."[50] But even during Tōjūrō's decade of supremacy, he was

not immune to criticism or to negative comparisons with Hanzaemon, and Kiseki pointed out that while "Tōjūrō's style is interesting, there are aspects of it that amateurs cannot enjoy. Hanzaemon's
style is such that rich and poor alike—even total unsophisticates—
like him."[51]

In his two-part record of Genroku kabuki titled "Dust in the
Ears" (Nijin Shū; contained in The Actors' Analects), Kaneko
Kichizaemon recorded anecdotes about Tōjūrō and quoted his
words of advice to other actors, while also making note of Tōjūrō
and Hanzaemon's critiques of one another. Each great actor
respected his rival, but had critical comments to make as well. At the
peak of Tōjūrō's dominance, for example, Hanzaemon admitted
that Tōjūrō was the better actor, but attributed Tōjūrō's skill to "natural genius"—and it was just this "genius," he argued, that prevented
Tōjūrō from being a skillful teacher. "Since Tōjūrō himself has no
experience of having been bent and shaped by others, he does not
know how to bend and shape others himself," Hanzaemon claimed.[52]
Teaching was an important duty for master actors and particularly
for zamoto, so this was harsh criticism, but it remains unclear how
accurate Hanzaemon's evaluation was. The Actors' Analects shows
that Tōjūrō gave plenty of useful advice to younger actors, but Dust
in the Ears and other geidan (collections of theatrical anecdotes and
advice for actors) suggest that he would have been opposed to teaching in the traditional sense—that is, to teaching which required students to mimic set patterns of movement and voice as closely as
possible. In those entries in Dust in the Ears in which Kaneko
describes Tōjūrō's teaching methods, he makes clear that the actor
never offered cut-and-dried solutions to acting problems, but used
trial and error, physical repetition, and intellectual analysis to help
actors devise their own, individual approaches.[53] By all accounts,
Tōjūrō's aversion to traditional methods of instruction stemmed not
from his own lack of formal training but from his belief that young
actors should develop their own styles early, in fact much earlier
than was typical in his day. Hanzaemon also belittled the praise that

Tōjūrō received for the convincing acting in roles which he had
carefully researched and prepared, saying that audiences were more
impressed when someone like he, Hanzaemon, did a fine job
onstage despite his habitual lack of pre-performance preparation.[54]
This entry suggests that Hanzaemon may have been intimidated by
Tōjūrō's almost obsessively thorough preparation for stage roles.

Tōjūrō was capable of sharp criticism of younger actors, but surviving geidan indicate that he rarely indulged in unsolicited criticism
of his peers. He noted his opinion of Hanzaemon's art in the course
of giving general words of advice. When Tōjūrō said that actors
should "forget about the audience and perform as if the events
onstage were real," or that they should not add impromptu "comic
twists to their acting,"[55] it was clear enough that he had Hanzaemon's style in mind. *The Actors' Analects* is filled with accounts
of Tōjūrō's evaluations of actors and acting styles in mind, but all his
criticism is constructive, and has a single purpose: encouraging people to create better kabuki.

Hanzaemon and Tōjūrō were both very successful zamoto.
Hanzaemon is famous for producing plays that helped other actors
achieve fame and fortune, but Tōjūrō achieved his greatest renown
in dramas he produced himself. Given this, it seems odd that all surviving geidan indicate that Tōjūrō was much easier to work with.
Yoshizawa Ayame put it cogently when he told a disciple that "working alongside Tōjūrō was like sailing smoothly along in a great ship.
Acting with Kyōemon [Hanzaemon], I was always tense and had to
work very hard."[56] One reason for this difference in their reputations
was that fellow actors could count on Tōjūrō to follow a play script,
but they never knew when Hanzaemon might threaten to "steal the
scene" with an impromptu change, forcing the actors around him to
improvise until they could return to the text. As zamoto, Tōjūrō
often cast himself as the biggest star of his plays, but his usual
method was to impress audiences with virtuoso monologs. In this
way he could garner the greatest acclaim without stealing the thunder of the actors working with him. Tōjūrō's strongest criticism of

Hanzaemon concerned this same issue. Hanzaemon had been praised by one and all for a certain opening-day performance, but Tōjūrō alone told Hanzaemon, without going into specifics, that the performance had been faulty. This upset Hanzaemon, and he strove to do better, but after the second day's show, Tōjūrō's opinion was unchanged. Hanzaemon finally pressed Tōjūrō to elaborate. Tōjūrō replied that the problem was that Hanzaemon's performance was too strong; he made it impossible for the young actor in the next scene to develop the confidence necessary to grow as an artist.[57]

What is significant about this episode is that Hanzaemon respected Tōjūrō's opinions so much that he endured discomfort in order to benefit from Tōjūrō's instruction. Hanzaemon knew that although Tōjūrō was his artistic and economic rival, Tōjūrō wanted, above all else, to see high-quality kabuki presented on every stage in the Kansai, even if this brought success to a rival actor. It is not surprising that Tōjūrō attended the opening of a rival theater's play. Tōjūrō realized that knowledge was power, and often sent his two playwrights all the way to Osaka to act as scouts to research the latest trends in kabuki there. Tōjūrō's method of instruction to Hanzaemon is also true to form. Rather than solve the problem for him right away, Tōjūrō first forced Hanzaemon to struggle with it himself. As we have seen, this was Tōjūrō's approach in teaching younger actors. But Tōjūrō was not a sadistic teacher; he did give instruction when a student's genuine efforts proved insufficient, just as he did with Hanzaemon.

This upstaging of a younger tachiyaku by Hanzaemon had been unintentional, and the acclaim that Ayame, Nakamura Shichisaburō, and even Tōjūrō himself won in Hanzaemon-produced plays attests to Hanzaemon's ability and selflessness as a zamoto. Where Tōjūrō apparently surpassed his rival as a zamoto was in the attention he paid to detail in regard to directing and producing. Like Hanzaemon, Tōjūrō refrained from setting himself up to be the star in every play that he produced. Kaneko, who worked with Tōjūrō for nearly twenty years, had this to say about him as a producer:

At that time any actor who worked with Tōjūrō seemed skillful. The reason was that Tōjūrō demonstrated proper breathing, good movement, and delivery. His company all followed his leadership and did not controvert his advice. His actors did so remarkably well precisely because they allowed themselves to be instructed by him. Moreover, Tōjūrō himself took few roles, and sometimes even stayed out of the public eye altogether. Someone said to him, "Your plays are entertaining and popular, but the one thing I regret is how few roles you take in them." Tōjūrō burst out laughing. "As long as my plays are good, I am sure you can forgive my absence from the stage. Audiences already know the qualities and defects of my acting. The work of my theater is not to present me, but to present plays."[58]

A final, telling difference between Hanzaemon and Tōjūrō as zamoto was the manner in which they assembled casts. In the 1680s and 1690s, Hanzaemon used family marriages to become the patriarch of a clan of kabuki actors. His casts consisted first and foremost of family members, to whom he gave the best roles. Ayame became his brother-in-law, and while Ayame may have found it difficult to work onstage with Hanzaemon, the zamoto did make sure that the best onnagata roles in his plays went to Ayame. This meant, of course, that Ayame would rarely have the opportunity to work opposite Tōjūrō, who was not a member of the clan. Tōjūrō assembled casts of unrelated actors—some veterans and others just starting out. Tōjūrō's authority was based entirely on his stature and personality; he did not serve as a family elder to his actors. In the decades and even centuries to follow, Hanzaemon's approach would be the model that powerful actors would emulate. Strong family ties among actors have helped kabuki maintain its best acting traditions through many generations, and ties to established acting families are essential to young actors hoping to play good roles on today's stage.

Hanzaemon Ups the Ante: Nakamura Shichisaburō's Victory in Kyoto

During the 1696–1697 season in Kyoto, Hanzaemon was zamoto of Kyoto's Hayakumo-za and Tōjūrō was in his second season as producer at the Mandayū-za. The actual theater buildings would have been across the street or around the corner from one another, on or near Shijō, or "fourth avenue."[59] In 1697 Tōjūrō had more than his requisite "two seasonal triumphs." *Yūgiri's Seventh Year Memorial Service (Yūgiri Shichinen Ki)* was part of a double bill for the second play of the year, in which Tōjūrō played his favorite character, Izaemon. Izaemon finds himself embroiled in love affairs, first with Yūgiri and then with two other courtesans: one looks just like Yūgiri and is thought to embody her reincarnated spirit, and another is Yūgiri's younger sister. Izaemon is so desperately in love with the look-alike that he sells his daughter by Yūgiri to the Ogiya (Yūgiri's former establishment) in order to continue the relationship with her. The work was a tour-de-force for Tōjūrō, and included a yatsushi scene in which he wore a paper kimono, numerous lovers' quarrels, a tearful scene depicting his parting from his daughter, and a rare episode in which the actor demonstrated his skill on the ko-tsuzumi shoulder-drum. As was usual in Tōjūrō's contemporary plays, a wealthy, human deus ex-machina—in this case a brothel owner—saves Izaemon and his ladies with a huge gift of cash.[60]

Later in the spring of 1697, Tōjūrō was presented with a windfall when a minor Mandayū-za actor who had gone to Ise Shrine on a pilgrimage happened to be staying at an Ise inn when a quadruple murder occurred there. This actor brought the story, in all its detail, back to Tōjūrō, who had Chikamatsu and Kaneko fashion it right away into a play titled *It Happened at Dawn on the Ninth Day of the Fourth Month at the Bright Star Inn (Uzuki Kokonoka sono Akatsuki no Akeboshigajaya).* Tōjūrō played a clerk at the inn, and in a long onstage speech (kōjō) as zamoto he explained how the material for the play had been discovered.[61]

In the summer Soga play, *A Soga Play to Entertain a Feudal Lord (Daimyō Nagusami Soga)*, Tōjūrō broke with precedent by playing a porter and the Soga family servant Onio, rather than Soga Jūrō. Chikamatsu conceived the entire play as a "play-within-a-play" and as a parody of his own first jōruri puppet play, *The Soga Heir* (*Yotsugi Soga*; 1683).[62] In the first act, a feudal lord's samurai retinue decides to entertain the master with an amateur production of *The Soga Heir*. In this act, Chikamatsu and Tōjūrō played with the concept of multiple identities, giving no fewer than three identities to each actor: his real-life, offstage identity; his character as a samurai in the play; and his role in the Soga play-within-a-play. Act One centers on rivalry, including that between actual actors, between samurai, and between characters in the embedded Soga story, with these three layers of conflict juxtaposed and interrclated so as to provide commentary on one another. Plays like this attest not only to the popularity of kabuki's top stars, but to the audience's craving for information on backstage rivalries and scandals. The Soga play was less a star vehicle for Tōjūrō than the spring double bill had been, and contained more scenes that showcased junior actors, including one involving an imitation of Danjūrō's aragoto. Children's roles were also prominent in this work.[63]

At the end of his very successful season, Tōjūrō produced a play in the fall of 1697 that was described as "a failure," and Hanzaemon outdrew Tōjūrō at the box office with a play he had adapted from Uji Kaganojō's puppet theater.[64] Records do not survive for most of the Hayakumo-za season, but given the scant attendance at Tōjūrō's last play, the competition that year between Kyoto's two top actor-producers seems to have ended as a slight victory for Tōjūrō.

For the 1697–1698 season, both Hanzaemon and Tōjūrō brought "heavy ammunition" down from Edo and elevated the level of their rivalry to a fever pitch. Tōjūrō's weapon was the onnagata Mizuki Tatsunosuke, a Kansai actor who had spent the previous two seasons awing Edo audiences with his spectacular dancing. In 1697 he was Japan's top-ranked onnagata. Hanzaemon engaged Edo's romantic-role superstar Nakamura Shichisaburō, and arranged for him to star in his plays.

Round One of the competition, the 1697 kaomise show, was a triumph for Tōjūrō's Mandayū-za. In the course of this play, Tōjūrō had Tatsunosuke perform the dance that had won him accolades in Edo; called "Seven Spirits" (*Shichibake*), this was a dance in which the girl Tatsunosuke played was murdered at the outset, but in which her will to live was so strong that she then went through multiple transformations as a spirit, becoming "a dog of carnal desire, a courtier, an old man, a vengeful ghost, and finally a woman again."[65]

By contrast, the kaomise show at the Hayakumo-za was a disaster. Hanzaemon had hoped to earn praise and profit by introducing Shichisaburō to Kyoto, but audiences reviled the actor as hopelessly untalented. A humorous poem (*kyōka*) was making the rounds in the streets, which went:

> Hanzaemon wanted to see Shichisaburō's beautiful eyelashes,
> so he went round to view the rear legs of the horse.[66]

Traditionally, the worst actor in a troupe played the rear legs of a horse, and cries of "you're a horse's ass" were among the most humiliating catcalls in Genroku-period theaters. The Hayakumo-za play that opened the New Year was no better received, and it began to look as if Shichisaburō's entire season in Kyoto might be a nightmare. Tōjūrō's company followed the crowd in disparaging Shichisaburō, but Tōjūrō himself countered that Kyoto audiences had simply proven that they did not recognize good acting when they saw it. Tōjūrō predicted that Shichisaburō would emerge as a "tougher opponent" in the coming months, and that everyone in the Mandayū-za company would improve as a result of the competition.[67]

Tōjūrō went to see every play in which Shichisaburō performed in Kyoto, and the two probably met frequently.[68] Having predicted that Shichisaburō would become a formidable opponent by the spring of 1698, Tōjūrō may well have gone to the aid of his rivals, to help them present him with tougher competition, for Tōjūrō clearly believed that the art of kabuki could only benefit from competition between fine actors.

Kabuki historian Tsuchiya Keiichirō posits that at about the time of the New Year's holiday, Tōjūrō went to visit Hanzaemon and Shichisaburō at Hanzaemon's home.[69] Tōjūrō explained to them the weaknesses in the kaomise play that had prevented Shichisaburō from showing his skill to best advantage, and persuaded Hanzaemon to stop relying on plays that had been successful for Shichisaburō in Edo. Tōjūrō explained that in Edo, Shichisaburō had benefited from the contrast between his style and the style of powerful aragoto actors like Danjūrō (he had worked onstage with Danjūrō just before coming to Kyoto), Denkurō, and master villain actor Yamanaka Heikurō (1642–1724). In Edo, Shichisaburō had "borrowed energy" from actors like these, but in the Kansai he would need entirely different plays if he were to succeed. Tōjūrō suggested that the two adapt a certain Chikamatsu puppet play to the stage, and incorporate into it the best confrontational and romantic business from Shichisaburō's previous work as Nagoya Sanzaemon.[70] Tōjūrō's two rivals took his advice. Shichisaburō likely wrote just one play during his career, *The Courtesan and the Peak of Asama (Keisei Asama ga Take)*, but it was a triumph and ran for 120 days starting early in 1698. This success vaulted Shichisaburō to a ranking among the top three actors in Japan.

> Shichisaburō's reception in *The Courtesan and the Peak of Asama* was directly opposite what it had been in the kaomise, and he had a great success. The cast of the Mandayū-za, as Tōjūrō had predicted, all said, with admiration, that his skill as an actor was truly frightening. Tōjūrō secretly summoned Kaneko Kichizaemon and gave him the following confidential injunction. "As I predicted during the kaomise we have a great competitor with us

this year, called Shichisaburō, and so all the actors will obviously have to do their best, but first and foremost we shall have to work hard on our material. You are our playwright and you must give it your best effort."

At every change of program Tōjūrō would go and see Shichisaburō perform, and invariably pronounced him a true master. Shichisaburō also saw Tōjūrō's acting, and exclaimed bitterly: "This actor Tōjūrō is far better even than I had heard. Had I seen his acting and studied it earlier, I should have achieved a much higher standard, but there is absolutely no point in my trying to do anything about it now." Tōjūrō's opinion of Shichisaburō, based on the performances he saw, was that his movements and posture on the stage were absolutely true to character. Tōjūrō derived great pleasure from this, and from the fact that the other actor's bearing was always extremely good. From then on the two men grew nearer together and very often had happy meetings.[71]

The Courtesan and the Peak of Asama was a complicated succession dispute play very much in the Chikamatsu-Tōjūrō mold, featuring the young samurai Ōzasa Tomoe no Jō, who must restore order to his domain while being involved in a complicated web of relationships with courtesans and other lovers. Shichisaburō received particular acclaim for "a scene in which he has a lovers' quarrel with the courtesan Ōshū while playing *go* by himself using fragments of a broken teacup for pieces on a coat decorated with a *go*-board pattern that he has spread out on the floor. In this scene he surprised everyone with his acting, which was inimitable, and the Kyoto audiences were in raptures."[72] The play was timed to coincide with a kaichō, and the entire story was linked to the worship of the god of the Asama volcano, then a very popular cult in Japan. Supernatural interventions occurred in each of the three acts. One occult scene proved remarkably influential; in it, the spirit of a cour-

Fig. 22 The most famous scene from *The Courtesan and Asama Peak*. Tomoe no Jō, played by Nakamura Shichisaburō (lower left), puts his hand to his sword when the angry spirit of his courtesan lover appears in the flames of the brazier. Artist unknown. 1698. Courtesy of The Theatre Museum of Waseda University.

tesan appears in the smoke of a brazier to reproach Tomoe no Jō for his infidelity (Figure 22). It seemed that after this triumph, no Genroku-period play could hope to succeed without a scene in which the spirit of a wronged or murdered woman appeared within a cloud of smoke. The women characters in *The Peak of Asama* had been sharply drawn and well acted, and virtuous and heroic courtesans named Ōshū and Miura (played at the Hayakumo-za by Ayame) would appear in many subsequent plays.

If Tōjūrō had indeed helped Shichisaburō achieve this great success, he was made to pay for his generosity with an exhausting theater season at the Mandayū-za. In his diary, Kaneko Kichizaemon described a year of constant activity and stress for that theater's playwrights, actors, and zamoto. No single one of Tōjūrō's plays could compete with *The Courtesan and the Peak of Asama*, and he was forced to run four plays to the Hayakumo-za's two, during the first six months of 1698. Tōjūrō had to endure two outright failures that season, with plays that closed after runs of fifteen days or less.[73] Perhaps the Mandayū-za's best play that year was an adaptation of a 1696 Danjūrō Seigen–Princess Sakura drama. In 1698 some Mandayū-za plays were written in two days and rehearsed in a week, but Tōjūrō, Tatsunosuke, and the two playwrights worked for two weeks adapting the Seigen-Sakura text, and the company rehearsed a full thirteen days.[74] The result was the Mandayū-za's longest run of the season, of forty-five days. Tōjūrō's summer Soga play also went well, but Hanzaemon and Shichisaburō had clearly prevailed in the 1697–1698 season.

The Courtesan on the Buddha Plain: *Tōjūrō's Most Rewarding Triumph*

Tōjūrō had told the members of his company that Shichisaburō's skill would force them all to improve. Whether the rank-and-file actors of the Mandayū-za actually improved, we cannot tell, but Tōjūrō and his two playwrights did set out to create a masterpiece of their own that would reestablish Tōjūrō as Japan's premiere actor of amorous heroes. The result was the play *The Courtesan on the Buddha Plain (Keisei Hotoke no Hara)*, which opened late in the first month of 1699. For eight months the Mandayu-za presented just this play and two sequels to it. *The Buddha Plain* was such an instant success that Osaka companies quickly had their own versions up and running.[75] The tables had turned, and in 1699 Hanzaemon's company, which had moved to the Nunobukuroya-za, was forced to present play after play, none of which could compete with *The Buddha Plain* or its sequels. Box office returns at the Mandayū-za in 1699 were unprecedentedly high, and Tōjūrō made so much money that he bought himself a spacious new villa downtown with as much frontage as a kabuki theater, a home so large and luxurious that it was a topic of immediate interest to everyone in Kyoto. It stood in Furoya-chō, just across the Kamo River from the theater district. It probably faced what is now Kiyamachi Street, a little south of where the Hankyū department store is located.[76]

In *The Courtesan on the Buddha Plain*, playwrights Chikamatsu and Kaneko created yet another succession dispute story, drawing some material from the nō play *The Buddha Plain (Hotoke no Hara)* and more from Shichisaburō's wildly successful *The Courtesan and the Peak of Asama*. The play was connected to a kaichō display of a rare statue of a "Buddha in shoes" from a temple in the town of Hotoke no Hara. Hyōbanki indicate that the scenes and characters adapted from Shichisaburō's play were particularly important to the success of *The Buddha Plain*.[77] The courtesan Ōshū in Tōjūrō's play was much like her *Asama* predecessor, a virtuous woman taken from the man she loves by a wealthy patron who secretly ransoms her from the pleasure district, leaving her whereabouts unknown to the hero. One scene inspired by Shichisaburō's play featured the jealous ghost of the hero's fiancée tormenting Ōshū.

Tōjūrō took the part of the play's hero, Umenaga Bunzō, a young samurai who spends too much time and money in the pleasure districts. Three women are deeply in love with him: his official fiancée Takehime, whom he ignores; the former courtesan Ōshū, whom he still loves but who has disappeared; and the courtesan Imagawa, his current love and the mother of his son. Bunzō's evil younger brother, Tatewaki, prevails upon their father to disown the wastrel Bunzō and instead make him, Tatewaki, heir to the family domain. The younger brother has allies inside and out the Umenaga house, and one of his confederates outside is none other than Imagawa's father, who has no idea that he is working first to discredit, and then to murder, the man his daughter loves. After expelling Bunzō, the villains murder Tatewaki's father, making the death look like a suicide, and Tatewaki becomes lord of the domain. But as long as Bunzō is alive, he remains a threat to Tatewaki, so the villains resolve to murder him too.

Making the hero's brother the primary villain was apparently a novel touch in 1699 (uncles and aunts had been stock villains in succession dispute stories until that point), but otherwise the story of the play is not all that different from *The Peak of Asama,* or earlier succession dispute plays. Tōjūrō and his writers added many comic scenes that were new to the genre—scenes that were intrinsically amusing and that called for "straight" acting. Two of the best of these were the "human washbasin in the dark" scene (see figure 21) and the "human kotatsu" scene mentioned above.

Early in Act One, Bunzō is disowned and turned out of his home. He wanders about, wearing Tōjūrō's trademark yatsushi costume, a thin paper kimono. By chance Bunzō finds his way into Ōshū's garden in the middle of the night. After Bunzō endures the indignity of being treated like a washbasin and is discovered, Ōshū and her ladies-in-waiting assemble to interrogate the handsome intruder. In a captivating monolog, Bunzō tells the story of the downfall he has suffered as a result of his love for two courtesans. His story moves the ladies and their mistress to tears, and the scene ends with Ōshū and Bunzō reunited. She reveals that she has remained true to him, and has never once been intimate with the husband who ransomed her. Later, Tatewaki and his men come to kill Bunzō, but Bunzō escapes into the crawl space between the ceiling and roof, and is able to make his escape. Ōshū demonstrates her mastery of some of the requisite skills of a samurai wife by fighting valiantly with a halberd; she even kills one of the attackers. She throws the dead body down a well, and convinces Tatewaki that the corpse was Bunzō's, thus putting the villain off Bunzō's trail for a time. Contemporary records show that the washbasin pantomime and Bunzō's account of his love life were among the highlights of the play.

Bunzō's kotatsu impersonation and the subsequent lovers' quarrel between Bunzō and Imagawa (Kirinami Senju, Tōjūrō's premiere leading "lady") was another favorite scene. The quarrel in particular demonstrates the sort of interplay between characters that earned

Tōjūrō his reputation as Japan's finest performer of amorous male roles. A translation of Chikamatsu's text follows.

We join the scene after Bunzō has crept surreptitiously into Imagawa's establishment and hidden himself under a kotatsu quilt. Two maids discover him there. Both fall in love with him on sight. He persuades the first to leave by promising to sleep with her later that night, but the second, a girl named Kozatsuma, is more persistent. Bunzō attempts to rebuff her with jokes and sarcasm, but the lovestruck girl mistakes these for expressions of love:

KOZATSUMA: We're in luck. Here's a futon all ready. Let's sleep together right now.

NARRATOR: She seizes Bunzō and pushes him down. Bunzō is perplexed.

BUNZŌ: Girl, wait. I'm thrilled that you feel this way, but you're a little too fast for me.

NARRATOR: Just as she jumps on top of him, Imagawa enters. Bunzō does not notice her until after he has uttered the words ...

BUNZŌ: I *am* grateful. Until I die I won't forget your love for me. (Bunzō sees Imagawa and gasps) But I think there's been a misunderstanding. This is terrible. Girl! See here! Why do you keep doing this to me? Please, let me go for today.

KOZATSUMA: What are you talking about?

NARRATOR: She looks up and sees Imagawa.

KOZATSUMA: Oh, now I know what's going on. You saw Imagawa looking at us and you got too embarrassed to sleep with me. Listen, Imagawa, you have to understand how much I love this man. I'd die for him. And he told me that cutting off his finger [a traditional sign of love] is old hat—he'd even pound all five fingers with a bamboo flute just to show how much he loves me. Imagawa, help me get him to stay with me.

BUNZŌ: Look here, girl. This is terrible. You're getting over-
              wrought.
KOZATSUMA: I love your face when it looks angry like that.
NARRATOR: She snuggles coquettishly against him.
IMAGAWA: All right, Kozatsuma, I'll help you with your lover.
NARRATOR: She puts the futon over Kozatsuma, pulls Bunzō out
              from under it, and begins to give Bunzō a piece of her
              mind, all the while kicking Kozatsuma, who remains
              under the covers. Kozatsuma then struggles out from
              beneath the quilts [Figure 23].
KOZATSUMA: Who did that?
BUNZŌ: Girl, I'm sorry. Now then, Imagawa, today we finally
              have a chance to spend some time together.
IMAGAWA: That's useless to me now.
KOZATSUMA: Yes, Imagawa, and this way you can have fun meeting
              your secret lover.
BUNZŌ: Girl, tell me, does she have a lover?
KOZATSUMA: She sure does. It's Shimbei, and they're really tight.[78]
IMAGAWA: There is a good explanation for all this.
BUNZŌ: Don't try to wriggle out of it. I've been ruined because
              of you. And we even had a child together. To think I
              believed in you until now. A dog is more honest—at
              least it wags its tail if it really likes you. No, no, go
              ahead. Be Shimbei's lover.
NARRATOR: He pushes her away. Then he seizes her and pushes
              her down.
BUNZŌ: Filthy bitch! Don't act so sorry for yourself.
NARRATOR: He moves away from her.
IMAGAWA: Is there nothing I can say? If you give me a chance, I
              can explain.
              Listen, Bunzō, I know you can't stand the fact that I
              met Shimbei, but it's *you* I want to be with.
BUNZŌ: Spare me your fine turns of phrase. You were intimate
              with Shimbei, weren't you?

Fig. 23 Scenes from *The Courtesan on the Buddha Plain*. Above, Bunzō (Tōjūrō) arrives at Imagawa's establishment in the pleasure district, disguised as a flute-playing priest, while Imagawa tells Bunzō's servant (upper right) how much she misses Bunzō. Below, Imagawa tramples her rival Kozatsuma, who is hiding under a quilt after failing in her attempt to seduce Bunzō (at left, still disguised as a priest). Book illustration, artist unknown, 1699. Courtesy of Osaka Prefectural Nakanoshima Library.

IMAGAWA: Just listen to me. Shimbei was totally obsessed with me. He said he was head over heels in love and was dying for his dreams to come true. It was all in the letters he sent me this year. But I have no feelings for him at all. I don't care what the master says—if I give him no sign of my approval, he can't have me. How can you possibly imagine that I would be untrue to you? It's too cruel!

NARRATOR: She breaks down in tears. Bunzō claps his hands in admiration.

BUNZŌ: You are a bodhisattva. I was wrong. Forgive me.

NARRATOR: Bunzō clasps his hands together, beseeching her.

IMAGAWA: Let's put this behind us. Hold me.

NARRATOR: They embrace, their love as true as ever.[79]

Fig. 24 The conclusion of *The Courtesan on the Buddha Plain*. At bottom, all the play's ladies dance at the kaichō display of the "shod Buddha" in Kyoto. Book illustration, artist unknown, 1699. Courtesy of Osaka Prefectural Nakanoshima Library .

This a typical Tōjūrō love scene, rich with doubts and accusations, anger and domestic violence, ribald humor and erotic suggestiveness, and with "true love" prevailing at the end. Imagawa and Bunzō's troubles do not end with this scene. When Bunzō learns that Imagawa's father is an ally of his evil brother Tatewaki, Bunzō breaks from her, although his feelings have not changed. He does this in order to spare her the agony of having to choose whether to betray her father or her lover. Imagawa later convinces her father of the folly of his actions, and her father kills Tatewaki to atone for his own past evil deeds. The play ends with a kaichō scene, in which the rare statue of the "shod Buddha" has been brought to Kyoto, and the whole city turns out to view it and to revel in the cherry blossoms. The scene concludes with all the onnagata singing and dancing among the gorgeous flowers (Figure 24).

Bunzō was far and away Tōjūrō's most popular role to that point. With this play, Tōjūrō was rated the finest actor in the Kansai, and he would stay at the top of the list until he died. In 1699 Tōjūrō was the unrivaled master of the young lover role. He was in fact fifty-three years old, yet he was capable of playing the sexiest, most desirable twenty-five year-old man in Japan. Perhaps more than anything else, this attests to his remarkable skill as an actor.

Tōjūrō Perfects His Art: Kabuki's Finest Actor at Work

Tōjūrō revolutionized the kabuki actor's art. He was the first who simply would not and did not dance. Most critics maintained that he was weak in roles that were physically demanding, "roles where one had to fight, jump, and leap about."[80] He had danced when he was young, and one hyōbanki says that "he could do roppō entrances, samurai strutting, and dance" if he thought that Kyoto audiences would enjoy this more than his own chosen style: "He could master it overnight. After all, you can learn these things working in front of a mirror."[81] This entry makes two important assumptions: that Tōjūrō's art is even more challenging than traditional dance-based acting, and that Kyoto audiences preferred Tōjūrō's style. Competition among Genroku kabuki actors was intense, and it was a time when theatrical innovation brought with it acclaim and financial rewards. All surviving records indicate that Tōjūrō was intelligent, clever, and diligent. He very likely created a new acting style deliberately, so that he would stand out.[82] He developed a style that suited his talents, but he may also have consciously limited the range of his performance precisely in order to create a clear, unmistakable image for himself.

Tōjūrō invented a stage art that contemporary records call "stationary acting" (i-kyōgen). Within this form, Tōjūrō demonstrated his mastery of dialog acting (ji-gei) and monologs (katari). This style of acting was broad and flexible enough to allow Tōjūrō's goals to differ from one scene to another. Sometimes he sought to amuse his audience, and sometimes he wanted them to weep along with the characters. Often he sought to impress audiences and critics alike with the realism of the action onstage. Critics described his acting in phrases like, "He looks like a real man when he quarrels with women," and "When he is engaged in discussions with a proprietor, it is totally convincing. Everyone in the audience agrees that this is just the way such conversations are."[83] This latter evaluation was written by Ejima Kiseki, and since this critic actually spent much of his adult life wasting his family's fortune in the pleasure district, his is no empty praise.

But Tōjūrō's realism was not for everyone, as the author of *An Actors' Hand-drum* (*Yakusha Itchō Tsuzumi*; 1702) noted:

> He is uninteresting to rank beginners and people from other provinces. There was once a man who came for the first time from a far-off province to go sightseeing in the capital. He wanted to see Tōjūrō, the pride of Kyoto, and he went with some of his friends to see kabuki.
>
> After he returned home from sightseeing, his friends in the country asked him if he had seen Kyoto's renowned Tōjūrō perform. The country man responded that he had indeed, and that he supposed that perhaps Tōjūrō was a skilled performer, but that he had not seen anything happen onstage to indicate this. All Tōjūrō had done was to come onstage and consult with people on various matters. The visitor from the country wished that Tōjūrō could have done his consulting in the dressing room and used the stage for a performance. "I guess my timing was off. I went to see him when he got involved in some discussion onstage which I never really did understand. It's too bad."[84]

This anecdote seems considerably embellished, but it is merely the most dramatic of many statements to the effect that provincial spectators did not enjoy Tōjūrō's work. The out-of-town tourist's disappointment suggests what a radical departure "realistic" acting was for the Japanese stage, and that it was, like any new innovation, difficult to understand at first. Spectators less familiar with the theater preferred kabuki of the sort that one Kyoto critic dismissed contemptuously as "waving peacock feathers and dancing angels."[85] Critics often referred to colorful, showy kabuki as "flower," a word that Zeami had used in his treatises on nō in the fifteenth century to describe the quality of beauty that performers should strive to achieve. What Zeami had meant by the metaphor was "something special in a performer that stands out from the supporting texture of the performance, the way that a colorful flower stands out against the greenery of a garden."[86] Kiseki wrote that Hanzaemon was "a flower in full bloom, but that Tōjūrō throws away his flower."[87] Others wrote that Tōjūrō was not flower, but fruit.[88] What all this "flowery" language meant was, in fact, complimentary to the actor: while the old, showy kabuki was good, Tōjūrō's new, consciously subdued, more realistic style was better. To be fair to the critics, even during Tōjūrō's heyday from 1699 through 1704, although they themselves considered Tōjūrō and his acting style the best in kabuki, they almost always mentioned in their commentary the opposing opinions that criticized realistic acting and sang the praises of dance and exaggerated martial heroics.

Until Tōjūrō, stage movement and posture in all forms of Japanese drama had been based on formal conventions derived from dance and mime, but Tōjūrō said:

> There are some actors who carefully study how to gesture effectively in plays. Of course, since actors appear before an audience, effective gestures are better than poor ones. I have not studied gesture myself. Gestures are not something that one can invent. They are a manifestation of the emotions. When one is joyful or angry, one's emotions show themselves naturally in the body.
>
> Can gestures be anything other than this?[89]

Tōjūrō approached realism by mastering the play text more thoroughly than any actor had before, and then remaining completely focused onstage, taking in all the words and physical expressions of the other actors, as aids in the creation of his own character. He told a fellow actor that it was his policy to:

> ... commit the words [of a play] to memory [during rehearsal] and on opening day forget them completely. However, I listen onstage to what the other actors say to me, and then I remember my lines and speak them. The reason I do this is that when we encounter people in daily life, and perhaps fight or argue with them, we cannot use lines prepared in advance.
>
> We hear what others have to say, and only then are we moved to reply. In acting, I think that everyday life should be the model, and that is why I memorize my lines thoroughly in rehearsal and forget them when I go onstage on the first day.[90]

Tōjūrō's insight as to what makes dialog seem real and not contrived is on the mark, and the analytical rigor that underlies his method of preparation shows the extent to which he was "a thinking man's actor." The modern director's oft-repeated admonition to actors that they must listen and react to other actors, rather than just delivering their own lines, is standard procedure in theater today, but the concept was revolutionary in Tōjūrō's day, and his total immersion in plays and characters made his art unique.

Hanzaemon, watching his rival at work onstage, pronounced Tōjūrō an intuitive actor, a one-of-a-kind genius whose style could neither be emulated nor taught. But to brand a person "a natural genius" is to belittle his efforts, and Hanzaemon probably did so out of misunderstanding, envy, or a combination of both. Fortunately, Kyoto's sophisticated critics realized the difficulty of the task Tōjūrō had set for himself. As early as 1693, the author of *Sumo Wrestling Actors (Yarō Seki Zumō)* had written of Tōjūrō:

He devotes careful study not only to his own lines, but to those of all the other actors in the play, and tries to bring out their various emotions. He does not interrupt the play with trifling asides. He concentrates on hearing and seeing what is happening onstage.

No one has ever paid as much attention to the fine points of acting as this man.[91]

This evaluation suggests how single-minded and controlled Tōjūrō must have been onstage, but his preparations always began long before the curtain rose and he walked down the bridgeway—even long before he started memorizing his lines. In order to portray different characters and a range of emotions realistically, Tōjūrō had to store up experiences and feelings inside him, so that they were ready to pour forth as if naturally when given the proper stimulus by an onstage situation. In his offstage life, he had to experience a wide range of activities and emotional situations.

All the contributors to *The Actors' Analects* agree that, for Tōjūrō, all of daily life was preparation for the stage. In Tōjūrō's own words, "The actor's art is like a beggar's bag. Regardless of whether you need it at the time or not, you should pick up everything you come across and take it away with you. There must not be anything about which you are entirely ignorant. Even purse-cutting should be carefully studied."[92] Tōjūrō was serious about this idea of "careful study." The writer Somekawa Jurōbei described how Tōjūrō once stopped at a tofu shop at Fourth Avenue and Kawara Street, and "stood at the entrance without going in, asking probing questions about how to make tofu."[93] Tōjūrō no doubt realized that he might someday have to play the proprietor of a tofu shop.

Tōjūrō did not believe that mere passive receptivity would be adequate preparation. He actively created situations in his offstage life that would enhance his skill as an actor. Thorough pre-performance preparation was more than a job or a pastime for Tōjūrō; if we are to believe the many accounts left by his colleagues in *The*

Actors' Analects, thorough preparation was a way of life, and perhaps even an obsession for him. He studied certain skills specifically
so that he could perform more realistically onstage. Kaneko, for
instance, noted how his proficiency in first aid stood him in excellent stead when he had to save a character who had attempted suicide in *The Ten Thousand Lanterns on Mount Kōya (Kōyasan
Mandō)* in 1696.[94] Tōjūrō played wealthy men whose generosity allowed their fortunes to flow quickly into the purses of friends and
clients, and justified his own extravagance and generosity as essential to his ability to portray millionaires convincingly. The young
men he played wasted their lives away in the pleasure district, and
Tōjūrō was praised for his realistic negotiations with brothel owners
and interactions with courtesans. Preparation for this sort of onstage
activity posed a problem for Tōjūrō because he was opposed, for
professional reasons, to the idea of kabuki actors' sporting in the
pleasure district. He wanted kabuki to become a more respectable
art form, and believed that for actors to be seen in the pleasure district would lower their professional credibility to the level of *taiko-
mochi,* the silly male jokesters and musicians who were hired to
enliven parties with courtesans, maids, and bathhouse girls.[95] Tōjūrō
apparently only went to the pleasure district a few times, for
research purposes, visiting each major establishment just once.[96]

When faced with an unfamiliar or particularly challenging role,
Tōjūrō endeavored to study it offstage first. Before he became
zamoto, Tōjūrō was faced with the particularly challenging role of a
man who betrays his wife. His method of preparing for this role is
perhaps the most famous of all the Tōjūrō anecdotes. The actor began a romantic dalliance with the proprietress of a restaurant in the
Gion, but after she had carefully prepared for their first night of
love, he hastily fled the scene. The following day Tōjūrō went to the
restaurant and thanked the woman, explaining that the aborted love
affair had been his way of preparing for the upcoming play and that,
thanks to her, he was now confident that his work onstage would go
well. "The people who were there and overheard his remarks

clapped their hands in astonishment, thinking how the methods of
true masters were beyond the grasp of ordinary men."[97] The fact that
Tōjūrō had betrayed the trust of the restaurant owner did not seem
to matter at all to the actor or his admirers, and modern readers' very
different reactions to this incident inspired Kikuchi Kan to write a
play called *Tōjūrō's Love*, in which the wronged woman commits
suicide in Tōjūrō's theater while the play is in progress.[98]

This single incident has had the unfortunate effect of typecast-
ing Tōjūrō as the sort of "coldhearted artistic genius" that Akuta-
gawa made famous with stories like "Hell Screen," but in fact most
anecdotes attest to his generosity and kindness. The demands of the
theater did not usually bring out Tōjūrō's heartless side, but rather
his graciousness.

Tōjūrō understood how easily the circumstances of an actor's
private life could help or hinder performances. When Tōjūrō became zamoto he made it his company's policy to aid onnagata in living as women offstage, and to treat them in the most courteous
manner that men could treat women in the Edo period. This same
appreciation of the influence of life offstage helped make Tōjūrō an
effective director. For example, when two skilled and high-ranking
onnagata were having trouble with one scene during a rehearsal of
The Story of Princess Jōruri (Jūnidan Zōshi), Tōjūrō recognized that
the two actors were unconsciously transferring their own identities
onto their characters, and so were injecting a completely inappropriate sense of equality and spirit of competitiveness into a play about a
princess and her subservient, loyal lady-in-waiting. Once Tōjūrō had
alerted the two onnagata to the source of the problem, they were
able to do a fine job with the scene.[99]

Tōjūrō tried never to take his skill as an actor for granted.
Whenever he became too contented, his acting suffered, and audiences let him know it. In the second sequel to *The Courtesan on the
Buddha Plain*, in the summer of 1699, Tōjūrō was riding on the
wave of his popularity as Bunzō. The play called for Tōjūrō to do a
solo comic interlude, while Bunzō waits for a chance to meet Ōshū

in private. On opening night Tōjūrō "hammed up" this scene, and met with heckling. Once again he had learned painfully that the only way to succeed was to "play the play." "'I realize now,' he said, 'that sincerity is paramount. I am fifty-three years old, and yet my art is not fully developed. Does that mean that it never will be?' There was a note of despair in his voice."[100] Tōjūrō remained ever the self-reflective superstar.

Creation of a Romantic Image

Tōjūrō's methodical, intellectual approach to his craft won him the admiration of the Genroku cultural elite, including not a few from the ranks of the samurai, but this does not explain why the ladies loved him so much. And love him they did. Early in 1700, *A Ten-Thousand-Year History of Actors (Yakusha Mannen Goyomi)* was breathless in its appraisal of him: "He is the founder of the Temple of Courtesan Love Scenes, Inspector of the Eight Sects of Love, the Saint Ippen of Heterosexual Love, the Grand Minister of Sexual Love. He's so masculine you want to exchange vows of love the minute you are introduced."[101] Ejima Kiseki wrote this hyōbanki, but for entries like this, he and other authors wrote in the guise of women, probably because more and more women were attending kabuki and reading the hyōbanki.

Tōjūrō was Japan's first romantic theater idol. The women of Kyoto and Osaka adored him much as American women of the 1920s adored Rudolph Valentino. But offstage Tōjūrō was definitely not a romantic ladies' man. He surrounded himself with theatrical colleagues, and let the women of the Kansai pine for him at a distance. It was not the real Tōjūrō that women yearned for, but the image that they saw in the characters he portrayed. Of course, the intensity of Tōjūrō's approach to his work would have been well known by the mid-1690s, and spectators might reasonably assume that there would be little difference between the private man and characters like Bunzō or Izaemon. But in fact Tōjūrō only needed to experience something once to make it a part of his actor's toolbox, and didn't have to actually live the profligate life of the young wastrels he depicted onstage.

Many scholars have set out to explain the tremendous appeal Tōjūrō held for women spectators when he was at the height of his career.[102] The key was not likely to have been his good looks. He was fifty-three years old in 1699, and many young tachiyaku actors must have been more handsome than he. Much of the sex appeal of Tōjūrō's characters was projected onto them by other characters. In most of his plays at least three beautiful, talented, and charming women go into raptures over Tōjūrō's hero and compete to win his love. If the performances of these onnagata were convincing and made the heroines' feelings seem genuine, then these feelings might well be shared by many women in the audience, despite their intellectual understanding that everything taking place onstage was fictionalized. Geidan accounts suggest that as a zamoto Tōjūrō was a master at helping the onnagata in his company prepare for their work onstage, and that this directorial talent was primarily motivated by the desire to see his colleagues become better actors, but it had the side effect of furthering his own image as a romantic paragon.

Tōjūrō's attractiveness to women characters onstage surely helped increase his mystique offstage, but his characters' power to attract was no one-way street: perhaps equally important to the actor's charm was the fact that the characters he played were entirely fascinated by women. Women, and love for women, dominated his heroes' lives. Most of his characters were samurai, but family honor meant nothing to them when their romantic lives were at stake. Each hero was willing to sacrifice his fortune and good name to remain true to the woman he loved. When it came to true love, even the man fallen from wealth had no use for pride, as the character Samon demonstrates in a 1700 play when he cheerfully goes off to borrow a cup of rice to make his own meal, without any concern for his status or reputation, thinking only of the woman he loves.[103] Tōjūrō's heroes never used women as a means of attaining something else of greater value to them, a practice that would have been all too common in real life. Instead women themselves were always of greater value to his heroes than anything else.

The classic Tōjūrō hero is intelligent and generous and has a winning sense of humor. He can be angry, petulant, and a little violent when he feels that a woman has betrayed him, but this is because love means so much to him. He is resourceful in the expression of love, and knows well that wit and originality can help win a woman's heart. In several plays, the shy but infatuated hero uses a pet monkey to convey his feelings to the girl he loves,[104] an endearing trick which Disney's bashful Aladdin was to use three centuries later.

Tōjūrō strove to create a mainstream heterosexual romantic hero, and this of course did not appeal to all women. Some liked their men "kinkier" than a Bunzō or Kamon, and Ejima Kiseki expressed the feelings of such women in the words of "one capricious young widow—a nun in service to the world of pleasure" who said, "He's too gentle and healthy, not capricious enough. It's a real flaw in the gem, and in this he is very unskilled. For this I would have to rate him very low."[105]

But most women had no objection to gentle and healthy men, and idolized Tōjūrō. If the women in the audience were to have paused and used their good judgment to consider the Bunzōs, Kamons, and Samons that Tōjūrō brought to life on the kabuki stage, they would have recognized what terrible husbands they would make. But what entertaining, chic, and sensitive lovers they would be. Tōjūrō created a fantasy man who was irresistible to most women, and he did this by using his own formidable skills in realistic acting, and reinforcing the appeal of his heroes by having Chikamatsu write into his plays a bevy of remarkable women who adore them.

The Inner Man: An Unsolved Mystery

In his personal life Tōjūrō was not the witty career lover-boy that he depicted onstage. Apart from his research-motivated near-affair with the restaurant owner described above, rumor attributed to him only one other lady paramour, the proprietress of the Yoshifumi-sha in Gion, with whom he was reputedly "very tight."[106] Tōjūrō never married, although he may have had two sons. It was remarkable for an actor of his stature to choose not to marry and establish a strong family line of actors. All the great tachiyaku, and even the onnagata of the age were doing it, including Arashi San'emon, Danjūrō, Hanzaemon, and Ayame. But not Tōjūrō.

In the Edo period a man who never married was most likely devoted to the pure way of male love, but there is no clear record of this either. In the same hyōbanki that published the rumor of his love affair with the Yoshifumi-sha proprietress, another commentator counters that rumor with the confident assertion that Tōjūrō is in fact "really close to Mr. Senju,"[107] meaning Kirinami Senju, the onnagata most frequently paired with Tōjūrō onstage. Entries in The Actors' Analects say that Tōjūrō was "particularly attached" to some of his onnagata and went on two- to three-day excursions with groups of them.[108] If the actor had truly been a devoted follower of homosexual love, there would have been no need to conceal that fact for any fear of stigma in the Genroku period. Of course, it would not have strengthened Tōjūrō's romantic appeal among women fans if definitive, widely-known information showed him to be a dedicated homosexual. Tōjūrō's sexual orientation will likely remain a matter of conjecture. If we accept all the above rumors as true, we can assume that Tōjūrō, like Danjūrō, partook of relations with both men and women. Unlike Danjūrō, however, there is no indication that Tōjūrō considered love affairs of any kind to be inimical to his effectiveness onstage.

An even greater mystery is Tōjūrō's aversion to marriage and family, institutions which, as Danjūrō had written, were (and are) the very foundation of Japanese society. Although there is no reason to believe that Tōjūrō ever married, he reputedly had two sons. Neither son appears at all in the geidan records. Because these accounts provide extensive details on Tōjūrō's life, the absence of references to children suggests that his sons were not very important to him. A single entry for each son in the hyōbanki states that he was fathered by Tōjūrō. This is slender evidence of Tōjūrō's paternity, but most Japanese historians accept it as true. Both sons had careers as kabuki actors, and although both used the name Sakata, there is no evidence that Tōjūrō personally raised or trained the boys when they were young. The older of the two, Tōkurō, was born in 1668. His first appearance in the hyōbanki shows him, at the age of eighteen, living separately from his father and earning a salary of fifteen ryō as an actor of wakashu roles. A later entry says that as a child he performed with minor troupes in the Kyoto region. It seems that Tōkurō had to struggle to make it into the list of rank-and-file kabuki actors. As a child he received no training or nurturing of the sort that Danjūrō lavished on his son Kuzō. Surviving records tell us that Tōkurō appeared with his father onstage just once, playing a priest in *The Courtesan on the Buddha Plain* in 1699. After this, Tōkurō disappears from the historical record; he either died or left kabuki.

Tōjūrō's second son was Sakata Heishichirō. We do not know the dates of his birth or death, but hyōbanki record his career in kabuki as spanning the years 1705 to 1712. In 1705, when Tōjūrō was at the Nunobukuroya-za, Heishichirō served as zamoto, even though he was still a wakashu actor. This is strong evidence for Heishichirō's close connection to Tōjūrō, since no wakashu actor could possibly rise to this position unless he were serving as the agent of a more powerful figure. Father and son worked in different companies in 1706, and in 1707 Heishichirō became an onnagata. In the same year Tōjūrō formally recognized Yamatoyama Jinzaemon (1667–1721), a promising disciple unrelated to him by blood, as the next generation's premiere actor of romantic leads. Jinzaemon had become a Tōjūrō disciple just three years before.

Since Tōjūrō remained unmarried, he would have likely arranged for his sons to be raised, during their early childhood, by married relatives. This would not have prevented him from taking the boys under his wing as disciples. As a teacher Tōjūrō could have prepared either of his sons to succeed him, but it appears that he did not. It would seem that Tōjūrō, unlike his peers, did not regard his art as family property. For Tōjūrō, acting in romantic lead roles did not require the mastery of a repertory of techniques, but was a matter of conviction and personality. If Heishichirō did not have the will or inclination to be a tachiyaku actor, and preferred instead to be an onnagata, Tōjūrō was content to let his son pursue that calling.

We can only speculate, but it is possible that Tōjūrō consciously structured his private life in a manner that he believed would increase his appeal to women spectators. By remaining unmarried and unconstrained by family ties, he preserved an illusion of availability to women admirers, and his ambiguous sexual orientation may have further fueled women's interest. This same pattern was repeated a century and a half later with Danjūrō VIII, the most popular kabuki heartthrob ever to work on the Edo stage. Like Tōjūrō, Danjūrō VIII remained unmarried throughout his life, and kept his love life a closely-guarded secret. The women of Edo adored him. In the 1840s and 1850s Danjūrō VIII look-alike dolls were being mass-produced for women fans, and the outpouring of women admirers' grief upon his death far surpassed even the Tōjūrō phenomenon.[109] The women of Edo brought so many gifts to Danjūrō VIII's grave that the temple had to maintain a twenty-four-hour guard to keep robbers away.[110] Even today in Japan it is apparent that women theatergoers empathize with warmhearted characters who nevertheless cannot enjoy family ties, and that they are intrigued by attractive performers of mysterious or ambiguous sexuality.[111] Tōjūrō's offstage persona almost seems to fit the heartthrob requirements too well for it to have been completely uncontrived.

The women of Kansai loved Tōjūrō while he graced the Kyoto stage and mourned him after his death, but it was male critics and colleagues who wrote the elegies praising his personal character. A careful scrutiny of surviving hyōbanki and geidan shows that, like any man, he had his strengths and foibles; he was a man of contradictions. Tōjūrō was sometimes virtuous to a fault. He was careful always to maintain his personal dignity, and continually sought to elevate kabuki's stature and reputation. He was convinced that this meant that he should not consort with courtesans in the pleasure district, but rumor had it that he lacked even the courtesy to reply to letters sent him by the courtesan Imagawa (a real woman, not the character from *The Buddha Plain*) who had fallen in love with him, and that his silence hurt her deeply.[112]

Tōjūrō was a "high liver," and remarkably open with his wealth. This was fine when it meant helping others, as when he gave the owner of his favorite restaurant money to build a teahouse, and handled the matter so discreetly that it was never apparent that large sums of money were changing hands.[113] When he invited colleagues to his home he made a point of serving only gourmet fare, and tailored the menu to suit the tastes of individual guests.[114] Tōjūrō sent his most famous gift, on the occasion of the New Year, to his good friend and sometime rival Nakamura Shichisaburō a few months after Shichisaburō's return to Edo. Rather than send something typical or something ostentatious, Tōjūrō had a barrel of pure Kyoto water shipped all the way to Edo for Shichisaburō to use in making his New Year's tea. The water was free, but the shipping charge would have been very expensive, and the gift demonstrated Tōjūrō's sensitivity not only to his friend's needs (by all accounts Edo water was not very tasty), but also to his friend's stature, since Kyoto water was the one thing that money could not buy in Edo. Shichisaburō said of the gift, "After my meetings in Kyoto with Tōjūrō I thought I had gotten to know him thoroughly, but obviously I had not. This present shows a depth of feeling which is hard to measure."[115] Somekawa Jūrōbei, who recounted the incident, was deeply impressed: "Even so sensitive a man as Shichisaburō had difficulty divining the depths of Tōjūrō's heart. Other people were incapable of even discussing him."[116]

Extravagance for the benefit of others is no fault, but Tōjūrō was extravagant in his own consumption too. The Genroku period was the era of the "big spender," and Japanese in Edo and the Kansai loved to read and listen to tales of spendthrift behavior. No doubt a certain amount of envy underlay the circulation of these stories, and Tōjūrō supplied plenty of grist for the rumor mills. After *The Buddha Plain* he lived in a veritable mansion, a house larger than that of any other actor. Ejima Kiseki wrote that as Tōjūrō grew older his taste for luxury increased. "He wouldn't wear a robe again after it had been laundered once. He lit his living room exclusively with candles, and wouldn't eat a meal unless it included fish or fowl. He drank strong tea after every meal and warmed his saké in a fire fueled by aloeswood. These are indications of the extent to which his extravagance had advanced."[117] When asked to account for his spendthrift ways, Tōjūrō laughed and said that he was making almost 1,000 ryō a year precisely because he managed his affairs so wastefully. "When one becomes well known and is acclaimed as one of the top three actors in the country, shouldn't one be large-hearted? It wouldn't do for me to concern myself over petty details, now would it?"[118] Kiseki noted that despite his high salary Tōjūrō had difficulty making ends meet, and that there was very little money to his name when he died in 1709.

One act that struck even his friends as unusually extravagant took place when a wealthy samurai admirer of Tōjūrō's sent him a gift of a full-grown pine tree to plant in his garden. When it became apparent that the tree was not going to fit through the gate in the garden wall, Tōjūrō nonchalantly told the workmen to tear the wall down. "A bit of plaster afterward will put it right," he said.[119] Rebuilding the wall would of course be time-consuming and expensive, but Tōjūrō enjoyed making a fine show of having money to burn.

Tōjūrō's strong sense of propriety usually impelled him to be kind and considerate to others, but he could be an unpleasant stick-in-the-mud if he felt that other people were not applying themselves seriously enough to their work. He had no qualms about criticizing even those of superior social status when he felt that they were not attending to business. Whenever an actor asked Tōjūrō for an evaluation of his work onstage, he could count, for better or for worse, on total honesty. Even actors whose performances had been very well received by audiences could not necessarily expect praise from Tōjūrō. Nor did it matter to the actor if a long, analytical reply might ruin the conviviality of a social gathering—he would speak his mind no matter what.[120] If his colleagues' geidan are to be trusted, it would seem that hypocrisy was foreign to him.

Taking on New Challenges

Tōjūrō followed his triumph in the *Buddha Plain* trilogy with starring roles in Chikamatsu plays for the 1699–1700 theater season, and he continued to be the toast of Kyoto. As one critic put it: "Just as innumerable hands stroke the back of the necks of teahouse girls or healing Buddha statues, so tens of thousands of people are talking about him, and everything they say is favorable."[121] The writer added that "he has become an icon of excellence to Kyotoites, and the merciful Kannon to women."[122]

For six years Tōjūrō had flourished as zamoto of the Mandayū-za theater, working with the capable Chikamatsu-Kaneko playwriting team. In the 1700–1701 season, for reasons that remain obscure, he gave up his zamoto rank and left the Mandayū-za to work under Yamatoya Jimbei as the leading tachiyaku at the Hayakumo-za. Initially he was to work alongside Hanzaemon, Mizuki Tatsunosuke, and Yoshizawa Ayame, and perhaps it was the chance to team up with the three best actors in Kyoto that lured him away. It turned out that Hanzaemon would leave the Hayakumo-za for the Ebisuya-za company even before the season opened, but this was still a rare opportunity to work with both Ayame and Tatsunosuke. It was a strange year for Kyoto kabuki, with Chikamatsu and Kaneko writing not for Tōjūrō, but for the newest, least experienced troupe in the city. Tōjūrō warned Jimbei and Ayame that their theater and the

Ebisuya-za—both old and established companies—could not afford to let down their guard; precisely because the Mandayu-za company seemed outmatched by the others it was likely to prove a dangerous rival.[123] Just as Tōjūrō had predicted, Kyotoites flocked to see "new blood" on the kabuki stage, and the Mandayū-za more than held its own. The other two companies were forced to showcase their young actors in order to stay competitive.

Tōjūrō played one notable role that season in a unique play entitled *Up-to-Date Kyōgen (Imayō Nō Kyōgen)*, a work in five acts which presented kabuki adaptations of five unrelated kyōgen farces. Tōjūrō starred, in the fourth act, as a stutterer embroiled in a trouble-ridden marriage. The challenge of the role as Tōjūrō conceived it was to do a convincing simulation of a speech disability that sounded silly, and yet to somehow induce spectators to empathize with the stutterer so fully that they would weep with him over his predicament.[124] Speech impediments were outside Tōjūrō's direct experience, so he had to rely on intellectual analysis alone to solve the problem. On opening day the audience laughed and praised Tōjūrō's acting, but Tōjūrō was chagrined at his failure. After a full night of rethinking and experimenting with his delivery he went back onstage the second night and had the audience in tears. Tōjūrō's success in this play was based on his intuitive understanding of stuttering.

> Stuttering may occur when a man remembers inwardly that he is a stutterer, and so, feeling ashamed that people are listening to him, stutters from embarrassment. But it can also happen that he forgets himself and stutters, as when he is happy or angry. Today I refrained from stuttering when I might have done so out of embarrassment, and stuttered only in moments of joy, and anger, and when I found things funny.[125]

Tōjūrō had met the challenge of this role brilliantly, but looking back at his achievement today, it becomes tinged with irony. In two years he would suffer a stroke and would himself need to overcome a very real speech impediment in order to continue his career.

Tōjūrō's Art in Full Flower: The Courtesan and the Great Buddhist Service at Mibu Temple

Late in 1701, Tōjūrō rejoined the Mandayū-za and playwrights Chika-matsu and Kaneko, all working under zamoto Arashi San'emon II. San'emon recognized that Tōjūrō was the foremost actor in the Kansai, and he arranged for his writers to work closely with Tōjūrō on the Mandayū-za plays. Texts do not survive for either the kaomise play or the New Year's play of 1702, but the hyōbanki offered the usual praise for Tōjūrō's work in them. The second play of 1702, *The Courtesan and the Great Buddhist Service at Mibu Temple (Keisei Mibu Dainenbutsu)* was the single greatest triumph of Tōjūrō's career. Critics had written that Tōjūrō consciously avoided "flower" onstage, meaning that he did not do "showy" per-formances, but he had long been developing his talent as a virtuoso monologist to such an extent that he could showcase his work in this area as "flower" when he chose to do so. In *Mibu Temple* his monologs were the undisputed highlights of the play.

Mibu Temple is a long, complex succession dispute play featur-ing a wealthy, dissolute young hero named Takatō Min'ya, much like Bunzō of *The Buddha Plain*. The new challenge for Tōjūrō was his disguise in Act I. He had to play a poor, bedraggled, habitually drunken peddler of saké lees (pungent dregs which were commonly used by housewives and servants to make pickled radishes). Despite Tōjūrō's espousal of realistic portrayals of onstage characters, he had not favored this approach to playing members of the lowest strata of society; he wanted greater verisimilitude in kabuki, but did not advo-cate unsightliness on the stage.[126] On the opening day of *Mibu Temple*, and on the second day as well, the spectators made clear that they did not like Tōjūrō's peddler, shouting at him to cut short his monologs. When the play ended at nightfall on the second day, Tōjūrō stayed behind at the theater with another actor to try to work out the problems. His solution started with a change to a more realistic, more disheveled costume. This was not the first time that costuming had been key to good acting for Tōjūrō,[127] and the fact that the mere donning of a costume could have such a profound effect on his ability to "become" a particular character links him to Japanese theatrical traditions that extend as far back as nō drama. The story of Tōjūrō's second rehearsal tells us that he dressed as shabbily as a real peddler would, and went through his entire routine on the empty stage in the darkened auditorium.[128] When he exited from the bridgeway and appeared backstage he was still so much "in character" that two men who happened to see him there passed out from fright, believing that a thief had broken in to the theater. Tōjūrō then went home and further refined his monolog. From the third day of the run, his saké lees peddler's impersonation was the hit of the show, and audiences clamored for him to continue the monolog indefinitely.

Tōjūrō's peddler was not a frightening figure. Let us now enter the play (as it was later published by Chikamatsu) to observe the actor in the most popular role of his career. Young Min'ya, impoverished by his own extravagant patronage of the pleasure district, wanders homeless, eking out a living by selling saké lees. The peddler supports two baskets on a shoulder pole, one of them containing a wooden saké bottle (Figure 25). He happens upon the mansion of Princess Katsu, his official fiancée, whom he has never met:

> Wearing an old straw hat and an old hemp kimono that is half falling off his shoulders, he enters.
> "Saké lees! Fine housemaids, do you want saké lees?" Drunk on saké, he totters along. He comes to a certain mansion; from inside he can hear the sounds of shamisen music and women singing popular songs. "Will you buy

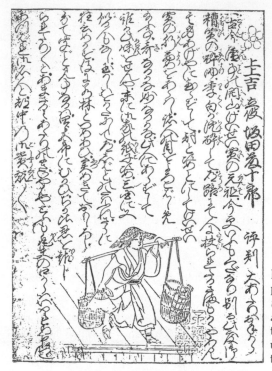

Fig. 25 Tōjūrō as the saké lees peddler in *The Courtesan and the Great Buddhist Service at Mibu Temple*. Book illustration (frontispiece), artist unknown, 1702. Courtesy of the National Diet Library.

the dregs of a song? Will you buy the leavings of a princess's aloeswood perfume?" He staggers about.

Shintarō's younger sister opens the garden gate and comes outside.[129] She trips on a rope hanging out of one of the baskets.

"I've caught one, I've caught one, I've caught a pretty girl!" He helps her get untangled and she goes back into the house.

The princess then steps out onto the verandah with all her ladies. "Where do all these drunks come from?" they wonder aloud, inspecting him. The peddler takes off his hat and sits down.

He pulls out his saké bottle [and speaks to it].

"It's the lofty courtesan! It's the lofty courtesan! If Your

Fig. 26   A scene from *The Courtesan and the Great Buddhist Service at Mibu Temple*. Min'ya (Tōjūrō), disguised as a saké lees peddler, lounges on the veranda of his fiancée's mansion. The two converse as the imposter claiming to be Min'ya looks on angrily from the right. Book illustration, artist unknown, 1702. Courtesy of the National Diet Library.

Highness should feel a bit queasy, just gulp this down." He pours some saké into a rice bowl. "Your Highness has now had four-fifths of a bowl of saké." He drains the saké, holds the bottle upside down and says, "It's time for her procession!" And, using the bottle, he imitates her walk.

"It's the bandy-legged walk of the courtesan! Now she is entering the brothel. 'Spread my quilts,' she says," and he lays out his hat, placing the cask into it. "There, the great courtesan is going to bed. Sleep well."

He embraces the bottle and lies down. He caresses the bottle. "Oh courtesan, what long ears you have! This is strange, there's a hole in the bottom. I guess it's the same hole as always." Cradling the cask, he falls asleep, dead drunk.[130]

Princess Katsu has no idea that this man is her fiancé. In fact, an evil faction seeking to usurp power from Min'ya's family, the Taka-tōs, has had one of its agents come to call, claiming to be the fiancé Min'ya; the imposter is now waiting in an inner room. Still, the princess is intrigued by the peddler (Figure 26). She senses that despite his appearance he must be a man of high birth who has fallen in the world. She tells her maids wake to him up and bring him inside, but he refuses to budge. He won't see any princess, he says; he is interested only in courtesans. Princess Katsu instructs her maids to tell him that she is a courtesan. On hearing this, the ped-dler grows enthusiastic and staggers inside. Princess Katsu attempts to determine his identity, but he is too drunk to answer her ques-tions correctly. He reveals, nevertheless, that it was love for the cour-tesan Michishiba that brought him to his present state. He is not too drunk to be witty, and soon finds himself completely smitten by the beautiful "courtesan" before him. He proposes marriage, saying that although he has a fiancée, she means nothing to him.

After a time, Princess Katsu learns that the shabby peddler is named Min'ya, and realizes that she now has two men named Min'ya in her house. Her ladies suspect that Takatō Min'ya must be such a famous playboy that all sorts of riffraff have taken to calling themselves by his name in tribute. The women do not for a moment imagine that this man is their mistress's fiancée. The princess leaves the room to ponder the situation. She returns and tells Min'ya that he should go back home and marry his fiancée. He adamantly refuses, insisting that the "courtesan" before him is the only woman he will marry. But he is penniless and cannot afford the huge sum needed to buy her out of prostitution. Min'ya longs for the kind of philanthropic intercession that by then had become standard in Tōjūrō's plays. "Why don't they send someone from home with money for me?" he asks, and weeps, grasping the "courtesan's" hand.[131] Then he falls into a reverie, and in a drunken hallucination sees the family's servants come to rescue him. This hallucinatory monolog was a parody of the felicitous conclusions of so many of

Tōjūrō's earlier plays—scenes in which the suddenly-wealthy hero pays off all his debts to pleasure district establishments and distributes gifts to everyone who has shown some kindness to the courtesan who is now to be his wife.

> "My goodness! Look! They've come all the way to Kyoto for me, all the way from home.
>
> "'Heave-ho, heave-ho,' they're hoisting money boxes on poles. 'One-two, one-two,' a long line of spearmen running in. So many of them have come to greet me. Ten thousand ryō in gold coins; it feels so good, *so* good! All right, it's time to buy out my courtesan. One and all, come and witness this. This will be splendid. Who are you? You're Yomoichi, who taught shamisen to my courtesan? Since you taught her the shamisen, here's a ryō for you.
>
> "'Who is this cat? You're the cat who will be the skin on my courtesan's next shamisen? In that case, here's a ryō for you too. Look, it's a mouse peeping out. What, you're the mouse who used to chew on my courtesan's combs? Well then, here's one ryō for you too. The brothel is in an uproar, the courtesans' women escorts are dumb with amazement.'"
>
> Before he can finish his monolog of love for his courtesan, he falls into a drunken sleep.[132]

Princess Katsu gazes at his sleeping form and decides that she wants him for her lover, not the stiff, formal Min'ya in the other room. The other Min'ya is revealed as an imposter when the Takatos' loyal retainer Hikoroku arrives at the mansion. Princess Katsu declares her love for her betrothed once he wakes, finally sober.

The two monologs quoted above may seem somewhat silly when we read them today, but it is also obvious how entertaining they could be in the hands of a master actor. They are perfect vehicles for

a "one-man show," with Tōjūrō using at least three distinctly different voices (Min'ya's, a narrator's, and a courtesan's) and are wonderfully suited to imaginative mimesis and expressive gesturing. Tōjūrō's
fans were particularly impressed with the way he managed to manip-
ulate the saké bottle so that it truly took on the qualities of a living
courtesan. General consensus among Tōjūrō's supporters held that
no other actor could possibly pull off a scene like that. As a monolog
it was very different from, and far more challenging than, anything
Tōjūrō had done previously. Elsewhere in the play Tōjūrō did fine
work in more conventional scenes, but the peddler scene proved far
and away the most memorable, and the image of a saké lees peddler
came to signify the actor himself (see figure 25).

Tōjūrō spent the remainder of the season playing Min'ya in
Mibu Temple and in two sequels to it. No dissenting voices from the
hyōbanki could now be heard to dispute Tōjūrō's superiority to all
other actors. Yet the anti-Tōjūrō camp found a new reason to dislike
him: his *Mibu Temple* was so superior that they feared that no one
would go see any other plays; they worried that rival theaters would
be bankrupted. These kabuki fans felt betrayed because Tōjūrō had
always advocated performing "without flower," and now his peddler
role, which everyone recognized as being "all flower,"[133] was relegat-
ing their own favorite actors to the shadows. Perhaps fate was reading the hyōbanki in 1702, because she quickly stepped in to "level
the playing field" in Kansai kabuki.

A Fight Against Two Tough New Rivals: Illness and Old Age

In the late fall of 1702, when Tōjūrō was at the height of his powers
and prestige, just nine months after the opening of *Mibu Temple*,
illness forced him to leave the theater for more than a month. He

probably suffered a mild stroke. Tōjūrō was back onstage at the
Mandayū-za for the first show of 1703, in a play about fox posses-
sion. He played a man forced by a fox spirit to speak nonsense, stage
business that may have been created to allude to his temporary

speech impairment. Tōjūrō was back in good form for the second play of the year, in which he portrayed a young man caught in a love triangle, but he did not garner the rave reviews that he had in *Mibu Temple* a year earlier.

While the 1703 season was something of a disappointment for Tōjūrō after his triumph in *Mibu Temple* in 1702, it was a milestone year for Chikamatsu. Chikamatsu wrote *The Love Suicides at Sonezaki (Sonezaki Shinjū)* for Takemoto Gidayū's puppet theater in Osaka. This was the first love suicide play written for puppets, and it was a resounding success. Chikamatsu broke from the pattern he had established for Tōjūrō's kabuki plays by creating a lowly romantic hero with no sense of humor, no sense of style, and no money, who was totally obsessed with the love of just one woman. Puppet theater audiences found it easy to sympathize with this new type of romantic hero. Chikamatsu would write for kabuki for several more years while also writing puppet plays, but soon he would leave Kyoto for Osaka to become Takemoto Gidayū's staff playwright at the Takemoto-za puppet theater. Tōjūrō was on the verge of losing one of the most important weapons in his artistic arsenal.

In the fall of 1703 Tōjūrō was stricken by a much more serious stroke, from which he took a full three months to recover. He made his comeback appearance in a revival of *Yūgiri's Last New Year,* playing Izacmon. In the 1704 version of the play Izaemon reveals that he has been ill and has spent some time convalescing at the Arima hot spring (about thirty miles from Osaka), surely a reference to Tōjūrō's own experience. Playing his favorite role in a play that had always brought him accolades was a wise move, and appears to have given Tōjūrō the confidence to perform at his best. The play had several memorable lines and some fine new shukō, or the free adaptation of well-known plots, including a scene in which Izaemon responds to the appearance of the spirit of his betrayed wife with calm and compassion, a refreshing change from the histrionics typical of such scenes of the occult.

Tōjūrō continued to be ranked at the top of the tachiyaku list in the Kansai, but the 1704 hyōbanki *Actors' Dance Fans (Yakusha Mai Ōgi)* used the metaphor of a pine tree seven times to describe the actor and his art. This hyōbanki states that he is "like a pine tree. Now and in ages past, it is impossible to tire of gazing on him. Tōjūrō is 'the pine' among the three actors of Japan."[134] The hyōbanki noted that audiences had loved his Yūgiri play, feeling that they had seen "Tōjūrō at his best," yet the author wondered if Tōjūrō's unsurpassed skill would "soon be buried by illness as snow covers a pine tree."[135] Of the three felicitous New Year's plants—the pine, the plum, and the bamboo—only the pine is associated with venerable old age; this is clearly not the ideal image for an actor specializing in the parts of romantic young men.

Even Ejima Kiseki, always one of Tōjūrō's most faithful supporters, admitted in 1705 that the actor was beginning to slur his words during the longer lines. This forced Kiseki to wonder if Tōjūrō would enjoy any more great successes on the stage.[136] While Tōjūrō remained at the top of the hierarchy of Kansai tachiyaku, the honor was beginning to mean something akin to that accorded to professors emeriti. A close look at the detailed evaluations in the hyōbanki shows Tōjūrō occasionally being outshone by younger actors. Kiseki observed that in an Osaka staging of the 1705 play *The Courtesan and the Pine of Inaba (Keisei Inaba no Matsu)* a younger actor's reprise of Tōjūrō's role had shown more strength and charm than Tōjūrō's original.[137] Tōjūrō continued to have his devoted supporters and to do solid work onstage, but Kiseki recognized that between 1699 and 1702 the general public had come to expect the remarkable from Tōjūrō, and was bound to be disappointed with anything less.[138] Tōjūrō would never again manage a play to rival the smash hits of *Mibu Temple* and *The Courtesan on the Buddha Plain*.

As he battled illness, even Tōjūrō, with his prodigious imagination and strength of will, was hard-pressed to narrow the gap between the reality of his aging physique and the youthful fantasies he sought to create onstage. Tōjūrō was perceptive, and certainly he recognized this contradiction and sensed his own powerlessness to resolve it. The very "realism" that he had brought to the kabuki stage now threatened his career. It would be a few more years before the hyōbanki published the brutal truth about the venerable old master, but in 1708 they finally did:

No one really believes that a woman would fall in love with such an old man. It is a sad metaphor, but imagine that a bamboo fire-blowing tube was a person. Once the tube was a soft, young shoot, but now it is brittle and hard, and still it asks us to think back on its younger days. No matter how much you may like bamboo shoots, the thing is a fire tube now, and you know very well that you can't take a bite out of it.

Now, there are some people who will say that everything in the theater is imaginary, so one needn't be concerned with the question of whether actors are young or old men. If they act skillfully we become absorbed in the play and are moved. Such gentlemen are remarkable connoisseurs, but foolish women like myself—no matter what play we see—feel that what is going on is real and true. We shed tears at the sad places, and our hearts race during frightening scenes. We are aroused by love scenes and our hearts are strangely moved. It is when we are so transported that plays are at their most enjoyable.

But how is a woman to fall in love with an old man who is surrounded by young men, even if only in a play? This is as unlikely as the idea that a grandfather, though hungry, would refrain from eating and go off to play hide-and-seek with his grandchildren instead. But perhaps it doesn't seem this way in the eyes of the gentlemen who are such connoisseurs. I present this critique merely as the feelings of a simple woman.[139]

As early as 1706, Sakata Tōjūrō had recognized his insurmount-

able dilemma, and in 1707, in a ritual onstage scene, passed the yatsushi art on to his most promising disciple, Yamatoyama Jinzaemon. In
a play called *Ishiyama Temple and the Lake of Lovers' Vows
(Ishiyamadera Chikai no Mizuumi),* an old night watchman (Tōjūrō)
tells a young samurai heir (Jinzaemon) about his romantic exploits of
years gone by, gives the young man some advice about how to win
the heart of the courtesan he loves, and hands over to him his old
paper kimono to wear when he travels incognito to the pleasure district.

> The difference between up-to-date acting and the older
> style is like that between cherry blossoms and maple
> leaves. This much Mr. Sakata must understand in his gut.
> This is why he encouraged Mr. Yamatoyama to soften his
> old style and bring it more up to date, and why he passed
> on to him his *haori* jacket and his paper kimono. Even
> craftsmen who instruct their children to carry on after
> them, and masters who pass their arts on to their disciples
> are following the natural laws of heaven and earth.[140]

The passing on of the paper kimono symbolized Tōjūrō's bequest
of his art to Jinzaemon. Tōjūrō must have believed that Jinzaemon
had the potential to develop his own effective approach to the roles
of young lovers. Tōjūrō did not expect or want his disciples to imitate their master in every particular. He made this very clear at
Murayama Heiemon's (d. 1718) farewell party in 1707, when he
rebuked the guest of honor for imitating the Tōjūrō style in order to
win acclaim in Edo:

> In reply to the actor's claims of indebtedness, Tōjūrō shook
> his head. "Your acting must be bad," he said. "It is fitting
> that a man's art should flow out, as an independent style,
> from his innermost being.
> "If you make me your model, you will be inferior to me.

Work a little harder to perfect your own style!" he concluded, and all the jollity went out of the party.[141]

Other great kabuki actors believed that young actors should train
by imitating master actors, and were flattered when peers imitated
them, but Tōjūrō maintained his rigorous stance on individual creativity to the very end of his career. As it happened, his was an out-
look which ensured that the particulars of his acting would not long
survive his death.

After he had handed over his paper kimono to Jinzaemon,
Tōjūrō tried to avoid young lover roles. He began to play older,
minor characters, although neither the fans nor he himself were sat-
isfied with this choice. When *Sansho the Bailiff (Sanshō Daiyū)* did
poorly because of a weak performance by the actor taking the role of
the young lover, Tōjūrō remarked that even at his advanced age he
could have made more of the part, and that perhaps the theater
would have been better off if he had tried. Many fans were disappointed that he had begun to take small roles, and Kyōemon
(Hanzaemon) suggested that Tōjūrō should act in the parts he did
best as long as he was able, particularly if he was going to keep
announcing that he could play them better than the young actors
who were actually doing them.

In 1708 the producer of the Kameya-za prevailed on Tōjūrō to
start playing young lovers again. Perhaps the zamoto realized that it
would be more entertaining to watch a famous old actor struggle
than to see him fade away in minor roles. The role of the young
lover was taken by Sawamura Chōjūrō (1675–1734) in the first play
of the new year, and by Tōjūrō in the second. Chōjūrō enjoyed his
first critical success with that first play, and was praised for "doing
keisei-kai like Sakata Tōjūrō."[142] One hyōbanki stated that "Chōjūrō
has a style that attracts a lot of women. He is good at everything:
roppō, yatsushi, and aragoto acting."[143] When his turn came, Tōjūrō
repeated all of the popular scenes from his past successes: "He went
crazy over courtesans, got disowned, disguised himself as a saké lees

seller and later as a night watchman, he wore a paper kimono, he played a *sasara*, and he sang on people's doorsteps."[144] All this effort earned him the comparison to the bamboo tube quoted above.

In the tenth month of 1708, the Kameya-za marquee announced Tōjūrō's final appearance as Izaemon in a Yūgiri play. "People were taken aback at the realization that his art was to vanish so soon, and thronged to the theater like birds in the late autumn sky."[145] Kabuki, which had been a brash, iconoclastic, upstart theater in 1680, had in just thirty years developed a sense of decorum and an appreciation of its own history. Audiences filled the Kameya-za for the last play of the 1708 season, not to see exciting, top-quality theater, but to witness a piece of theater history in the making, and to bid farewell to an ailing old actor.

Tōjūrō was listed in the Mandayū-za company for the 1708–1709 season, but he did not appear onstage for the kaomise and made only one minor appearance during the season, in the role of a priest. The reason he took that part was to show the audience that he was still alive.[146] Tōjūrō died on the opening day of the 1709 kaomise at the age of sixty-three.

Tōjūrō's Uncertain Legacy: The Vicissitudes of Kamigata Wagoto

After Danjūrō's murder in 1704, his son Kuzō observed just one month of mourning before taking the name Danjūrō II. He knew that the title would be critical to his success as a tachiyaku actor in Edo. In the Kansai too, prestigious names lent actors wealth and stature; the Arashi San'emon dynasty in Osaka stood as proof of this. Despite the outpouring of grief over the death of Tōjūrō, no actor made a move to take the Tōjūrō name. His son Heishichirō, working as an onnagata, either felt that the name should go to a tachiyaku actor, or sensed his own limitations and feared that he could not live up to his father's reputation. Although Tōjūrō had designated Yamatoyama Jinzaemon his artistic successor, Jinzaemon chose to continue to use his own name in his pursuit of wealth and fame as an actor of romantic leads.

For over a year the Tōjūrō name sat beckoning, like a dangerous gold mine that no one dared enter. Then one Sakata Chōzaemon (formerly Kuwanaya Chōzaemon; 1669–1724) moved to Kyoto from the provincial theaters of Fushimi and Nara, and in early 1711 pronounced himself Sakata Tōjūrō II. He said that he was Tōjūrō's younger brother, and although people sometimes remarked that he did bear an uncanny resemblance to the late master, hyōbanki authors looked skeptically on Chōzaemon's claim. More likely he had been a provincial actor who had studied under Tōjūrō and been given the right to use the Sakata surname. Nakamura Ichirōji, producer of the Nunobukuroya-za, probably felt that the name of Sakata Tōjūrō alone would draw fans, no matter who worked under it, and he lent his support to the new Tōjūrō. Fans and critics enjoyed comparing the two Tōjūrōs, and although Tōjūrō II never fared well in the comparison, he was rewarded for his audacity in that he was able to build a much more lucrative career in kabuki in Kyoto and Osaka than would have been possible in the provinces. Tōjūrō II attracted some promising disciples but never became a leading actor, and in several geidan anecdotes he is portrayed as something of a laughingstock.

Kabuki aficionados agreed that Tōjūrō's real successors were Yamatoya Jinzaemon and Sawamura Chōjūrō. Jinzaemon was particularly skilled at keisei-kai scenes, and hyōbanki entries commented that on several occasions his acting was nearly indistinguishable from the late Tōjūrō's. Chōjūrō began his career as a musician and made the shift to acting when he was twenty-six years old, receiving his first rave reviews in 1708, while he was acting in the same company as Tōjūrō. During the two years after Tōjūrō's death, Chōjūrō emerged as one of the Kansai's top actors, while working as the romantic lead in revivals of two of the best plays of the Genroku period: as Yūgiri's Izaemon and as the hero of *The Courtesan and the Peak of Asama*.

It was in the era of Jinzaemon and Chōjūrō that kabuki critics felt the need to categorize more clearly the kind of acting and sce-

nography that Tōjūrō had perfected and that his two successors
were now using as the basis of their careers. In the 1710s they called
it the "soft style" *(yawarakagoto)* and in the 1720s they began to use
the term "gentle style" (wagoto).[147] The word wagoto included within
it keisei-kai and other scenes showcasing love and the tender emotions, as well as all the business that had made Tōjūrō famous:
expressions of devotion or prevarication to the beloved, lovers' quarrels and reconciliations, erotic innuendo, monologs recounting past
romantic exploits, humorous interactions with women whose infatuation with the hero is markedly one-sided, and so on. Critics had
begun to make a clear distinction between acting or scenes done in
the wagoto style and those done in the aragoto or jitsugoto styles.

By the 1720s wagoto kabuki was changing. "Stationary acting" (i-
kyōgen), an innovation that Tōjūrō had made as one part of a new
brand of realism, was dying out. Critics wrote that it no longer entertained even Kyoto audiences.[148] Chikamatsu's puppet plays were
being adapted more frequently to kabuki and, from 1714 on, kabuki
theaters used the gidayū narrator and the shamisen player of the
puppet theater to accompany and guide performances by actors
working in adaptations of puppet plays. This gave kabuki versions of
Chikamatsu's *The Love Suicides at Sonezaki* and *The Courier for
Hell* (Meidō no Hikyaku; 1711) an important musical component
that had not been part of Genroku-period wagoto plays. The appeal
of gidayū recitation and gidayū-based acting was part of the reason
for the demise of stationary acting, and actors came to rely on the
narrator and shamisen to provide them with the timing and cues
that actors working onstage to that point had formerly been obliged
to devise themselves.

In the Ichikawa Danjūrō tradition, from the 1750s through the
present, actors have continued to perform many of the same plays
and roles that were invented by Danjūrōs I and II. While most of the
physical movements and vocal qualities have changed over the centuries, certain elements of these actors' performance style have been
preserved, thanks to the "body-to-body" and "voice-to-voice" instruc-

tion that they handed down within the family. Tōjūrō's relationship to his sons and his admonition of Murayama Heiemon show that he was opposed to the kind of rote imitation that was required if specific movements and vocal business were to be preserved over long periods of time. While the spirit of Tōjūrō's characters survives in play texts, and his personality and philosophy are known to us from the geidan and hyōbanki, his bequest to his fellow Kansai tachiyaku actors was a tradition of the nontransmission of specific acting techniques across generations. Each great Kansai wagoto actor has since needed to develop his own style, and the work of great masters has tended to die out with the second generation. By way of contrast, the Sawamura family went to Edo where, thanks to the influence of strong family acting traditions *(ie no gei)*, they were able to create their own family wagoto and jitsugoto styles, as well as approaches to certain great roles that have been passed down from generation to generation.

The only Tōjūrō role that has been performed with any regularity from the eighteenth century through the modern day is Yūgiri's lover Izaemon, but the staging of the version still performed today, called *A Love Letter from the Licensed Quarter (Kuruwa Bunsho)*, bears little resemblance to the approach taken in the Genroku period. Three years after Tōjūrō's death, Chikamatsu memorialized the great actor by adapting the most popular scene from Tōjūrō's first big hit into the puppet play *Yūgiri and the Straits of Naruto (Yūgiri Awa no Naruto)* (see page 113 for a synopsis of this scene). For the next seventy years, the romance of Yūgiri and Izaemon survived primarily as a puppet play until, in 1780, playwrights, musicians, and actors began to experiment with adaptations back to the kabuki stage. Since 1780, the Yūgiri-Izaemon reconciliation has been played as a dance drama, and the current staging of *A Love Letter from the Licensed Quarter*, first done in 1873, is a lavish musical number featuring the integration of three musical ensembles, each specializing in a different tradition—the gidayū and *tokiwazu* forms of narrative chanting and the *nagauta* lyrical song. Nevertheless, thanks to Izaemon's wild fluctuations in mood, *Love Letter* requires virtuoso acting on the part of whoever takes the leading role: Izaemon longs for Yūgiri, then comes to despise her for her "betrayal" of his love; only later does he recognize her devotion and succeed in reconciling with her. Only a first-rate dancer and actor can do justice to this role. *A Love Letter from the Licensed Quarter* has been very popular, and has been performed at least once a year since 1805, when the present title of the play first came into use.[149] When the part of Izaemon is well acted, it still conveys something of the spirit of the stylish, petulant, self-absorbed young master who, in the capable hands of Sakata Tōjūrō, charmed and amused Osaka and Kyoto audiences through the three decades of the Genroku period.

Tōjūrō's contributions to kabuki extend far beyond the one great role he has bequeathed to the modern stage. His legacy survives today primarily in *The Actors' Analects* (*Yakusha Banashi*), where his devotion to the twin arts of acting and directing, and his analytical approach separate him from all his peers. Tōjūrō gave pure acting—devoid of any dance or music—a place on the kabuki stage. While pure acting and kabuki realism have never eclipsed the popularity of dance- or music-based drama, Tōjūrō broadened the range of what was possible and acceptable in kabuki. He provided inspiration for later actors struggling to establish their own individual styles early in their careers, and for reform-minded actors and directors of succeeding generations who sought to return verisimilitude to the kabuki stage.

4

YOSHIZAWA AYAME
Patron Saint of Kabuki's Onnagata

Looking, Moving, Thinking, and Feeling Like a Woman

By the end of the first decade of the eighteenth century, all the hyōbanki were agreed that one man was the "temple founder" (*kaizan*) and "patron saint" (*ujigami*) of the onnagata profession. This was Yoshizawa Ayame, and in 1711 Ejima Kiseki deemed him the finest actor, bar none, in Japan. No other hyōbanki disputed the claim. His rise to preeminence is even more remarkable an achievement given the desperate poverty of his childhood.

Ayame took his cue from Sakata Tōjūrō and made acting, not dance, the focus of his art. This was more daring for an onnagata than for an actor of male roles because dance had always been at the very heart of the onnagata's performance. Ayame's rivalry with Mizuki Tatsunosuke, the greatest dancing onnagata of all time, energized Genroku kabuki throughout the country, from Edo to Osaka. Ayame believed, like Tōjūrō, that convincing portrayals onstage needed to begin with psychological and physical preparation offstage. Roles had to be created from the inside, by actors' duplicating the emotions of their characters. As we have seen, Tōjūrō had achieved, at

the peak of his powers, the remarkable feat of convincing audiences
that he was thirty years younger than he really was, and possessed of
a much more romantic, capricious personality than was actually the
case. But the challenge that Tōjūrō faced was small in comparison
with Ayame's. Ayame set out to convince both the men and women
in the audience that they were watching a woman onstage. Given
Ayame's conviction that he could do this only if his heart, mind, and
body were one with his characters', he realized that he had set himself a daunting task. Nevertheless, he devoted his career to overcoming the formidable physical and social barriers separating the
genders, and the hyōbanki record that he was more successful in this
than any actor had been before. Many actors of the Genroku period
had already taken to wearing women's clothing offstage, but for
Ayame this was not enough. Onnagata had to look, move, think, and
feel as women did at all times. His approach to his craft was so
clearly effective that it had a tremendous impact on his colleagues
and successors.

Ayame's stature as the best onnagata and the finest actor in
Japan gave him the right to speak with authority on the nature of the
onnagata's art. *The Words of Ayame*, recorded by a colleague (Fukuoka Yagoshirō; fl. 1700–1730), represents the first and, even today,
the most authoritative source on the preparation and the philosophy
necessary for success as an onnagata. While many later onnagata
wrote their own geidan, none ever supplanted *The Words of Ayame*.
All that was left for Ayame's great onnagata successors to do was to
try to find a new and unique approach to his "way of the onnagata."[1]
The difficulties inherent in the onnagata's task, Ayame's constitu-
tional inability to "coast along on his past successes," and the pres-
sures facing actors in the 1710s and the 1720s all conspired to send
Ayame down dangerous artistic paths late in his career; his own
actions sometimes seemed to contradict his convictions as he
expressed them in *The Words of Ayame*. But the record shows that
Ayame learned from his mistakes, and he departed kabuki a veritable
"god" of the theater.

Thanks largely to Tōjūrō and Ayame, women became an important part of the kabuki audience. From late Genroku on, producers,
actors, and critics would regard women patrons as essential and irre-
placeable, not only in terms of box office receipts, but as judges of an
actor's skill and appeal. Tōjūrō and his wagoto successors drew to
the kabuki theaters women who wanted to see the most stylish,
attractive men in the city. Ayame's women fans identified with the
characters he created, and were able to accept them as women
involved in a wide range of human relationships. Onstage Ayame
was a wife and mother, a romantic lover, a maidservant, and a stern
samurai matron—acting and reacting believably to various situations, from the pedestrian to the fanciful or macabre. And as many
onnagata have done since the Genroku period, he attracted both
men and women fans who came to the theater to gaze in wonder at
this man who was able to evoke so convincingly the essence of wom-
anliness.

From Prostitution to the Stage: A True-Life Rags-to-Riches Story

Yoshizawa Ayame was born in 1673, probably in Osaka, although a
counter-theory contends that he was born the son of a farmer from
Kii Province (now Wakayama Prefecture).[2] In either case, he was
born to an impoverished family. The Osaka biography states that Ayame was the oldest of three children (he probably had two younger
brothers) and that his father died when he was five years old. His
mother tried to makes ends meet by working as a seamstress, but
when this did not allow her to keep food on the family's table, she
sold her oldest boy to an establishment that would raise him and then
eventually begin to hire him out as an *iroko*, or boy prostitute. Whether
Ayame came from Wakayama or Osaka, scholars agree that by the
time he was about eight years old, he was living with a family of shamisen players who performed on the kabuki stage. He would have
received shamisen lessons from the time he arrived at his proprietor's
home. When he reached puberty, his proprietor would have hired

him out to entertain at parties and to entertain individual clients.

In 1673 another child was born, a boy who would become the renowned onnagata Mizuki Tatsunosuke, Ayame's greatest rival. Tatsunosuke was born into much more favorable circumstances—he was the nephew of Yamatoya Jimbei, a leading Osaka tachiyaku who sometimes worked as a zamoto. Tatsunosuke's childhood was free of worry or want, and the boy was groomed for the stage from an early age; he almost certainly never worked as an iroko.

Iroko were the pretty "walk-on" actors of kabuki. They began appearing in plays even before they could work as entertainers, and while many managed to build careers on the stage, others who were less talented or less fortunate disappeared into obscurity in their twenties, after difficult careers as male prostitutes. Young Ayame was one of the luckiest iroko in the history of the trade. During his teenage years, he acquired a long-term patron, one Tachibanaya Gorozaemon, a wealthy, landed gentleman from a small city west of Kyoto. Gorozaemon was like a father to Ayame, paying for all of his performance lessons and giving him sound career advice. Gorozaemon was a skilled amateur nō performer and Ayame was at first attracted to that art, but Gorozaemon wisely kept his charge from wasting his effort on an art that had no use for outsiders. On the kabuki stage, lineage did not matter if one had talent and charm, and Gorozaemon knew that kabuki held the best hope for the future for this promising lad. So he arranged for Ayame to study under Arashi San'emon I, then the finest kabuki tachiyaku in Osaka.[3]

As a teenager, Ayame performed bit parts onstage as a wakashu and also in female roles, while studying the arts of the onnagata (including dance and music) and the tachiyaku. He seemed on the verge of following his teacher into tachiyaku roles, but San'emon I died in 1690. Perhaps Gorozaemon suggested that Ayame make his career as an onnagata. In any case, in 1690, at age seventeen, the young man who had earlier been called Ayanosuke changed his name to Ayame, which means "iris"—a wonderful choice for an onnagata, thanks to its hermaphroditic juxtaposition of male leaves

and female flowers. In the same year Ayame ended his formal relationship with his patron and set out to make his own way in kabuki.
He was always grateful for Gorozaemon's kindness. To Ayame, his
patron had been a surrogate for the father he had lost when he was a
small boy. Ayame took as his "house name"[4] his patron's last name,
Tachibanaya, and used his patron's nickname, Gonshichi, when he
was required by law or custom to provide a masculine name.

Traveling the Tōkaidō in Search of a Place in Kabuki

Both Ayame and Tatsunosuke embarked on their careers in 1690,
and spent their early years working all three of Japan's largest cities.
In the early Genroku period, onnagata traveled between Edo and
the Kansai more frequently than did specialists in the other roles.
The force of the perception of Kyoto women as more refined and
beautiful than any others, together with the flourishing industry of
male love in Osaka, resulted in a situation in which all of Edo's onnagata had to be imported there from the West. Edo was a good place
for a young onnagata to start a career because most of the best specialists in the field eventually returned to the Kansai to settle down,
leaving Edo less competitive than the Kansai. At the tender age of
eighteen, in 1691, Mizuki Tatsunosuke made a splashy debut at
Edo's Nakamura-za, transforming a well-known warrior's spear
dance into an athletic woman's dance that excited and amazed Edo
audiences (Figure 27). Tatsunosuke also did very competent work as
a girl who is stabbed to death and then returns as a ghost to torment
her murderer. After a single play, Tatsunosuke was rated the second-
best onnagata in Edo.[5] In 1691 his star was shining brighter even
than Danjūrō's, although Danjūrō had been appearing on the Edo
stage for fifteen years. "Housewives in wealthy establishments gave
up their books to study the spear dance, tradesmen changed their
names to Tatsunosuke in order to attract customers, and those shops
that simply added the name Tatsunosuke to their signs invariably
saw their sales increase."[6] After one more year of glory in Edo,

Fig. 27 Mizuki Tatsunosuke's spear dance. Print by Torii Kiyonobu, from the series *Fūryū Yomo Byōbu*. From a copy held in the collection of the Tokyo Central Metropolitan Library.

Tatsunosuke went to Kyoto. For an onnagata, Kyoto was the real proving-ground, much as New York is for stage actors today. The crowds in Kyoto were as enthralled by Tatsunosuke's dancing as their Edo cousins had been, and at the age of just twenty, in 1693, he topped the list of onnagata in Kyoto.

For Ayame, meanwhile, the early 1690s were equally peripatetic, but he enjoyed none of the glory and prosperity that Tatsunosuke did. For at least two years, between 1690 and 1692, he worked at two Edo theaters, trying to establish his name as an onnagata. His work went all but unnoticed.[7] Ayame was probably back in the Kansai in

1692, because his first surviving reviews are in *The Fully Colored Great Mirror of Actors*, which came out that year. These were written by the same hyōbanki author who had roasted Tōjūrō, and who had few words of praise for any actor. Ayame fared no better than anyone else. The only favorable comment the author made was about his looks: "Whatever angle you look at him from, his eyes are very cute ... He's the kind of person I would like to spend some time with if I had enough money."[8] This comment, of course, harks back to Ayame's iroko days, and the hyōbanki's second line refers to his erotic appeal as a wakashu, suggesting that Ayame was having some difficulty shedding his wakashu persona for that of a woman. *The Fully Colored Great Mirror of Actors* was consistent in its dismissal of Ayame's acting, calling it "inexperienced," "uncertain," "grating," "hard to follow," and "over-reliant on the use of his face as an acting tool."[9] This and other early hyōbanki give us our first physical descriptions of Ayame. He had a lotus-like complexion, and in addition to his attractive face and "cute eyes" he was tall and slender, with cheeks that were a little too thin. He had a warm, disarming sort of erotic appeal that won quite a few hearts among his fans, including "a certain priest who became so obsessed with Ayame that he fled the temple and fell into a life of degradation."[10]

It was probably during the 1692–1693 season that Ayame was first able to work with Tōjūrō and to observe his work carefully and regularly. That year, Ayame worked at the Mandayu-za in Kyoto, in a company led by Hanzaemon and starring Tōjūrō. The hit of the season was Chikamatsu's first surviving kabuki play, *The Festive Display of Statuary at the Temple of Maya, Mother of the Buddha.* Ayame took the fourth or fifth most important onnagata role. The typical starring roles for onnagata at the time were high-ranking courtesans, who epitomized the height of feminine beauty and fashion of the period; onnagata could only establish first-rate careers by excelling in the courtesan roles. There were three courtesans in *The Temple of Maya*, but Ayame played the part of Kofuji, a girl in her twenties who had recently been promoted from courtesan to courtesan's handler (Figure 28; see also figure 19). For all the brevity of the role, Kofuji is a spirited character who becomes involved in two short but rancorous arguments, proving that she can not only take but also dish out physical and verbal abuse. Ayame then joined the three "leading ladies" for the celebratory dance at the Maya Temple festival that concluded the play. Best of all, Ayame was able, probably for the first time, to spend a few minutes acting directly opposite Tōjūrō. Tōjūrō would remain Ayame's inspiration for many years.

Ayame's main appeal still seemed to be his good looks, but by several accounts he was improving as an actor. He "had received roles that suited him, and his care in their execution was beyond description," said one hyōbanki, although that same reviewer then went on to note that some sections of the plays were poorly performed.[11] Ayame probably remained in Kyoto the next two seasons,

Fig. 28 Yoshizawa Ayame in 1693 as pictured in *Sumo Wrestling Actors* in the role of Kofuji in *The Festive Display of Imagery at the Temple of Maya, Mother of Buddha.* Courtesy of Tokyo Central Metropolitan Library.

moving with Hanzaemon to the Hayakumo-za and then back to the Mandayū-za. His name was appearing regularly on programs in a variety of roles: princesses, wives, and his first documented role as a heroic woman who dies and returns to earth as a ghost.

Despite his artistic growth, Ayame was still a rank-and-file actor. No critic ever mentioned him in the same breath with Tatsunosuke. In the 1693–1694 season, Tōjūrō was in Osaka, and the Danjūrō-Tatsunosuke team overshadowed everyone else in Kyoto. Tatsunosuke's subsequent year with Tōjūrō and Chikamatsu at the Hayakumo- za was even more triumphant. Chikamatsu unabashedly interrupted the flow of his plays so they could feature Tatsunosuke's dances, and Chikamatsu even used Tatsunosuke's name for the title of a play that closed the 1695 season and served as the gala send-off for Tatsunosuke, who was to return for a second stint in Edo; this was *Mizuki Tatsunosuke's Farewell Gift and Celebration (Mizuki Tatsunosuke Tachi Furumai)*. Tatsunosuke's biggest hit of the season was the cat dance in Chikamatsu's *An Up-to-Date Tale of Genji in Sixty Chapters (Ima Genji Rokujū Jō)*. In this play, Tatsunosuke's character falls in love with a man who proves to be her brother, and so someone she can never hope to marry. She happens to see a pair of sibling cats mating and becomes so jealous and distraught that she is transformed into a cat driven by butterflies into a dancing frenzy.[12]

While Tatsunosuke had all of Japan eating out of the palm of his hand, and was garnering praise for the flashiest, most dramatic onna-gata acting to be seen on the stage—featuring ghosts, sword-fighting lady avengers and haughty courtesans—slow and steady Ayame was beginning to get increasingly good reviews. Descriptions of his skills begin to suggest the directions that Ayame would take as a more accomplished, mature actor. Praise for his attention to detail and his single-mindedness mirror similar descriptions of Tōjūrō's work onstage.[13] Emotional scenes and expressions of grief and loss were his strong suit, and his vocal style was improving.[14] *The Great Mirror of the Stage* noted his "unassuming, clean-cut attractiveness," and concluded that "he has the erotic appeal of his namesake, the iris, and is skilled in all the arts."[15]

Tatsunosuke went to the Ichimura-za in Edo for the 1695 kaomise, and Ayame may have made yet another trip to Edo at this time too. If so, Ayame was at the Yamamura-za with Danjūrō,[16] but he would have had just six weeks to work with Danjūrō before fire destroyed the theater at the year's end (see pages 58–59). Later records show Ayame in one play in Osaka in 1696. Perhaps he returned to the Kansai after the fire, reasoning that Edo was an unlucky place for him. After working in Edo, Osaka and Kyoto, Ayame had yet to find his niche in the kabuki world.

A Strategic Marriage and a Very Big Role

As of the 1696 season, Ayame's best years on the stage had been the three he spent in Kyoto under the leadership of Yamashita Hanzae-mon. Hanzaemon may well have "discovered" Ayame, and it is clear that he respected the young onnagata, both personally and as an actor. Ayame certainly realized that one key to Tatsunosuke's success had been the powerful uncle who had guaranteed him excellent roles from early on in his career. At some point in the mid-1690s Aya-me cast his lot decisively with Hanzaemon by marrying the younger sister of Hanzaemon's wife. We know that Ayame preferred Tōjūrō to Hanzaemon as an acting partner, and that Tōjūrō's work inspired Ayame to make innovations in onnagata acting, but in 1695 Tōjūrō had no experience as a producer. Further, Ayame may have sensed that Tōjūrō worked best with onnagata like Kirinami Senju who looked beautiful as women, but were more passive and less strong-willed than himself. Ayame's marriage proved to be a very strategic move. Hanzaemon welcomed him into his family troupe, and from 1697 on, Ayame's roles improved steadily. Ayame made a point of preventing people from learning anything about his married life, but the strange union between a real woman and a man who always dressed and acted as a woman, proved durable and productive.

Ayame's wife bore him four sons, and this made it possible for Ayame to begin his own acting dynasty.

Anticipation was at a fever pitch for the 1697–1698 theater season in Kyoto because it was to feature a direct confrontation between teams comprising the best talent in all of kabuki: Tōjūrō, Tatsunosuke, and the Chikamatsu-Kaneko playwriting duo headed the Mandayū-za company, while Hanzaemon, Ayame, and Nakamura Shichisaburō were at the forefront of the Hayakumo-za troupe. This meant that the two most popular actors and the two best playwrights in kabuki had joined forces against the stage's savviest producer, the relatively unknown Ayame, and a wagoto star from Edo whom audiences in the Kansai had never seen. Ayame took the leading onnagata role in every Hayakumo-za play that season. The Hayakumo-za kaomise and New Year's shows drew scant crowds as Kyotoites flocked to the rival theater, but Ayame was not to blame for these failures. He was praised for his subtle and erotic solo work (see page 196), whereas Shichisaburō did so poorly that Kyoto spectators joked that he should be playing the rear legs of a horse. The main reason for the Mandayū-za's success was Tatsunosuke's "Seven Spirits." This was the most exciting dance he had ever performed, and unprecedented in kabuki history in terms of its concept and the scale of its spectacle.[17]

The second play of the year, however, turned the tables decisively. This was *The Courtesan and the Peak of Asama*, written by Shichisaburō, with secret assistance, perhaps, from Tōjūrō, who wished to see his rivals offer him stiffer competition. *The Courtesan and the Peak of Asama* solidified Shichisaburō's stature as one of the two best wagoto actors in Japan, but the play had an even more dramatic impact on Ayame's career, launching him decisively into the competition for the status of "best onnagata in kabuki."

Ayame took the role of the courtesan Miura, unquestionably the most important woman character in the play; many of his best scenes were played opposite Hanzaemon. Miura makes her grand entrance in the first act, doing the courtesan's languid figure-eight sashay right into the mansion of a feudal lord.[18] The boorish heir to a feudal domain has fallen in love with her, but she wants nothing to do with him. The feudal lord's wife is impressed by Miura's beauty and says she will make a fine consort to the heir, but Miura will only marry the man she truly loves, who turns out to be none other than Wada, the reigning lord of the domain (played by Hanzaemon). This of course infuriates Wada's wife, who conspires with her son to re-move the reigning lord. But Wada's devotion to Miura is as strong as her love for him, and he willingly suffers banishment to be with her. The two live together as man and wife in the commoners' district of the city, with Wada working as a palanquin-bearer. In all the scenes between Wada and Miura, the courtesan is depicted as the stronger-willed and more intelligent of the two, and records of the reception of the play tell that the actor who most moved the audiences was Ayame, not Hanzaemon. Hanzaemon, famous for his upstaging of other actors, had found his equal in Ayame.

One of Ayame's finest scenes was in Act Two. The action takes place fourteen years later; Miura and Wada have a thirteen-year-old daughter named Osan who is attacked while her mother is out; the girl is fatally stabbed by her own tutor, who then steals a large sum of money from the house. The hard-earned money had been intended to redeem the honor of the story's hero, Tomoe no Jō, played by Shichisaburō. Miura returns and has a poignant last encounter with her dying daughter, who identifies the murderer and pleads to be avenged. Miura then conceals Osan's death from her husband while she stoically negotiates with a brothel owner over the terms of her own return to service in the quarter (Figure 29). The purpose of her self-sacrifice is of course to replace the stolen money. Suddenly, after thirteen years as the wife of the man she loves, Miura again finds herself working as a prostitute, but this time it is a choice she has made herself, for a noble cause. Miura in *The Courtesan and the Peak of Asama* was the epitome of the idealized Genroku-period courtesan: beautiful, virtuous, intelligent. Ayame later played this same role three more times; his sons performed it after him; and

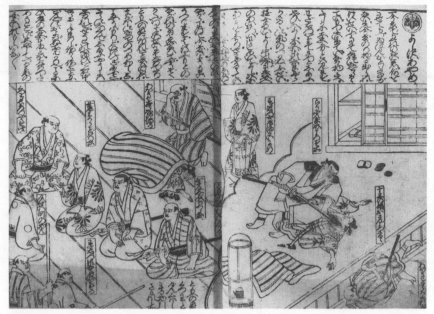

Fig. 29 Yoshizawa Ayame as Miura in *The Courtesan and Asama Peak*. Right panel: Miura goes to buy saké while the tutor murders her daughter. Left panel: Miura (third from left) negotiates the terms of her return to service in the pleasure district. Her murdered daughter is concealed in bedding as her servant weeps. Courtesy of The Theatre Museum of Waseda University.

other leading onnagata tried their hand at Miura in the 1710s through the 1730s. Miura was a very popular character and she was also lifted many times from *The Courtesan and the Peak of Asama* to appear in totally unrelated plays. This original version, in 1698, played for a remarkable 120 days, nullifying the best efforts of Tatsunosuke, Tōjūrō, and Chikamatsu to draw larger crowds to their shows. Finally, an onnagata had appeared in Kyoto who was capable of giving Tatsunosuke a run for his money.

The Glory Days of the Genroku Onnagata: Six Years of Rivalry with Tatsunosuke

Prior to *The Peak of Asama*, the hyōbanki had never mentioned Ayame in the same breath with Tatsunosuke, but after Ayame's stunning success in that play, no discussion of one man seemed possible without making a comparison to the other. Ayame received his first jō-jō-kichi rating in 1699, along with just three other onnagata, and was listed as second in Kyoto to Tatsunosuke.[19] By 1704 it was clear that "there were only two great onnagata, Ayame and Tatsunosuke,"[20] but every observer recognized that in their style of performance they were complete opposites. The success of two such different actors is testimony to the richness and variety of the onnagata arts at the turn of the eighteenth century. Together Ayame and Tatsunosuke embodied everything that an onnagata could be or strive to attain.

Tatsunosuke was an all-around performer, but excelled in dance, the onnagata's traditional "flower." His background, however, was a harbinger of things to come in kabuki. He had never been an iroko; instead he was the relative of a prominent actor and producer. He was given the title of top onnagata despite his lack of erotic appeal.[21] He had a round face, large jowls, and a long nose, and he danced with an expression of pride and smugness. When compared to a flower, he was called the "plum blossom" among his onnagata peers;[22] the plum is a hardy flower that blooms through snow and cold, and one with many masculine connotations in kabuki and in Japanese culture in general. The hyōbanki record shows that on occasion his acting was affecting enough to draw sympathetic tears,[23] but in most cases Tatsunosuke thrilled crowds with spectacular roles and virtuosic dance. In their evaluations of tachiyaku actors the Kansai connoisseurs seemed to favor subdued acting over histrionics and dance, but they never lowered Tatsunosuke's rating for this reason.

Ayame took a different approach to his craft—one that won him many steadfast admirers. His experience as an iroko and early praise of his good looks link him to the onnagata traditions of the mid-seventeenth century, but he was innovative in his focus on acting rather than dance. He never went as far as Tōjūrō did in ignoring dance because dance was simply too well established as an onnagata art. Ayame believed that the courtesan's erotic appeal was central to the onnagata's creation of a feminine persona, but he began to relegate eroticism and courtesan roles to a secondary place in his art relatively early in his career, disappointing some observers. In the late Genroku period Ayame was compared to more feminine flowers—including the iris, of course, and the cherry,[24] with its delicate scent and vulnerability (Figure 30). Like Tōjūrō, he strove to create believable characters onstage, and took pride in his ability to make an audience feel the emotions of the women he played. He was recognized as the undisputed master of emotional and tearful scenes, but at the same time he was thought a much subtler actor than his two major

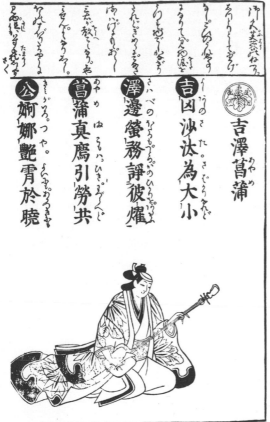

Fig. 30 Yoshizawa Ayame playing the shamisen, from the hyōbanki *Amayo no San-pai Kigen* (1693). Courtesy of The Theater Museum of Waseda University.

rivals: "He doesn't go overboard in expressions of love the way Ogino (Samanojō) (1656–1704) does and he doesn't look as haughty as Mizuki."[25]

There is no record of what Tatsunosuke thought of Ayame, but Ayame is critical of Tatsunosuke in one entry in *The Words of Ayame*; he notes Tatsunosuke's brilliance in dance but calls him "deficient" as an actor and attributes this to a lack of hard work.[26] Ayame and Tatsunosuke were almost always employed by different theater companies and sometimes worked in different cities. Even when they were in the same company, they were rarely onstage together, although in Osaka in 1704, they played samurai wives who vie to marry their daughters to the same man, and later Ayame played the ko-tsuzumi drum in accompaniment to Tatsunosuke's dance.[27] Their arts were almost always compared at some distance. Ayame was capable of upstaging other leading actors with his brilliant work, but observers noted that instead he usually made fellow actors look good. One noteworthy exception was in 1700 when, as the courtesan Sango in *The Courtesan and the Rope of Virtue (Keisei Zen no Tsuna)*, he allowed his tachiyaku counterpart, Yamatoya Jimbei, to "quite disappear from the scene" (Figure 31).[28] Jimbei was Tatsunosuke's powerful uncle, and Ayame's stealing the show may have been a rather overt form of thumbing his nose at his rival.

Ayame wrote that achieving the "languor," "charm," and "erotic appeal" of the courtesan was the first basic step in creating a feminine persona. Beginning in 1697, Ayame played courtesan roles to wide acclaim. In this, as in all his work, Ayame's attention to detail served him well:

> His toilette in a solo scene during the kaomise with Shichisaburō [in 1697], when he trimmed his nails and so on, and then when he glanced up to see that Shichisaburō had arrived ... the use of his eyes and his attention to posture were the essence of eroticism. And he does this again and again.[29]

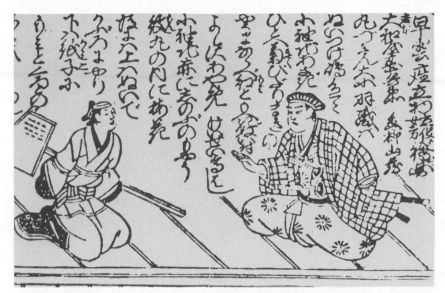

Fig. 31   Illustration from the hyōbanki *Yakusha Yatsushi Ukejō*, 1701. Ayame, tied up with ropes, plays the courtesan Takahashi, with Yamatoya Jimbei as Sanzō, in *Keisei Saganohara*. Courtesy of The Theatre Museum of Waseda University.

It became apparent as early as 1700 that Ayame's main interest did not lie in exuding feminine eroticism and charm. One critic said that "sometimes he gets so into the action onstage that he loses his erotic appeal as an onnagata," and another observed that "there is a severity to Ayame that detracts from love scenes but makes him excellent in scenes of argument or lamentation."[30] In the Genroku period, frequent criticism for lack of erotic appeal or poor work in romantic scenes normally signaled the demise of an onnagata's career, but Ayame sought to expand the artistic boundaries of the profession. He wanted to make women characters come alive onstage, even when beauty and eroticism were not central to a character or a scene. Emotional scenes had become Ayame's forte by late Genroku, and the hyōbanki of that time consistently refer to him with sobriquets like "the founder of the Temple of Tears." "He never weeps alone," one critic wrote, "but always with a crowd of one hundred or two hundred. The tissue sellers love him—their sales go up whenever his name is on the boards to appear in a play. My, how the tears fall. They cry 'boo hoo!' and blow their noses. This is Ayame's chief and most remarkable skill."[31]

For centuries, Japanese performers, whatever their art, had striven to "bloom" onstage, to appeal to audiences much the way beautiful flowers attract the eye in a garden. From the time that onnagata first took to the kabuki stage they had sought to achieve "flower" in their effeminate good looks and their skill in dance. Ayame was attractive when he was young, and he of course recognized that dance was the onnagata's "flower." Like any onnagata, Ayame did dance onstage, but evaluations of his ability in this area range widely, from so poor that "I had to cover my eyes when he danced the duet with Takashima" to "It is true his dancing cannot compare with Tatsunosuke's, but he is still way ahead of the young onnagata."[32] But for Ayame the "flower" of dance was only a means to a higher goal, the "fruit" of convincing acting. Ayame told young actors to work hard on their dance because healthy flowers are necessary to produce healthy fruit.[33]

When he referred to acting as "fruit," Ayame was borrowing terminology used by critics in their praise of Tōjūrō, but in the highly competitive and highly charged environment of Genroku kabuki an actor needed to possess something extraordinary if he was to rise to the top of the profession. For audiences, what Ayame called "fruit" was in fact a new and remarkable kind of flower—the flower of verisimilitude in a man's depiction of women. One observer wrote that "he seems born to play women. He has the same easy skill in natural acting as Tōjūrō and Hanzaemon; it's as if real people come alive when he plays them."[34] Many onnagata, today as in the Genroku period, seem more convincing when their masculine features are blurred by distance, but not Ayame: "His facial expressions are excellent. The closer you sit to the stage, the more enjoyable is his performance."[35] "His main skill lies in being so like a woman that one wonders what is actually under his loincloth. No matter what

role he is playing—a lady-in-waiting, a samurai wife, or whatever—
he is never ambiguous, but always convincingly real. So much so
that one is moved to cry out, 'It is she! It is she!'"[36] Ejima Kiseki gives
a vivid description of the way an audience in 1700 responded to
Ayame's "flower" of verisimilitude in the play *The Courtesan and
the Rope of Virtue*:

> At times Ayame laughed and at times he wept, and it all
> seemed to come from a real woman.
>   "Do it in the nude!" someone shouted. "Well done, well
> done!" the cries rang out. Then the crowd was speechless
> and there was a period of silence in the galleries and the
> pit. Then all at once the spectators erupted, "Bravo!
> Bravo!"[37]

This description of Ayame's triumph as an actor contains one
particularly troubling remark, the spectator's cry of "Do it in the
nude!" This catcall is not unsettling for its rudeness, but because it
represents a cruel reality of the Genroku stage: audiences quickly
grew bored with even the most innovative and virtuoso performances, and were unimpressed when actors made even outstanding
work look easy. They wanted to see actors face and surmount nearly
impossible challenges. In 1698 Tatsunosuke received rave reviews
for playing a crippled samurai wife who defends herself skillfully
with a sword against a host of attackers—all while being confined to
the medieval equivalent of a wheelchair.[38] The audience was most
impressed because the great dancer had performed fabulously without ever using his legs. Although Ayame had worked for decades to
become a convincing woman onstage, and despite the years of effort
that this mastery represented, it was unlikely that his remarkable
achievement of verisimilitude would continue to seem remarkable
for long.

The Secret to Becoming a Woman Onstage

Ayame believed even more strongly than did Tōjūrō that the quality of an actor's life offstage determined his ability to create convincing characters. "If he does not live his normal life as if he was a woman, it will not be possible for him to be called a skillful onnagata. The more an actor believes that his time spent on the stage is the most important to his career as an onnagata, the more masculine his performance will be. It is better for him to consider his everyday life the most important."[39] Living like a woman in everyday life meant copying the externals of women's behavior; wearing women's clothes, speaking in the more polite, deferential language of women, eating the kinds of foods that women preferred, and so on, but it also meant conducting oneself like a virtuous woman and accepting the standards society applied to women.[40]

Ayame's prescription for living like a woman went far beyond the externals mentioned above, extending to an effort to respond emotionally as a woman would to all the situations faced in daily life. Ayame believed, with Tōjūrō, that characters needed to arise naturally from an actor's soul. *The Words of Ayame* contains many anecdotes that attest to Ayame's success in this effort. Inappropriate food and behavior dismayed him as they would a well-bred lady. Like any true onnagata, he would feel offended if someone forgot to use the word "young" before the word "onnagata," since he noted that real women are disturbed by evidence of aging.[41] Ayame believed that any open reference to the fact that an onnagata was a man with a family should provoke real, acute embarrassment—and that any onnagata who did not feel this way did not belong in the profession.[42] Ayame took active steps to refine his feminine sensibilities, taking lessons in such quintessentially feminine arts as incense appreciation.[43] As all Japanese know, serious pursuit of any traditional art does far more than impart skill or knowledge; it helps to develop a sense of values and finer aesthetic and emotional responses.

When the psychology of a woman character was simply too far removed from his daily experience, Ayame relied—again, like Tōjūrō—on analysis of characters' motivations and feelings. *The Words of Ayame* suggests that characters who most often presented Ayame with this kind of challenge were the wives of samurai or feudal lords in historical plays who were entrusted with duties of grave historical import, or left with no choice but to kill themselves and their families in order to remain faithful to the warrior code which governed their lives and actions just as sternly as it did the men of the ruling class. Several entries attest to the challenge of balancing the samurai wife's ingrained sense of femininity against the violence and cruelty inherent in her social position. Careful character analysis helped Ayame win praise for his believable handling of even the thorniest of roles:

> In the case of the wife of an elder counselor threatening an enemy, the actor bears in mind that she is the wife of a samurai, and so always has her place her hand on her sword in a haughty fashion. To play her as being very bold in her handling of a sword when, considering that she is a samurai's wife, she does not normally even wear such a weapon, would be bad acting. The best way to portray her is that she should not be afraid of the sword. But to have her indulge in argument, and challenge her adversary, striking the stage, slapping her hand to her sword-hilt, would be to play her as if she were a tachiyaku in an onnagata's cap.[44]

Acting as a woman offstage was important at all times, but perhaps never more so than in the theater dressing room. As Ayame put it, "To sit alongside a tachiyaku who is to play the part of one's lover, and chew away at one's food without any charm whatsoever, then go straight out onto the stage and try to play a love scene with that same man is sure to lead to failure on both sides, for the tachiyaku's heart will not actually be ready to fall in love."[45] We have seen that Tōjūrō also impressed on the actors in his company the need to treat onnagata as if they were real women, and set an excellent example with his own conduct. The onnagata's offstage persona was equally critical in preparing the ground for the proper audience response. If people of the Kansai were accustomed to seeing Ayame as a woman offstage, this would make it easier for them to accept him as the women he portrayed.

For Ayame, total commitment to working as an onnagata was key:

> If an onnagata has the notion that he can always switch over to tachiyaku roles if things are not going well in his chosen field, this is a sure indication that he no longer has any sense of artistry. Any real woman must accept the fact that she cannot become a man. Can you imagine a woman's being able to turn into a man simply because she cannot live with things as they are? "If an onnagata thinks this way," the Master used to say, "he is ignorant of a woman's feelings."[46]

Ayame believed that women are by nature more nurturing and cooperative than men, so he emphasized ensemble acting and the need to make weaker artists seem better when they worked with him.[47] Yet he was a kabuki actor, and is known to have said, "Kabuki isn't court kickball—one should not sacrifice personal success to help other actors with their performances."[48] There were times, as we have seen, when Ayame eclipsed the performance of a tachiyaku partner, but he did so only when necessary, and did not make a habit of it. In 1698 hyōbanki writers noted that Ayame outshone Hanzaemon in *The Courtesan and the Peak of Asama*, but that lesser actors looked uncommonly good working alongside Ayame.[49] Hanzaemon was Ayame's chief supporter, and was himself an actor and a producer with a reputation so solid that it could not be hurt by a dazzling performance by Ayame. In fact, Ayame's stardom would please Hanzaemon and redound to his profit since he was Ayame's producer and brother-in-law. In the same play, Ayame was careful to support the efforts of the more vulnerable actors. This combination of ambition and "feminine" sensitivity was at the heart of Ayame's personal character and his craft.

This approach to the profession was shared by other actors of the Genroku period, but because Ayame dominated the onnagata hierarchy for so long, and left the first written collection of advice for actors who would follow, it was he who exerted the most powerful impact on the field in his own time and over the generations since. Wearing women's dress had become ubiquitous practice by mid-Genroku, but Ayame called for a far stronger commitment, and most onnagata responded enthusiastically. One actor seems to have carried Ayame's principles to excess. According to one anecdote, Sawamura Kodenji (1665–1705) refused to appear in a play in which the script called for the villain to refer to him as "a little monkey," which Kodenji declared was a fatal insult to anyone with even the least sense of pride in "her" beauty.[50] According to another, Kodenji was once traveling the Tokaidō Road in a palanquin, when the ride became so rough that he stopped the bearers, climbed out, and chastised them for bouncing him so severely that they brought about the early onset of his monthly bleeding.[51]

Ayame went to such pains to cultivate a feminine public persona that the character of his private, family life remains a secret. No rumors even survive to suggest what he was like as a husband or father. His four sons were born in 1702, 1711, 1719, and 1720, but while extensive records survive documenting their stage careers, we know nothing at all about their relationships with their father. _The Actors' Analects_ is full of stories that give clues about the private lives of other actors, but no such anecdotes were recorded about Ayame. In the 1720s Ayame's change to tachiyaku roles suggests that he may have undergone some sort of mid-life crisis, but the hyōbanki offer no hard evidence, nor even any rumors, but only speculation. How did Ayame feel personally about having to work so hard every day, playing challenging roles onstage and off? We cannot be sure, but Japanese scholars assume that it was never easy, and that he suffered and struggled all his life to raise the art of the onnagata to new heights. However, there is for the most part no hard evidence to substantiate his suffering. Living in public as a woman may well have seemed more natural to him than living as a man. The only evidence to the contrary comes near the end of his life. In the last two years of his career, he occasionally wore the haori jacket and kimono appropriate to an elderly man, and after his retirement he began to use his male name, Gonshichi.

The Best Actor in Japan

In 1704 Mizuki Tatsunosuke, Ayame's long-standing rival, retired from the kabuki stage. He was just thirty-one years old at the time. Three decades before, retiring by about the age of thirty had been the norm for onnagata, but those were the days when a young man's looks were all that mattered. In 1704, Tatsunosuke's retirement shocked the kabuki world. The rival actor's beloved uncle, Jimbei, died that same year, but Tatsunosuke, who still received nothing but top ratings, no longer needed his uncle's support to get good roles or to dominate the stage. Tatsunosuke left kabuki at the peak of his career, perhaps because he sensed that his work would soon go into decline, and he preferred to leave while his impressive reputation was still untarnished. One factor behind his decision may have been the heavy physical toll placed on him by the sort of dancing he did. Tatsunosuke was the only one of Japan's onnagata ever to be described as doing "acrobatic" (*karuwaza*) dance,[52] which certainly increased the risk of injuries, especially to the knees. Or perhaps Tatsunosuke sensed that Ayame, who specialized in a much less physically punishing art, was about to overtake him in the onnagata hierarchy. Tatsunosuke and Ayame had performed together in 1704, so Tatsunosuke would have had opportunity to observe his rival carefully. But whatever the reason, Tatsunosuke changed his name to Yamatoya Uzaemon and left the stage, spending the rest of his life in retirement. He would outlive Ayame by sixteen years.

By 1704, Ayame had invariably been the top-rated onnagata in any city provided that Tatsunosuke was not working there, but Ayame had never been able to best his rival when they were in the same town or in the same company. Now, with Tatsunosuke gone, no onnagata could challenge Ayame's ranking. Still, this did not mean that Ayame now lacked artistic challenges. In fact, the opposite was true. With Tatsunosuke's retirement, Ayame became obliged to take on the dramatic, histrionic women's roles that had always been the other man's forte. Toward the end of the Genroku period, critics were agreed that Ayame's acting style was gentle and subdued, and Ayame himself maintained that "unaffected acting wins renown. He who tries to be extraordinary, unusual, or too strong will achieve rare, but short-lasting artistic flowers."[53] The oft-cited metaphor for this conviction is an account that describes Ayame's blossom-viewing trip to Tennōji in Osaka. Crowds at the temple flocked to see rare flowers in outlandish arrangements instead of admiring, as the actor did, "the skill with which ordinary flowers were arranged."[54] If we accept as true Ayame's professions of love for the beauty and elegance of the simple and the ordinary, then he cannot have been pleased with many of the roles that he began to play at this time. But neither would the situation have surprised him, because he knew that the taste of most of the people he was paid to entertain was no different from that of people who flocked to see the rare, exotic flowers at Tennōji. For the next twenty years, Ayame proved fabulously successful at creating the kabuki equivalents of the extraordinary and rare flowers that he believed were destined to be short-lived.

Kabuki audiences in the early 1700s craved novelty, and producers and playwrights attempted to satisfy them by creating new, challenging pieces for Ayame. In 1705, Ayame amazed audiences with his portrayal of a samurai girl from Kyushu, speaking in a regional accent so authentic that even the fans from Kyushu were convinced. When the girl and her family fell on hard times and the character was on the verge of being sold to the pleasure district, she turned kabuki convention upside-down with a damning attack on the institution of prostitution. She objected strongly—in the end unsuccessfully—to being forced to participate in it, even for the good of her clan.[55]

Ayame appeared in more macabre and outré scenes than ever before. He played a samurai wife who transforms herself into a fox in a desperate bid to escape a cruel husband, and in another work pulled a bloody dagger and a letter from a recently dispatched corpse.[56] Clearly, Ayame had begun to fill in for Tatsunosuke in the kinds of roles the other man had always played.

It was after 1705 that Ayame turned to Tōjūrō for inspiration and added a new kind of "flower" to the repertory of onnagata arts—the dramatic monolog. In 1706, in Osaka, while playing the role of a female hairdresser, Ayame did a long monolog during which the woman reminisces about her lost love, placing a conical hat on her futon, manipulating it and complaining to it as if it were her lover.[57] This was a scene clearly inspired by Tōjūrō's saké lees peddler in *Mibu Temple*. Ayame did fine work in this, and many other monologs.

Finally, Ayame began to depict more and more women pressed by dint of circumstance to imitate men. Onnagata had played women who impersonate men from early in the history of men's kabuki, but this type of role would have been particularly challenging for Ayame, given his professional commitment to somehow preserving a character's female "reality" even while wearing men's clothing. He began by portraying women who engage in activities generally associated with men. In 1709 he played a woman who takes a job as a palanquin-bearer to enter the pleasure district to search for her young son who had been abducted there and was being forced to wear women's clothing and work as a courtesan's apprentice (*kamuro*).[58] His earliest attempts at "male impersonation" met with mixed reviews,[59] but in the 1710–1711 season his success in this kind of role was part of the reason that Ejima Kiseki felt he had to invent a whole new rating for Ayame, *goku-jō-jō-kichi* ("extreme high-high good fortune"), a rating above that ever accorded any other actor in Japan.

The hit of the 1711 season was *An Account of the Courtesan's Original Vows (Keisei Honganki)*. For the two preceding decades Ayame's emotional scenes had been guaranteed to induce tears in women spectators, but Ejima Kiseki noted that during the 1711 play "even the young toughs in the audience were weeping so hard that the tears loosened their fake beards, which all fell to the floor."[60] In *The Courtesan's Original Vows*, Ayame played a courtesan-turned-samurai wife who, in order to buy medicine to cure her lord's daughter's blindness, has no recourse but to sell her own daughter into prostitution. The situation was typical tearjerker, and it induced the beard-wetting incident quoted above. Later in the play the wife disguises herself as a man and goes to the pleasure district to visit her daughter. She arrives just in the nick of time because the daughter has fallen in love with a poor man who cannot afford to buy her out of the quarter, and the two are planning to commit double suicide. The mother, still incognito, shadows the pair, then forcibly disarms and subdues them just when they are on the verge of killing one another.[61]

At this stage in his career, Ayame began to devote particular attention to honing his ability in the martial arts and to improving his skills in wagoto tachiyaku acting—such as negotiating for and to entertaining courtesans, disputing with lovers or family members, moving and speaking as if drunk, and performing monologs of all types, from humorous routines such as the conical hat solo to dramatic recounting of samurai battles. He used all these routines when playing women who impersonate men.

In the 1710–1711 season Ayame's zamoto was Yamashita Karumo (1686–1718), a middle-ranking onnagata who was a disciple of Yamashita Kyōemon (the new name which Hanzaemon had taken to honor his Kyoto audiences). Karumo was only twenty-five years old, and did not have sufficient stature to work as a zamoto in his own right, but Kyōemon was with the same theater company and probably cooperated closely with young man. It was very rare to see an onnagata to take on such weighty managerial responsibilities, partly because this ran counter to the notion that onnagata should, in their offstage lives, emulate more-or-less average women, but Karumo did not have a glittering reputation to protect, and Kyōemon may well have urged Karumo to take the position because the young onnagata possessed some special skills as a negotiator and facilitator of artistic collaborations.

The 1711–1712 season was the first and the only one in which Ayame himself served as a zamoto. During this season he managed the theater company at Kyoto's Ebisuya-za. Like Karumo, Ayame continued to play women's roles throughout his appointment as zamoto, but unfortunately there are no surviving hyōbanki records to tell us how he fared. His popularity with Kyoto audiences had certainly not diminished, but the fact that he never again worked in this capacity may indicate that he felt that the duties of the position indeed detracted from his performance. He certainly did not need the additional income that came with being a successful zamoto. In the 1710s, his salary was in the vicinity of 1,000 ryō a year,[62] probably the highest paid to any kabuki actor.

For almost ten years Ayame had stood alone at the top of the ranks of Japan's onnagata, and for two years he had been rated the finest actor in Japan. Edo audiences were dying to see him perform, and a gala season in Edo was planned. He was to travel the fifty-three stages of the Tokaidō Road and work at Edo's most prestigious theater, the Nakamura-za, for the 1713–1714 season. Ayame was scheduled to play opposite Edo's top tachiyaku, Nakamura Denkurō (Nakamura Shichisaburō had passed away in 1708 and Danjūrō II had not yet emerged as the dominant figure on the Edo stage).

A Tumultuous Year in Edo: The Iris in Full Bloom

In the 1690s Ayame had traveled the Tokaidō unnoticed by anyone, an obscure actor awaiting his first big break. In 1713 he was Japan's most popular celebrity and his journey this time was triumphal. It was customary for the kabuki fans in Edo to meet visiting actors at Shinagawa, just south of the city, and join them there for a parade-like entry into the heart of the city, where various welcoming festivities would take place. But the throng of Ayame's well-wishers —largely women—was as huge "as for a Zenkōji kaichō,"[63] and Naka-mura Kanzaburō, the Nakamura-za producer, fearing the sort of public disturbance that so frequently brought swift government punishment down on the art, decided to spirit Ayame into the city by a different route, and disguised as a man. "Ayame wore a cotton kimono, striped hakama trousers, and concealed his face in a cloth scarf. He looked just like a young man from the fish market. Thus Ayame was forced into disguise in Edo even before he played his first role."[64] Ayame's persona as a woman was by then so persuasive that the world at large considered his dressing in men's clothing a form of disguise, and scholars count his secret entrance into Edo among his successful "male impersonation" roles.

Ayame arrived safely at the Nakamura-za around dusk and hoped to visit Denkurō that evening to discuss their upcoming performance, but Denkurō had other guests and sent a message to Ayame deferring the meeting. Denkurō died suddenly that same night, and so was never able to welcome Ayame to Edo. The pairing of this wildly popular onnagata and tachiyaku that the city had so anticipated was not destined to take place. This was considered by many a frightening omen for a season that had held out such high hopes.

If Ayame had disappointed his fans by sneaking into the city, he did not disappoint them the night before the opening of the kaomise. It was a cold night but throngs had again gathered, hours before the theater was due to open. Kanzaburō arranged for hot drinks to be distributed to the crowd free of charge and then opened the theater at midnight so that spectators could wait until morning in relative warmth. Edo fans believed that Ayame had himself suggested these thoughtful measures, and his reputation rose even higher.[65]

Despite Denkurō's absence, the kaomise play was every bit the smash success that Ayame and his producers and fans had hoped for. Audiences jammed the Nakamura-za beyond capacity for the duration of the kaomise, and one account tells us that "even the children and the dogs of Edo were shouting, 'Ayame! Ayame!' in the streets."[66] In the kaomise, Ayame played Kikusui, wife of the warrior hero Kusunoki Masashige, in *A Woman Kusunoki and the Chronicle of the Great Pacification (Onna Kusunoki Taiheiki)*, treating Edo to the kind of acting for which he had achieved renown: he enacted Kikusui in "straight" scenes in which he embodied the look and the mannerisms of a real samurai matron with uncanny authenticity. In this play, he fought skillfully with samurai weapons and killed a villain; he told the story of Kusunoki's battles in the dynamic style of a tachiyaku; he wore a magical "disappearing raincoat" to break into a house to commit burglary; he cut off his finger in a love pledge and bandaged the wound himself while enduring the pain stoically; and he was transformed into a female demon in a scene that recalled the nō play *The Maple Viewing (Momijigari).*

By far the most popular scene in the play, and one of the finest moments in Ayame's career, came when Kikusui disguised herself as a ladies' maid named Otake who chattered on about her beloved while engaged in a very quotidian chore: pickling *daikon* and other vegetables (the daikon is a giant white radish). Her ingenious, playful, pun-laden monolog went like this:

> "How embarrassing, as a woman, to be seen pickling vegetables. This daikon is the man and this turnip is the woman. We put them to bed, pat, pat, pat!" She covers the vegetables with a coarse cloth. "And throw on a little salt."

She picks up a daikon and looks at it. "From the beginning, you weren't a daikon root, you weren't even a carrot.
But if you will be my cool, vinegared greens on hot summer days and my spicy *miso* companion pickle on the coldest nights of winter; if you're the rhubarb pickle who helps
me clean the bath, and you're with me every morning like
breakfast pickles and help me clean the house for the New
Year; if you stick with me like the pickles that go with
sticky rice cakes in sweet bean soup—then how happy I
will be! Oh, how happy I will be!"[67]

Ayame ended by throwing the vegetables into the vat, and perhaps
occasionally into the audience, to thunderous applause.

The monolog is a humorous, virtuoso performance employing
humble items from daily life as "found object puppets" and derived
from the Tōjūrō tradition of wagoto tachiyaku acting. The attitudes
expressed by Otake in her virtuoso discourse demonstrate why
Ayame so captured the hearts of the women in the audience. What
Otake thinks about her man, and what she wants from him, are not
likely to spark in him any sense of masculine pride. She begins the
main section of the monolog with a humorous belittling of his viril-
ity, then goes on to say that constancy and companionship are what
she most wants. She may want a little spice too on cold, winter
nights, but more than that she needs someone who will be with her
each morning and who will help her scrub the bathtub and clean the
house for the New Year. Almost any woman in the audience would
have been delighted to have a mate like this—an ideal male companion of a sort that is hard to find even today, and very different from
Danjūrō's superheroes or the flighty wastrels of Tōjūrō's kabuki.

In 1709, all four Edo kabuki theaters had begun the custom
(which they would continue for nearly two hundred years) of doing a
play about the Soga brothers for their first show of each new year.
Ayame's name was written into the title of the Nakamura-za's New
Year's play for 1714. In *The Felicitous Soga Iris (Kotobuki Ayame*

Soga), Ayame impressed Edo audiences by excelling at Tōjūrō-style "stationary acting" and impersonating a male millionaire, all within the context of his role as the Soga brothers' older sister.[68] Ejima Kiseki wrote, "Ayame seized the aragoto-addicted audience by the scruff of their necks. That's a master for you."[69]

The Soga Iris had been running almost two months when a terrible scandal broke that put a stop to all the performances of kabuki shows in Edo. Lady Ejima (1681–1741), a high-ranking female official in service to the shogun's mother, was discovered partying at the Yamamura-za theater in the company of Edo's most attractive, sought-after wagoto actor, Ikushima Shingorō (1670?–1743).[70] Ejima had taken a detour from a pious pilgrimage to the Tokugawa graves, taking eleven women attendants with her to the theater. A full investigation followed, and revealed that her secret romantic relationship with Shingorō had been going on for nine years. All the ladies involved were sentenced to live the rest of their lives under house arrest, and the actor was exiled to distant Miyake Island. He remained there for twenty-eight years and was granted amnesty just one year before he died. The Yamamura-za was shut down forever: the building was demolished and the owner's assets were sold at auction.[71] For the next 150 years, Edo would have three, not four, kabuki theaters. All theatrical events were canceled for the duration of the investigation, and the authorities summoned most of Edo's leading actors for questioning. The Ichimura-za and Morita-za began production in the fourth and fifth months respectively, but the Nakamura-za was not permitted to reopen until the seventh month. At the very pinnacle of his career, Ayame was forced to spend four months in idleness, as a result of the worst scandal in the history of Edo-period kabuki. Ill fortune seemed to befall Ayame whenever he worked in Edo.

Ayame performed in one last play in Edo before returning to the Kansai, and he was superb. Ejima Kiseki wrote that "when he did his farewell play, *Onna Karukaya,* it would not have mattered if the tachiyaku had never come onstage. He did all sorts of solo work, all of it successfully. Even now, all the people of Edo talk about is Ayame, and they are full of regret that he has left them."[72] But much as Edoitcs had loved Ayame, no producer was likely to bring him back. His year in Edo had started with an ill omen, and then the theater had been brought to a standstill. Edo-period Japanese were too superstitious to risk the disaster that Ayame seemed to bring with him to the city. There was never again any discussion of an Edo tour for Ayame.

Because Ayame's work in Edo in 1713–1714 had been his first there as a leading onnagata, the three hyōbanki that dealt with those performances contained more heated debate about his style than had been typical in the years following Tatsunosuke's retirement. Debate between fictional characters was a popular convention in hyōbanki, and Ayame inspired much discussion. One writer asked, "Has he lost his erotic appeal, or has he maintained it, but just chosen not to display it most of the time?" and another wrote, "Was the fact that he did danced so rarely a weakness or a strength?" One sophisticated fictional spectator created by Ejima Kiseki responded to the latter question in the voice of a Tōjūrō fan of old: "With an onnagata as remarkable as Ayame, I don't want to see him dance. All I want to do is see how well he can act. I certainly don't want to see him start dancing suddenly, just for the sake of entertaining some hicks from the distant provinces."[73] A fictional woman connoisseur set the record straight for a young man who complained that forty-year-old Ayame was no longer the most attractive onnagata on the stage: "Ayame's work when he was young is what has made it possible for today's young onnagata to be as erotic and appealing as they are."[74] Just as Tōjūrō had done late in his carccr, when he performed his last Izaemon, Ayame induced spectators and critics alike to think about the theater they loved in a historical context. Ayame may have suffered ill luck in Edo, but he also taught Edo audiences what to look for in a great onnagata, and it would only be a matter of time before great onnagata would finally emerge from Edo as well.

Ayame Breaks His Own Rules

Back in Kyoto in late 1714, Ayame presented his own onnagata version of the Edo aragoto roppō dance, as a kind of "souvenir" from Edo. He also did the pickling monolog, and variations on it, again and again in his plays, but his innovative work in the years following the Edo tour revolved around gender confusion. His women characters impersonated men of all stations, from street vendors to feudal lords. Ejima was particularly impressed by a challenging role that called for Ayame's woman character to live disguised as a man. The woman conceives a child and is forced to work harder and harder to conceal her true identity, returning to female dress only near the end of her pregnancy.[75] From 1710 on, Ayame received nothing but praise for his women's impersonation of male characters, as well as for his work in the tachiyaku style. Between 1714 and 1719 all the authors of the hyōbanki vied to come up with new, effusive ratings that they could assign to Ayame and to no other actor. The gist of each was: "Ayame is peerless, easily the finest actor in all Japan."

As late as 1718, at age forty-six, Ayame was praised for his youthful appearance as a young woman, but in the two seasons between 1718 and 1720, when he left Kyoto to perform at two different theaters in Osaka, his plays began to suffer from mediocre attendance.[76] He was still ranked as the finest kabuki actor in Japan, but his exalted status was beginning to take on a somewhat hollow ring.[77] The women's roles that Ayame played in these years were exclusively older women, mostly stern samurai wives and matrons. Ayame's obvious skill at the tachiyaku arts, coupled with the deaths of so many great tachiyaku in the Kansai influenced him to consider making a risky, late-career change to tachiyaku roles, and his recent lukewarm reception in Osaka may have persuaded him that he would have to take extraordinary steps if he wanted to save his career and his reputation.

Returning to Kyoto, Ayame edged closer to making this shift. He sought to demonstrate his virtuosity in a dramatic way in *The*

Courtesan and Sanemori at Ōhara (Keisei Ōhara Sanemori), his first play of 1721, by playing two roles, a sister and brother, in the same play. According to the play's story, the brother and sister closely resemble one another, so the double role was more than just a stunt. Ayame used quick changes of costume in the wings to switch from one character to the other. Kyoto audiences, and Ayame's women fans in particular,[78] flocked to the Ebisuya-za to see his performances. In terms of attendance the experiment was a success, but critical reviews were mixed. The play itself was patched together from old, stereotypical routines, and only Ayame's male role and quick costume changes gave the play any originality.[79] One critic wrote that all the gender-switching was "too hectic and overly tedious," and that the play contained too much buffoonery for an actor of Ayame's stature.[80] Ejima also had his doubts. He believed that Ayame's onnagata acting in 1719 and 1720 had been good despite the mediocre attendance. Ejima loved to populate his hyōbanki with loquacious spectators, and their comments on Ayame's work as the brother in *The Courtesan and Sanemori at Ōhara* were decidedly critical: "Ayame looked much worse in male roles than as an onnagata," and "he who was so wise has unexpectedly stumbled into confusion."[81]

Perhaps the good attendance and lively discussion mattered more to Ayame than did the criticism of the pundits, because for the 1721–1722 season he made a total break with the onnagata profession. He changed his stage name to Yoshizawa Gonshichi and set out to become a tachiyaku actor. He knew his own skills, so the tachiyaku whom he sought to emulate was Tōjūrō. Ayame would play gentle, stylish men and try to lend his roles the humorous touch that had served him so well as an onnagata. He acted in scenes that would take advantage of his established strengths. For example, ever since *The Courtesan and the Peak of Asama,* Ayame had excelled in scenes in which a samurai mother had to suffer the pain of losing a child while completing an important mission. In his kaomise play of 1721 he took the role of a young father forced to do the same thing.[82]

The choice of this play—with its familiar, though slightly altered plot—suggests an actor making a careful, deliberate first step into new artistic territory. Again audiences flocked to the theater, but the weight of critical opinion held that the play was popular "because people wanted to see Ayame try something extraordinary, not because he was all that good as a tachiyaku."[83] Most critics were ambivalent. They praised Ayame's timing onstage and his humorous acting, but found it difficult to compare him to other tachiyaku actors. When the hyōbanki appeared in the third month of 1722, he was ranked as a better than average (jō-jō) tachiyaku actor, but the experts expected Ayame to persist in his new calling, and eventually to become a fine tachiyaku actor.[84]

Had Ayame broken the most basic rule of commitment to the onnagata profession, the rule he himself had made? None of the contemporary critics were concerned with this question. *The Words of Ayame* had yet to be published, and other actors had made changes in role specialization, although few so late in their careers. But later scholars would hotly debate the point. Unfortunately, we have no clue to Ayame's personal motives for making this change. Nothing survives to tell what he might have written or said on the subject, nor did any observers close to him offer a record of their own thoughts. Many scholars today assume that Ayame made the change at a time of emotional vulnerability and weakness induced by the fear that he was losing his physical appeal as a woman. But Ayame apologists emphasize the fact that his admonition in *The Words of Ayame* is addressed to young onnagata who feel the urge to shift to tachiyaku acting when "things are not going well" in their chosen field. This could hardly describe an actor who stood at the top of the onnagata hierarchy for nearly twenty years and whom the world was happy to regard as virtually a woman. No, they argue, Ayame made the change simply because he had explored the onnagata role to its fullest and wanted to move on to new challenges. The nonapologists counter that Ayame may well have been the highest-ranking onnagata, but that his fear for his professional future placed

him in the same position psychologically as a young onnagata lacking confidence in his abilities. And so the debate continues, even
today.

Ayame took tachiyaku roles in two plays in the spring of 1722,
but no play texts or hyōbanki survive to tell us anything about either.
Then, suddenly, in the play that opened on the twenty-second day
of the fourth month, he appeared as an onnagata once more, and
was never again to try his hand at tachiyaku roles. The circumstances clearly suggest that Ayame himself viewed the experiment as
a failure. He changed specialties in the middle of the season, and at
the end of the season left Kyoto for Osaka. He would never again act
in Kyoto.

No one has ever suggested that the reason Ayame changed to
the tachiyaku specialty was because he believed he was not getting
the respect and adulation he deserved as a "peerless" actor. But
when he returned to the ranks of onnagata, audiences' and critics'
expressions of joy and relief were overwhelming. Ejima, in his 1724
hyōbanki *An Evaluation of the Quality and Art of Actors in the Year
of the Dragon (Yakusha Tatsugoyomi Gei Shina Sadame)*, put it suc-
cinctly: "I want to tell those of you who didn't see him while he was a
tachiyaku that Ayame is back, and he is getting ten times the acclaim
he did before his tachiyaku stint."[85] In the same hyōbanki, a fictional
kabuki-loving priest and a townsman spectator, both created by
Ejima, expressed the sentiments of all the hyōbanki writers:

PRIEST: I pray that he plays onnagata roles until he has to use a
            walking stick onstage, that he doesn't tamper with his
            onnagata art, and that he won't find anything again to
            attract him to the tachiyaku roles.

SABURŌ: He should take his lesson from nō actors who keep on
            playing Yang Guei Fei and Komachi [the two most beau-
            tiful women in the histories of China and Japan respec-
            tively] until they're one hundred years old, even after
            they've shaved their heads like priests. What is essential

is natural feelings. There are things they call wigs that he
can use to hide his gray hair. I want to see his renowned
art continue for ten thousand years.[86]

There were also a few critical voices in the hyōbanki—fans who
felt that Ayame should never have made the change in the first
place—and one character in Ejima's hyōbanki dared express the
opinion that the art of any onnagata, even Ayame's, was bound to
suffer if the actor began to take male roles.[87] Another critic made the
observation that, from a commercial standpoint, it was probably a
good idea for established onnagata to switch over to tachiyaku roles
since people would come in droves out of sheer curiosity.[88] But the
presiding sentiments were joy and sympathy, and Ayame's stature as
the "the best actor in Japan" was assured until his retirement.

Ayame returned to the same kinds of women's roles that had
begun to bring him acclaim from the time of Tatsunosuke's retirement. Ayame no longer played young women, but his samurai wives
and mothers engaged in a wide range of activities, from swordplay,
tearful partings, and painful family sacrifices, to humorous adaptations of the pickling monolog. After his return to Osaka and to onnagata roles, Ayame invariably drew large crowds and garnered
breathless praise from the critics.

In 1727, one hyōbanki notes that the elderly Ayame had taken to
wearing men's clothes when he came to meetings in the theater and
that he looked like any other elderly gentleman.[89] It would seem that
Ayame was breaking yet another of his essential rules for onnagata.
But there is no indication that this hurt his performances. Beginning
in 1726, his appearances onstage grew less frequent, and for a time
he did nothing but his old, famous routines. Still, the critics were
delighted with everything Ayame did. In 1727 and 1728, detailed
records of two plays show Ayame once again in important onnagata
roles, with multiple appearances in multi-act plays. In his last stage
appearance for which we have definitive records, in the spring of
1728, he played the determined nurse of a feudal lord. The nurse

tells a moving story about her lord's last fight and, in the last act, disguised as a nun, uses a rope to strangle two samurai villains to death.[90] We cannot verify whether this was Ayame's final stage appearance, but he retired after the 1728 season and passed away on the fifteenth day of the seventh month in 1729.

Ayame's Impact on the Art of the Onnagata

In the 1720s, Japanese sensed that a historic era was coming to an end. The opulence and exuberance of Genroku culture were suddenly reined in by the Kyōhō reforms of the 1720s. This was as true in theater as in other realms of culture and city life. One nostalgic observer expressed his sense of impending loss: "The most remarkable men alive today are the jōruri playwright Chikamatsu and the onnagata Ayame. They are so special it is unlikely we will ever see their equal again."[91] By 1729, both men were dead. But long before Ayame had appeared in kabuki there had been beguiling onnagata, and the theater was assured of a continuing supply of beautiful young men. Ayame had given these actors the confidence to aspire to convincing women characters by demonstrating himself that the way to do this was by harmonizing one's appearance and one's inner life. He had added new flowers to the repertory of skills that could help make an onnagata rich and famous. The flowers that he had borrowed from Tōjūrō and used so successfully in women's roles— the humorous "found object" monologs and brilliantly recited tales of adventure—declined in importance for later onnagata, but elements of the art that he introduced and that remained essential over the succeeding generations included evoking tears during emotional scenes, depicting strong samurai women, and most of all, amazing audiences with uncannily realistic gender transformation.

Ayame, through his first- and fourth-born sons, founded the Yoshizawa acting line that was to last throughout the Edo period. His second son became a tachiyaku actor and successor to the Yamashita Kyōemon line. Most of Ayame's descendants were onnagata, but no one else working under the name Yoshizawa Ayame would ever reach the pinnacle of renown that the first Ayame achieved.

The two great onnagata of the next generation were Segawa Kikunojō I (1693–1749) and Ayame's third son, Nakamura Tomijūrō I (1719–1786). Each opened new territory in the profession and put his own stamp on the art of the onnagata. Like Ayame, Kikunojō started out as an iroko and was assisted in his early years by a kindly patron who made it possible for him to become a kabuki actor. Kikunojō was famous for striking good looks: "His beauty was such that it seemed all the erotic appeal in the world had been concentrated in one man."[92] Kikunojō recognized that to be successful he would have to win acclaim in both major forms of onnagata "flower"—dance and convincing portrayals of women. The three greatest hits of Kikunojō's career were dance plays,[93] but to become a skilled performer of women's roles, he lived Ayame's "way of the onnagata" even more fully than the great founder had done himself. Kikunojō never contemplated changing to male roles, and he insisted on playing young, attractive women until the end of his career. He recorded his own thoughts on the way of the onnagata, and modified *The Words of Ayame,* criticizing "the master" for depicting characters with whom older women would identify so strongly:

> It is very bad for an onnagata to have too many women fans, and bad to even consider playing wives or matrons. An onnagata should have many male fans, and his goal should be to make them wish they could have a woman like him. In women fans, the onnagata should instill a desire to have the same things he does—the same combs, hairpins, scarves, and sashes; women should like the styles he likes. It is most important to have samurai girls, female entertainers, and townsmen's daughters imitating you. The only women fans that one should have are young women.[94]

Later generations of onnagata were inspired by Kikunojō's advice and became the arbiters of fashion for the women of Japan's big cities. They soon began to exploit the commercial possibilities of their adulation, and by the mid- to late 1700s, onnagata were enjoying huge supplemental income generated by product endorsements of cosmetics, ornaments, and tea, and by retail franchises which sold patented lines of clothing decorated in distinctive, personalized patterns. Of all the tachiyaku acting lines, only the Danjūrōs could compete with the great onnagata in terms of their marketability and their influence on the world of fashion.

Kikunojō had been born exactly twenty years after Ayame, whereas Ayame's third son, Nakamura Tomijūrō—who would be his most successful—was born when Ayame was forty-six. Ayame, Kikunojō, and Tomijūrō can in fact be said to represent three different generations of onnagata. Perhaps the most remarkable point about Tomijūrō's career is how different it was from his father's. He was, of course, never an iroko, and from the time he was very young he trained under the finest actors in the Kansai, including Ayame. Like Kikunojō, he excelled in both acting and dance, and the stellar achievement of his early career was bringing Tatsunosuke-style spectacular spirit-transformation dances (*hengemono*) back to kabuki's center spotlight. In 1752 his *The Maiden at Dōjōji (Kyōganoko Musume Dōjōji)* electrified Kyoto audiences, and in 1753 it played for a remarkable six months at the Nakamura-za in Edo. *The Maiden at Dōjōji* is now an icon in the repertory of Japanese dance, with a mystique and a rich body of history and lore that ranks it far above any other dance play. Of Ayame's sons, Tomijūrō was the only one to match his father's remarkable rating of "peerless in Japan." Tomijūrō was able to accomplish this because he was even more skilled as an actor than he was in dance.

While working as an onnagata, Tomijūrō lived by his father's dicta, dressing and behaving as a woman and practicing numerous feminine arts.[95] But later in his career he played tachiyaku roles, including aragoto staples like Soga Gorō, and did so with skill and to great acclaim.[96] Traditionalists criticized him for his unladylike behavior, and complained that his onnagata acting suffered because of his performance of male roles, but the critics did not deter Tomijūrō. Audiences loved actors who presented themselves with, and then surmounted, artistic challenges. Tomijūrō paved the way for actors to play roles outside their specialties; men who did this came to be called kaneru yakusha (multitalented actors). This soon became the norm, not the exception, in kabuki. Tomijūrō also founded an acting line that has survived to this day (the currently-active descendant is Tomijūrō V) and which is still noted for its versatility and breadth.

Over the years, onnagata traditions have changed and developed. Edo began to raise and train its own onnagata specialists, and eventually was no longer obliged to import them from the Kansai, as had been done during the Genroku period. Onnagata kaneru yakusha played a wide range of women, including members of the lower classes, not just fine ladies in disguise. Their roles ranged from criminals and outcasts to serving girls. Most onnagata in the Edo period tried to live by the dicta of *The Words of Ayame* through at least part of their careers, and people in the country's three largest cities generally understood why these young men cross-dressed and behaved like women, and supported them in their efforts. It is even said that women tolerated onnagata using the women's section of public baths, because they recognized how crucial it was for young actors to participate in every possible facet of female life. Some successful onnagata discovered that they did not in fact need to dress and live as women offstage in order to enact women's roles to their own satisfaction and that of their audiences. For these onnagata, mastery of art and technique served better than more internalized forms of preparation.

Today, as in the Edo period, whatever approach an individual onnagata may employ, his goal is the same daunting one that Ayame spoke of early in his career and sought for the rest of his life to achieve: to convince everyone in the audience, male or female, that he is a member of the opposite sex. Much of the magic and thrill of kabuki today comes from watching onnagata attempt and achieve this remarkable transformation.

5

FOUR LEADING ACTORS IN KABUKI TODAY

Danjūrō, Ganjirō, Ennosuke, Tamasaburō

Energy and Experiment: Genroku Kabuki and Today's Kabuki Stage

It was almost exactly three hundred years ago that Danjūrō, Tōjūrō, and Ayame emerged from the ranks of their fellow actors to lead kabuki into a new era. The Genroku period was a time of cultural ferment and of intense competition between actors and playwrights. It was an age when an actor could achieve success only if he dared take the theater in new directions and then had the luck to win praise, and not condemnation, for his audacity. Today Japan is once again in the midst of an era of intense cultural creativity. As in the Genroku period, the stage is just one of many forums for artistic experimentation, and kabuki maintains vital links to many other genres of performance.

Kabuki is now one of Japan's classical theaters, an impressive edifice built of three centuries of stage tradition. Yet few of kabuki's top actors feel that traditional kabuki can remain exactly as it is today if it is to thrive in the coming century. Most feel that the energy and the spirit of creativity and adventure that were intrinsic to Edo-period kabuki have been lost. Actors seek to remedy this situation in

224

different ways. Some focus on infusing their acting with more energy and immediacy. Some revive lost plays that they feel recapture the spirit of the great actors of the past. Others strike out in completely new directions, commissioning new works, introducing new dramatic traditions, and creating new links with other theatrical forms. While many fine actors are at work on the kabuki stage today, four of them in particular—Ichikawa Danjūrō XII, Nakamura Ganjirō III, Ichikawa Ennosuke III, and Bandō Tamasaburō V—can be called the inheritors of the legacy of Genroku kabuki. Danjūrō and Ganjirō are striving to recapture the essence of Edo-period aragoto and wagoto kabuki, and Ennosuke and Tamasaburō, like the three remarkable actors of three centuries ago, are engaging in more radical experiments and forging new connections that have begun to bring kabuki back to mass audiences.

Today's Danjūrō: A Spiritual Actor Imbued with Family History

Danjūrō XII (b. 1946) has a strong sense of connection to the eleven Danjūrōs who preceded him. Before he took that illustrious name in 1985 he told an interviewer that he wanted to be a Danjūrō who would call to mind the image of every member of the family line who went before him, and that he wanted to be remembered as a Danjūrō whose consciousness was rooted in Edo culture.[1] For Danjūrō XII this does not mean doing exactly what his father did. He has searched the past for exciting plays that over time were lost to the kabuki stage and has revived them, one with such great success that it has since been performed again several times since. Of all the Edo-period Danjūrōs, Danjūrō I is his greatest inspiration. Danjūrō XII seeks to recapture the charisma and heroism that the pioneering actor brought to the Genroku stage, and to revive the spiritual, even the healing, power of Danjūrō I's acting.[2]

Danjūrō XII's affinity with his forebears is so intense perhaps because it is a matter of conviction rather than direct kinship. Beginning early this century, fifty-nine years passed with no Danjūrō on the kabuki stage. Fine actors in collateral families and the legacy of great Danjūrōs of the past prevented kabuki actors, fans, and producers from allowing the main branch of the Ichikawa line to die out as so many acting families had done over the centuries. When Danjūrō XII's father, Danjūrō XI, finally took that illustrious name in 1962, it was at the advanced age of fifty-three, and although he was a popular and respected actor, living up to the inflated expectations of critics and audiences proved to be no easy task. As so often occurred in the history of the Danjūrōs, tragedy struck swiftly and unexpectedly—cancer struck down Danjūrō XI in 1965, when his son and heir was just nineteen years old. Danjūrō XI was one of Tokyo's top actors, but his tenure as Danjūrō was too short for him to regain much of the power and prestige that was last enjoyed by Danjūrō IX, who had been instrumental in making kabuki into an enduring, classical art form.

In 1965 the nineteen year-old Shinnosuke, the young man who would become Danjūrō XII, found himself in a difficult position. He was heir to the most prestigious name in kabuki, but his father had given him detailed instruction in only three roles. Of these, just one, that of Benkei in *Kanjinchō,* was from the repertory of the family's hereditary plays (the "Eighteen Great Plays"). Shinnosuke would have to rely on older colleagues and relatives to train him in the great roles of his own heritage as well as in other roles; he would have to study under teachers whose own sons were rivals his own age. Danjūrō XI had been called "too serious an actor,"[3] and the young man inherited from him the qualities of perseverance and dedication that were essential to his success in building a career even in the absence of a powerful father.

Shinnosuke was fortunate to begin his career in kabuki in the 1960s, when the lean postwar years were coming to a close and there were ample opportunities for young actors to play good roles at such nontraditional theaters as the Toyoko Department Store Hall. He was able to work with talented actors his own age and, in lesser roles, with the best senior actors in kabuki. He founded his own recital series and used it to perform challenging roles and to begin his first experiments in reviving kabuki plays that had not been staged for decades or, in some cases, for centuries. Like many actors of his generation he occasionally worked outside kabuki, in modern theater (*shimpa*, or melodramatic, contemporary plays sometimes featuring *onnagata*; and *shingeki*, or modern, largely Westernized theater), in films, and in television. These experiments, along with the extensive work he did in kabuki, broadened his skill and increased his confidence, until in 1969 he took the Ichikawa family's second-most prestigious name, Ebizō.

Today in kabuki the ideal of the versatile, multitalented actor has largely replaced the notion of the brilliant but narrow specialist in a single kind of tachiyaku role. This broadening of the actor's repertory had begun in earnest in the mid-1700s, and actors like Danjūrō VIII then added popular wagoto roles to the Ichikawa family aragoto tradition in the mid-1800s. Danjūrō XII has said that he was most in awe of his father when he saw him act in wagoto plays.[4] A Danjūrō today is expected to excel in aragoto acting but to be able to play all sorts of roles. As a young man, Danjūrō XII performed in a wide variety of tachiyaku roles. He studied aragoto under his uncle, Onoe Shōroku II (1913–1989), the finest aragoto actor in postwar kabuki, but the performance record shows that he did not have a strong affinity for the straightforward heroics of the majority of the "Eighteen Great Plays." He favored three particular works in the aragoto tradition: *Narukami, Sukeroku,* and *Kanjinchō.* None of these plays feature simple characters: Sukeroku is more a commoner than a samurai, and he has vexed relationships with his brother and mother; Benkei is wracked by guilt about striking his lord; and Priest Narukami has a power-hungry, lecherous streak. Complex heroes and complex emotions interest and attract Danjūrō XII, perhaps because they suit his personal style, which combines striking good looks with a gravelly voice that he can modulate to sound uncanny, frightening, or even tortured.

While taking on varied work as a young actor, Danjūrō XII continued to return to his historical roots. In the postwar years, some kabuki actors went to college, and Danjūrō XII was one of these. For many young men, the college years were a time for radical thinking, both politically and artistically, but Danjūrō XII chose to delve into history, and wrote his graduation thesis on Danjūrō V. Four years after taking the name Ebizō, he organized and starred in his most successful revival to date of a lost aragoto classic, *Kagekiyo*, including the jail-smashing scene that was the signature work of Danjūrō IV. The part suited him: Kagekiyo is a wonderfully conflicted hero. The test of a successful revival, as Danjūrō XII has said himself, is whether it is performed a second and a third time. *Kagekiyo* has passed this test. In 1997, when Danjūrō XII played Kakegiyo in a revival of another long-unperformed play, he explained why he so enjoys the challenge of this role: "Kakegiyo is the only fully adult aragoto hero, but he is a total failure. He is an invincible warrior, but fails utterly in his quest for revenge."[5]

As early as 1976, when he was thirty years old, Ebizō began to seriously consider whether or not he should take the Danjūrō name. The Shōchiku corporation pledged to support him if he felt himself equal to the responsibility. He gave the matter very serious thought over the next few years and his deliberations, revealed in an interview with Suzuki Haruhiko,[6] tell us much about his character. The stature and authority of his Edo-period forebears weighed heavily on his mind, but he also considered his own ability as an actor, and the impact that his Danjūrō *shūmei* (accession or name-taking ritual) would have on his colleagues and teachers, and on contemporary kabuki as an art and an industry. The timing had to be right for everybody. Earlier Danjūrōs had taken the prestigious name in their teens, twenties, and thirties, but his own father had been fifty-three, and Ebizō did not want to offend his father's memory by performing the shūmei too soon. Ebizō recognized that his art needed further growth, but he hoped that the new name would stimulate him to greater achievements. He decided to become Danjūrō XII in 1985, when he would be thirty-eight years old. Shōchiku supported this decision, and arranged for three months of celebratory kabuki performances, along with other ritual and felicitous events to commemorate the occasion. To increase Japanese awareness of the Danjūrō tradition, a televised historical drama depicting the tumultuous life of Danjūrō I (with Ebizō playing his famous ancestor) preceded the three-month gala. The spring of 1985 was a grueling but exciting time for the current Danjūrō.

Danjūrō XII might be termed "the gentleman Danjūrō." He has none of the combativeness of Danjūrōs I and IV, none of the hauteur of Danjūrō V, none of the quirky vulnerability of Danjūrō VIII, and thanks to the half-century hiatus in Danjūrō history, he is in no position to act the "willful autocrat of kabuki" as did Danjūrōs II and IX. Danjūrō XII has never been embroiled in the sorts of controversy or scandals—stormy love affairs, broken marriages, or succession disputes—that have beset many of his colleagues. Danjūrō XII exercises no autocratic control over fellow actors, and his upright, considerate nature has served him well.

Danjūrō XII is sustained by religious faith, as were so many of his ancestors, and like Danjūrōs of the past he has celebrated his faith publicly onstage and at religious sites. Danjūrō XII's home in Meguro contains two Buddhist altars—one of the Lotus Sect, reflecting Danjūrō IX's conversion to that faith in the Meiji period, and the other dedicated to Fudō of Shinshōji Temple in Narita. It is to the latter that Danjūrō XII seems most devoted. He makes twice-yearly pilgrimages to Shinshōji, and additionally to special events at the temple.[7] Religious austerities and prayers at Shinshōji were an important part of the ritual preparation for taking the name Danjūrō in 1985, and the actor also led two chartered trains full of kabuki fans and Buddhist faithful on a pilgrimage to the temple that year as part of the shūmei festivities.

Danjūrō XII has personally produced eleven kabuki shows, four of which have been dedicated to the deities of Shinshōji and supported by the temple. By far the most ambitious to date was the August 1992 revival of one of Danjūrō I's most successful plays, *The*

Avatars of the Narita Temple Fudō. Danjūrō XII was attracted to the play largely because it contains an early version of the Narukami scene. He was also fascinated by the play's conflicted hero,[8] Ōtomo Kuronushi, who is torn between lust for the beautiful Ono no Komachi and envy of her skill as a poet (for a synopsis of the play, see pages 88–89). The play has many exciting scenes, including one where Kuronushi transforms himself into a huge praying mantis, as well as an early version of the seduction of the lecherous priest Narukami (Figure 32). Most kabuki revivals use staging conventions that were introduced in the mid-eighteenth through the mid-twentieth centuries—use of the *hanamichi,* elaborate stage sets, large musical ensembles—but for *The Narita Temple Fudō* Danjūrō wanted to recreate the atmosphere of the Genroku-period stage. Theater scholars helped Danjūrō and his team produce a play text, actors' style of physical movement, musical accompaniment, and costume designs and coloring that were as true as possible to those of the Genroku period. In most scenes, he used the modified nō stage design and minimalist properties of Genroku theaters.

The play commemorated the 850th anniversary of the death of an important Shingon saint, and for the last scene Danjūrō XII and his son Shinnosuke emulated Danjūrō I and his son Kuzō who, in 1703, had depicted motionless, standing twin avatars of the Narita Fudō. Audience members at the Kabuki-za in 1992 prayed to Fudō and threw offerings onto the stage, just as people had done three hundred years before at Edo theaters. *The Narita Temple Fudō* proved to be a fascinating recreation of Genroku-period dramaturgy, style, and stage energy, and was a wonderful tribute to the first Danjūrō.

Danjūrō XII's following has been increasing through the mid-1990s as his art matures and he makes a name for himself as a multi-talented actor. He is by nature a serious actor of serious roles, and his intimate, understated approach to the blustery, hard-drinking fish vendor Sōgorō in 1996 surprised and pleased his fans. His goals for the future include strengthening his heroic style in his favorite

Fig. 32 Ichikawa Danjūrō XII doing a pillar-entwining mie pose in the Narukami scene, in his role as Ōtomo Kuronushi in *The Avatars of the Narita Temple Fudō*, 1992. Photo courtesy of Ichikawa Danjūrō XII.

aragoto plays, and performing the most complex heroes in kabuki— including wagoto heroes, aragoto heroes, and villains. He will work on revivals only if plays have the potential to be performed regularly, as *Kagekiyo* has been. He is considering a reworking of the scene "Pulling the Elephant" (*Zōhiki*), a rarely-performed work from the "Eighteen Great Plays," and also hopes to do a full-length revival of a gidayū history play if he can put together a capable production team.[9] Kabuki fans can count on Danjūrō XII to keep the traditions of his forefathers alive, to work actively to reclaim the energy and spirit of Edo-period kabuki, and to diligently train his son to be a strong successor to the Danjūrō line.

Nakamura Ganjirō: Iconclastic Inheritor of the Wagoto Tradition

While Danjūrō works to recapture the energy of Ichikawa family aragoto, Nakamura Ganjirō III (b. 1931) has almost singlehandedly brought about the rebirth of kabuki in the Kansai. He has done this by breathing new life into kamigata wagoto, drawing inspiration from the energy and culture of the Genroku period. He takes Chikamatsu and Sakata Tōjūrō as his guiding lights in this endeavor. At work on the kabuki stage, he does almost seem a later incarnation of Tōjūrō: at age sixty-six, in the glare of the footlights, he truly becomes a handsome, vulnerable thirty-year-old man.

Ganjirō's family boasts only four generations on the kabuki stage, but his recent pedigree is unsurpassed. His grandfather, Ganjirō I (1860–1934), was the romantic idol of the Kansai who dominated the stage in Kyoto and Osaka from the time he was thirty years old until his death. Ganjirō II (1902–1982), the current Ganjirō's father, endeavored to step out from the shadow of his father's fame by reinterpreting his father's best roles and, further, by performing in roles his father had never taken. He left kabuki for a decade after the war to work as a film star but, following his return to the stage in 1965, became the most beloved actor in kamigata kabuki. Both early Ganjirōs began their careers doing considerable work as onnagata, but made their fame in male wagoto roles.

Ganjirō III came of age during a bad time for kabuki—the immediate postwar years. Kabuki audiences were dangerously reduced by the American occupation's restrictions on kabuki performances, and by the privations suffered in cities destroyed by bombing coupled with a new national inclination to reject old customs and vestiges of traditional culture. At this critical juncture former theater scholar and theorist Takechi Tetsuji (1912–1988) entered the Japanese theatrical arena as a financial backer, producer, director, and teacher. He spent much time and effort training young kabuki actors, and produced and directed shows that thoroughly energized Japanese traditional theater. He brought together actors from kabuki, nō, kyōgen, and modern theater and dance troupes in experimental dramas, and produced exciting new kabuki plays that were dubbed "Takechi kabuki."

At this time Ganjirō III was using the stage name Senjaku. He was Takechi's most devoted, hard-working pupil, and would go on to become Takechi's greatest success story. Takechi's instruction was both intellectual and physical. He had great respect for the best playwrights of the Edo period and believed that modern-day kabuki actors were not paying enough attention to play texts. Takechi taught his pupils to respect original texts and to work hard to understand the motivations and psychologies of their characters. He believed that kabuki needed more energy and more power. Actors needed to understand, and not to understate, the powerful emotions of the characters in their plays; meanwhile, they also needed new physical tools—new ways of breathing, moving, and using their voices. Takechi believed that artists from the different classical forms had much to teach each other, so he worked to break down the old, encrusted barriers that separate kabuki, nō, kyōgen, and dance, and to resolve the schisms among the mutually suspicious, traditionally incompatible schools within each of these arts. Thanks to Takechi, Senjaku was able to study under the finest nō and kyōgen actors, gidayū reciters, and classical dancers of the day— teachers whom he never would have met without Takechi's intercession.[10]

Senjaku's first big success came in 1953, with his powerful and startling new interpretation of Ohatsu, the courtesan heroine of Chikamatsu's *The Love Suicides at Sonezaki*. In his perceptive reading of Chikamatsu's play, Senjaku saw Ohatsu as a passionate woman, stronger and more decisive than her lover Tokubei. As Ohatsu, Senjaku spoke his lines with more intensity than was normally used by contemporary onnagata. Ohatsu sat closer to Tokubei than in earlier versions of the play, focusing her gaze on him with rapt attention. This simple change made palpable the strength of her love for him.[11] Senjaku's focus on the performance itself, and not on audience response, resembles Tōjūrō's approach. Facial expressions showing carnal ecstasy and physical desire for Tokubei excited audiences who were accustomed to onnagata exhibiting a more formal beauty which was based on the restrained charm of an ideal chaste and virtuous woman.[12] Senjaku rejected the mincing, pointed-toe walk of contemporary onnagata for a more deliberate, smoother gait, with feet sliding parallel to each other—the "slide-step" *(suri-ashi)* walk he had learned from his teacher of nō drama.[13] Throughout the play, Ohatsu dominated her lover Tokubei (who was played by Senjaku's father) with her will, presence, and physical action. *The Love Suicides at Sonezaki* (in which he sometimes played Ohatsu and, at other times, Tokubei) would become Ganjirō's signature play, as the Yūgiri-Izaemon plays had been for Tōjūrō. On January 16, 1995, in Osaka's Naka-za, Ganjirō appeared in *The Love Suicides at Sonezaki* for the thousandth time. In one of those frightening coincidences that seem to color the lives of great kabuki actors, the thousandth *Sonezaki* proved to be quite literally an earth-shattering event: just a few hours after the show, Kobe and Osaka were rocked by the most destructive earthquake to strike the Kansai region in several centuries.

Senjaku's *Love Suicides* was Takechi kabuki as it was meant to be performed, and a new star was born in Japan. His uninhibited, self-directed women characters appealed to younger women fans who were enjoying new rights and freedoms granted them by the postwar constitution and by changing social mores. In the early to mid-1950s, many new plays were written expressly for Senjaku, featuring vital, even dangerous women. But Senjaku's successes notwithstanding, kabuki producers feared that amid the climate of cultural modernization, the idea of using onnagata, as opposed to actresses, might come to seem anachronistic to the public at large, and they seized on Senjaku as the one actor who could prove decisively that onnagata could be as beautiful and feminine as the most alluring of actresses. Senjaku did not let them down: he even played in movies alongside actresses and was utterly convincing as a woman.[14]

Despite forays into modern theater and film, Senjaku remained first and foremost a kabuki actor, and by the late 1950s he had become a consummate kaneru yakusha and was taking on a remarkable variety of roles. He was slowly changing his primary focus from female to male characters, learning from the great tachiyaku actors of the Kansai (Kataoka Nizaemon XIII and Jitsukawa Enjaku) as well as from Hasegawa Kazuo, the greatest star of the region's lowbrow *taishū engeki*.[15] Senjaku believed that Hasegawa best embodied the wagoto style of his late grandfather.[16]

By 1975 Senjaku had developed his own individual approach to wagoto roles, a synthesis of Takechi kabuki and various elements absorbed from the actors mentioned above. In 1982, a year after his father's death, he founded the Chikamatsu Theater, with the ambitious plan of performing one original Chikamatsu play each year for the foreseeable future. The mid-1970s and early 1980s were lean years for Kansai kabuki, since many of the region's great actors died or moved to Tokyo at that time, and Shōchiku considerably reduced the number of kabuki shows held in both Kyoto and Osaka. Senjaku's Chikamatsu Theater was meant to revive enthusiasm for kabuki in the Kansai through the rediscovery of a local cultural treasure—the art of wagoto kabuki. Senjaku knew that his focus on Chikamatsu plays would enhance his own fame and popularity as an actor. His own career had "taken off" with his performance in Chikamatsu's *The Love Suicides. at Sonezaki*. Chikamatsu had had a reputation during the Genroku period for writing works that showed performers at their best, and Senjaku reasoned that this quality would not have changed with the passage of time.

In the course of his research on Chikamatsu, Senjaku "discovered" Tōjūrō, and found that he had a strong affinity for the man and his art. One of Senjaku's most exciting Chikamatsu Theater plays was his full-length revival of *The Courtesan on the Buddha Plain* in 1986. This had been a blockbuster for Tōjūrō in 1699, but had gone unperformed since then. It was the most ambitious project Senjaku had ever undertaken, and he enlisted the aid of some of

Japan's best artists in order to make it work: Kinoshita Junji turned the illustrated playbook into a usable script, and Takechi Tetsuji agreed to direct. *The Courtesan on the Buddha Plain* was a critical success and a wonderful showcase for Senjaku's talents as a wagoto actor (Figure 33), but it has not been performed by other actors since, probably because it is so difficult. According to Ganjirō, the role of Bunzō in this play presents a unique challenge because *The Buddha Plain* is a dialog play that dates from before the introduction of jōruri music and narration to kabuki. While there is some background music, it is up to the lead actor to control the timing of every scene he is in, and to convey both story and emotions without the

Fig. 33   Nakamura Ganjirō III as Bunzō in *The Courtesan on the Buddha Plain*, 1986. Photo courtesy of Nakamura Ganjirō III.

aid of a running narrative explanation. To facilitate this, Ganjirō has turned to the art of *katari* (storytelling) as performed by kyōgen actors.[17] In this he follows the lead of both Takechi and Tōjūrō, who enriched kabuki by incorporating techniques and values from other performing arts.

In 1992 Senjaku became Ganjirō III, taking the name his father and grandfather had used, and he is now one of the top stars of contemporary kabuki. Today he takes onnagata roles about half of the time, but he seems most excited with his endeavor to revive the spirit of kamigata wagoto kabuki. Ganjirō sees a crucial difference in the Edo aragoto and kamigata wagoto traditions: the former is based on *kata*, or fixed patterns of physical movement and voice that were preserved as accurately as possible over many generations, while the latter has relied on a less concrete transmission of spirit, in which every actor is forced to devise his own personal style of movement and delivery.[18] Takechi Tetsuji's unorthodox teachings had a strong impact on Ganjirō's style, but Ganjirō regards his own style as more traditional, not more modern, than those of other kabuki actors.[19] For example, Ganjirō still uses elements of the onnagata walk which he devised for Takechi kabuki, and he argues convincingly that the standard pigeon-toed gait was a relatively late development in kabuki, and that onnagata would not have walked that way on the Genroku stage, but in a manner closer to that of nō actors playing women's roles.[20]

Ganjirō's projection of youth onstage is remarkable, and reminiscent of descriptions of Tōjūrō at the height of his powers. Ganjirō says that the secret to this is not to attempt to create an image of youthfulness by any superficial means, but to let youthfulness flow from the heart. He strives to feel the vulnerability and the lack of control characteristic of a young man, and, in Chikamatsu's love suicide plays, to feel the tragedy of a young couple who unintentionally but inevitably proceed to destroy their own lives and the lives of the people around them.[21]

Ganjirō's Chikamatsu Theater led the way in the revival of

kabuki in the Kansai. From the mid-1980s through the mid-1990s, more and more kabuki plays were performed in Osaka and Kyoto. The Shōchiku corporation, which was founded in the late nineteenth century by two brothers from Kyoto, became convinced that the situation merited a major new investment in the region, and in March 1997 it opened a gorgeous new theater, the Shōchiku-za, in Osaka. Ganjirō headed the bill in the opening two months, and thanks to the Shōchiku-za, in 1997, for the first time in many decades Ganjirō worked more than half the year in Kansai. This was very gratifying to him,[22] and proof of the success of one of the goals of the Chikamatsu Theater.

Danjūrō partnered Ganjirō in *The Love Suicides at Sonezaki* in Chikamatsu Theater's 1997 production and in 1998 Ganjirō will appear in his most ambitious revival project ever; he will play Takatō Min'ya in *The Courtesan and the Great Buddhist Service at Mibu Temple,* the work that raised Tōjūrō to the status of a god in the world of kamigata kabuki. *Mibu Temple* has not been performed for three hundred years, but Ganjirō has dedicated himself to embodying the energy and spirit of Genroku kabuki, and if any living actor can pull off the role of Tōjūrō's saké lees seller, it is he. In fact, Ganjirō is so dedicated to the spirit of Tōjūrō that it is his dream to take the name Sakata Tōjūrō sometime in the next few years.[23] It still remains to be seen whether the management of Shōchiku will support such a move, but a triumph in *Mibu Temple* would certainly bring the dream closer. The kabuki world waits with great expectation for this event, but Ganjirō's supporters are praying that *Mibu Temple* will be less cataclysmic than was his thousandth *Love Suicides,* and that, unlike Tōjūrō, Ganjirō will enjoy a healthy, productive career for many years after the play. Ganjirō is now training his two talented sons, Ganjaku and Senjaku, to follow in his footsteps as leaders of kabuki in the Kansai.

Ichikawa Ennosuke—Bringing High-Tech, High-Energy Kabuki to the Masses

The biggest superstar on the kabuki stage today is Ichikawa Enno-suke III (b. 1939). His breathtaking aerial routines have made him well-known even among Japanese who do not attend kabuki perfor-mances, and his fabulously popular, high-tech "Super Kabuki" shows have packed halls for months at a time and have attracted new audi-ences to kabuki theaters. Ennosuke's innovations are a large part of the reason that in the 1990s kabuki has a wider appeal than it has at any time over the last one hundred years. While Danjūrō and Ganjirō strive to recapture the spirit of Genroku-period kabuki through play revivals and refinement of acting styles, Ennosuke alone among today's actors works in the manner of the great zamoto (actor-producers) of the Genroku period.[24] He has his own produc-tion company (Omodaka, Inc.) with a large number of actors—from minor actors trained in acrobatics, to promising young onnagata and tachiyaku whom he has scouted and recruited himself, to his right-hand man, his younger brother Danshirō IV (b. 1946), a premiere actor of villain roles. The company owns numerous properties and costumes, and hires its own technical staff for productions, includ-ing costumers, property men, stage designers, wig specialists, and computer experts. As head of this company, Ennosuke chooses and directs plays, takes the leading role in most productions, and com-missions play texts from leading authors, later rewriting them exten-sively to suit the needs of his theater. The Shōchiku corporation is a financial backer and coproducer for Ennosuke's original produc-tions, and Ennosuke is a partner in these projects, not merely a Shōchiku employee. Ennosuke's *modus vivendi* in kabuki is not the only thing he shares with the great actors of the Edo period. Like Danjūrō, Tōjūrō, and Ayame before him, he has built his career on introducing innovations that have mass appeal.

For the past decade, Ennosuke's new kabuki projects have been so successful and unfailingly profitable that Shōchiku gives him virtually guaranteed financial backing and a free hand to do more or less as he likes. But his relationships with authority figures in the world of kabuki were not always as harmonious as they are today. In fact, Ennosuke comes from a long line of feisty, upstart kabuki actors who have made a family tradition of challenging authority. His great-grandfather, Ennosuke I (1855–1922), was the son of a minor actor and choreographer. After some years as a talented disciple of Danjūrō IX, Ennosuke I "betrayed" his master by breaking most of the traditional rules of conduct that were intended to keep actors who lacked the proper lineage in positions of inferiority. Ennosuke I's transgressions included performing Benkei in *Kanjinchō* without permission at a minor theater in Tokyo, and he went on to build his reputation over the next two decades in Tokyo and the Kansai. In Kansai kabuki he became known for performing in the *keren* or "stunt" style, which featured "quick changes, tree-climbing, roof stunts, and tumbling, and which finished with tachimawari battle scenes of immense proportions."[25] Ennosuke I later returned to Tokyo and was reconciled with Danjūrō IX, but rather than rejoining his former master, he established a new and very distinctive acting family.[26]

Ennosuke II (1888–1963), grandfather of the current Ennosuke, was one of the great experimental kabuki actors of the prewar period, but whereas most kabuki innovators were aligned with the *shin-kabuki* ("new kabuki") movement which sought to create a modern dramaturgy that would downplay music and dance and focus on acting influenced by Western notions of psychological realism, Ennosuke II continued in his father's tradition of offering exciting, artistic performances full of music and dance. Ennosuke II's signature work is the dance drama *The Black Tomb (Kurozuka),* which premiered in 1939. This dance is based on an oft-dramatized folktale, but Ennosuke II incorporated into it avant-garde lighting effects and elements from contemporary dance, and he was the first actor in centuries to portray the old ogress of the play in a sympathetic light.

At the age of fifteen, the current Ennosuke moved to the home of his grandfather, who doted on the boy and gave him long hours of intense instruction. Ennosuke matriculated at Keio University where, in student theater clubs, he participated in a wide range of modern and avant-garde productions. Ennosuke notes that his college years were critical because they exposed him to Western drama theory and experiment, enabling him to look at kabuki from outside the tradition.[27] He recognized the physical power and technical brilliance of kabuki, but saw that modern audiences were put off by the tediousness of many plays and by the feudal moral system that guided the actions and beliefs of characters in the plays.

Ennosuke was a young actor in a hurry, and he prevailed upon his grandfather, then called En'ō, to support his accession to the Ennosuke name. The twenty-three-year-old upstart was audacious enough to attempt the role of the aged crone in The Black Tomb for the play that celebrated his shūmei, and despite performing daily under the skeptical, disapproving gaze of the elders of the kabuki world, he did splendidly. That same year, both his father (Danshirō III [1908–1963]) and his grandfather died. Leading figures in the kabuki world urged the young man to take another leading actor as a master and to build his career slowly and carefully, but Ennosuke told them that he would manage his career in his own way. His twenties were a time of struggle and conflict. For some years after his shūmei, he was not given roles commensurate with his abilities in the main kabuki forums, and had to scramble to produce his own, smaller-scale shows in unorthodox venues. He fought with Danjūrō XI over his right to perform material that Danjūrō IX had taught Ennosuke's ancestor, and in this dispute Ennosuke refused to bow to the authority of the distinguished Ichikawa line.[28] At twenty-five, Ennosuke married a famous actress, but this union ended in acrimonious divorce three years later. The divorce dominated the sensationalist press, and Ennosuke was invariably portrayed as the guilty party.[29]

But Ennosuke overcame all these obstacles, and he did it by performing exciting and original kabuki. He was aided by the completion of construction of the National Theater in 1966. In its early

years, the National Theater became a forum for younger actors'
experiments with full-length kabuki plays and revivals of long-
neglected masterpieces. By the 1970s, audiences were flocking to
"Ennosuke kabuki" at a variety of venues, including Shōchiku's
Kabuki-za, to enjoy a refreshing new approach to classical drama.

From the 1960s through the mid-1980s, Ennosuke focused his
creative energies on two kinds of activities: restaging and reinterpreting classical plays, and doing full-length revivals of lost plays. Of the
former category, his definitive work is surely *Yoshitsune and the
The Thousand Cherry Trees (Yoshitsune Senbon Zakura)*. In this
play, he became famous nationwide for his "flying fox" scene, and in
1968 he was the first postwar actor to use cables to "fly" from the
stage to the top of the balcony at the rear of the house. This was a
revival of an Edo-period custom that had fallen into disuse. *The
Thousand Cherry Trees* was so successful that Ennosuke performed
it again and again, refining and modifying the work with each new
production, culminating with a full-length, five-act version in 1981.
The flight scene was just one of many improvements he made in the
play's production. His first priority was to increase the play's tempo.
He did this by cutting redundant narration throughout, and by
speeding up the pace of actors' delivery.[30] He also cut the time lost in
scene transitions. He recognized that two or three minutes of boring
"deadly theater" (to borrow Peter Brook's expression) seem longer to
an audience than does half an hour of exciting, high-quality drama,
and that elimination of any tedious sections, no matter how brief,
could greatly affect the audience's sense of the tempo.[31] Ennosuke
juxtaposed action-packed, spectacular scenes with slower ones that
revealed character and emotion, creating the variety and pacing
essential to successful drama.

Ennosuke's flying scenes (*chū nori*) have remained a personal
trademark. These scenes are neither dangerous nor acrobatic, nor
does Ennosuke attempt to convey a realistic illusion of flight, but his
chū nori have been fabulously popular because Ennosuke fully under-
stands the psychological requisites of the flying hero. The develop-

ment of the story has to necessitate a magical defiance of gravity—the audience must be thinking, "Oh, if only the hero could take flight" before the magic occurs.[32] As long as this happens, it does not matter if the actor's cable is visible to all; the audience's emotions will soar with the hero to triumph or liberation. Other actors have done more modest chū nori since Ennosuke restored flying to the kabuki stage, but none have flown from stage to balcony, and none have used chū nori as often or as successfully as Ennosuke. In 1993 he recorded his three-thousandth flight to the balcony, and he has used flying scenes in all but one of his Super Kabuki plays.

Revival of lost plays proved to be a critical training ground for the Super Kabuki blockbusters of the mid-1980s through the 1990s. Between 1966 and 1984, Ennosuke produced fifteen revivals of lost plays, twelve of them full-length, multi-act plays. Most of the revivals required a tremendous amount of original work, enabling Ennosuke to hone his skills as producer, scenographer, director, and actor. He assembled a team of scholars and playwrights to search out lost plays that had potential to succeed on the modern stage, and to collaborate with him on refashioning them into new scripts. Each revival presented unique challenges, but one problem common to all was performance time: each play had taken ten to twelve hours during the Edo period, and so needed to be cut at least in half. Ennosuke's first task was always to create a detailed original storyboard. He cut subplots and tangential business, and strengthened the main plots. He restructured and reordered acts and scenes, decided on casting, and determined where to incorporate action like quick costume changes or flying scenes.[33] In some plays he experimented with the use of film. After all these decisions were made, playwrights wrote the scripts. Ennosuke always reserved the leading roles for himself. In one of his most successful revivals, *The Ten Role Date Play* (*Date no Jūyaku*; 1979), Ennosuke reconstructed a play whose text had been lost by fusing together stock scenes from several surviving Date plays, and by having his playwrights recreate material that was described in accounts of the original work. He emulated Danjūrō VII who, in 1815,[34] had thrilled Edo audiences by playing ten different roles in the play, many requiring athletic or even acrobatic quick changes of costume.

While most of Ennosuke's revivals proved very popular with audiences, shin-kabuki advocates and many kabuki traditionalists argued that they were weak in plot and characterization, and overly reliant on "technique"—by which Ennosuke's critics meant virtuoso acting and dancing as well as spectacular stage effects. Ennosuke recognized that the fabulous technique of actors of the nineteenth century did in fact dominate plays of that era.[35] He came to realize that the only way to marry technique and strong literary texts was to create his own original kabuki. He would not go in the direction of shin-kabuki, however, because he believed that this form eliminated from kabuki the "ka" and the "bu"—"ka" being the music and "bu" being the dance—that give it much of its expressive power.

From the very beginning of his career, Ennosuke has sought to bring large audiences to the theaters. To recreate the mass appeal that kabuki had lost late in the nineteenth century, he would have to create an updated form that would attract Japanese who had never seen kabuki before, a style that would be understandable and entertaining for people who came to the theater totally unprepared. Ennosuke's unique approach to kabuki's traditional "deformation" of historical antecedents was central to his strategy for creating this kind of theater. During the Edo period, playwrights and actors often recast characters and even moral systems from Japan's remote past to suit the norms of the time, and they used gorgeous costumes that were "deformed" just enough to seem exotic and historical while still reflecting up-to-the-minute fashionability. But by the 1980s, these Edo-period deformations were themselves archaic and unintelligible to most Japanese. Rather than continue to present them religiously to a small population of cognoscenti, Ennosuke resolved to remain true to the spirit of kabuki by creating original, modernized deformations of the past for his kabuki.[36] This meant writing scripts whose language and plots could be immediately understood by contemporary audiences, populating the stage with characters whose feelings and actions would make sense, and creating costumes that would suggest the past but would be gorgeous in the eyes of anyone attuned to the latest trends in fashion. To his contemporary deformations of historical moral values and staging conventions, Ennosuke added what he calls the three S's: "story, speed, and spectacle." The entire concept was theoretically brilliant but, as Ennosuke has noted, it was one thing to talk about original kabuki performance, and quite another to bring it off onstage. His first Super Kabuki would take years of preparation and tremendous dedication from the entire production team.

In 1986 Ennosuke's first Super Kabuki, *Yamato Takeru*, the story of Japan's earliest warrior hero, opened to huge popular acclaim in Tokyo. *Yamato Takeru* played for six months in three cities, making it the longest-running of any twentieth-century kabuki work. Renowned anthropologist Umehara Takeshi wrote the original text of this play, basing it on the *Kojiki*, Japan's oldest surviving work of history and legend, and Ennosuke adapted this text to the stage. The *Kojiki's* Yamato Takeru is a contradictory, dangerous man whose psychology remains a mystery, but the Umehara/ Ennosuke hero's romantic passions and military strategems make sense to the audience, and his tragedy elicits its sympathy. The opulent costumes by Mōri Tomio, a top designer for world-famous Issey Miyake, realized Ennosuke's goal of making Super Kabuki productions into nonstop fashion shows. Along with the fantastic costumes, Ennosuke used a lavish set, and lighting that was more dynamic and more emotionally effective than anything ever seen before on the kabuki stage. In one especially daring innovation, a huge, raging wildfire was enacted by performers doing vigorous modern dance while wielding flame-colored flags. *Yamato Takeru* is replete with scenes of combat and self-sacrifice, and after Takeru's tragic death at the hands of the wild boar–god of Mount Ibuki, following in the tradition of the *Kojiki,* he is reincarnated as a great white bird who flies off to parts unknown (Figure 34).

Fig. 34 Ichikawa Ennosuke III as Yamato Takeru incarnated as a great white bird in the Super Kabuki *Yamato Takeru*. Photo courtesy of Ichikawa Ennosuke III.

In *Yamato Takeru,* Ennosuke had sought to create "kabuki that transcends kabuki," and the cries of conservatives critics that "*Yamato Takeru* is not kabuki" were enough to prove to him that he had been successful.[37] In 1988 Ennosuke proclaimed his own "Ennosuke's Eighteen Great Plays" ("Ennosuke Jūhachiban"), including in this category major revivals and reworked classics. He still performs in these plays and in standard, Shochiku-produced kabuki shows, but his original work is now mainly in Super Kabuki. Ennosuke has revived and improved *Yamato Takeru* several times since 1986, always to full and enthusiastic houses, and between 1989 and 1993 he did three additional Super Kabuki plays: *The Dragon King* (*Ryūō*; 1989), a fusion of Peking opera and kabuki; *Oguri* (1991), which featured medieval romantic hero Oguri Hangan and which Ennosuke regards as one of his own best works in terms of character and spectacle;[38] and *The Tale of Eight Dogs (Hakkenden)*, based on a fantastic nineteenth-century tale of romance, adventure, and inter-species love. In these plays Ennosuke retained the dramaturgical formulae that had made *Yamato Takeru* so successful, but also made various innovations. In *Eight Dogs* he used live music emanating from an orchestra "pit" located in one of the auditorium's balconies, and in *Oguri* and *Eight Dogs* he contrasted sumptuous costumes with sparse, symbolic sets that relied on dramatic lighting effects to create mood and heighten emotion.

The 1996 and 1997 seasons saw Ennosuke turn out major new creative works at an almost frenetic pace. In the spring of 1996, he directed and starred in his fifth Super Kabuki play, *Kaguya*. Based on Japan's best-known fairy tale about a dazzlingly beautiful moon girl who sojourns on earth, and the misadventures of the suitors who seek to win her hand in marriage, it was the first of Ennosuke's Super Kabuki plays to center on a love story rather than on martial conflict. With many scenes set on the moon or in the heavens, it had the simplest stage sets of any Super Kabuki play to date. Ennosuke and his playwright, Yokouchi Kensuke, converted the maiden's tragic departure from earth in the original tale into a joyful reuniting of the maiden with her true love, the emperor, and a triumphal final exit with him on the back of a flying horse.

In the spring of 1997, Ennosuke quickened the pace of his production schedule, for the first time premiering a new Super Kabuki play just one year after the opening of the last. *Ōkuninushi* is set even further in the depths of Japan's mythic past than *Yamato Takeru*, and its hero, the god Ōkuninushi, is an indigenous Shintō deity of great bravery and kindness who unites the land under benevolent rule, but witnesses the destruction of his family and his own authority at the hands of the gods of Heaven who, at the play's end, force him into exile on the coast of the Japan Sea. For the text Ennosuke turned once again to Umehara Takeshi, author of *Yamato Takeru*, and Umehara produced what to Ennosuke is the least emotional in style, but the most moving, and the most "Shakespearean" Super Kabuki text yet produced.[39] Umehara too felt very proud of the literary quality of this play and had it published in book form by a commercial press.[40] In notable contrast with *Kaguya*, for which a long original tale exists, the author of *Ōkuninushi* took sparse genealogical and poetic source material and converted it into high tragedy. The tragedy seems calculated to move Japanese who remember World War II, thanks to Ōkuninushi's loss of all his children, his voluntary abdication in order to prevent further bloodshed, and his attempt to pass on his wisdom and his heritage to a lone grandson. This last scene especially strikes a sympathetic chord with Ennosuke, who owes so much to his own grandfather.

Each of Ennosuke's Super Kabuki plays have required tremendous investments of time, energy and money, but since the success of *Yamato Takeru* in 1986, Ennosuke has enjoyed the financial support of Shōchiku, Japan's most powerful entertainment corporation. And Shōchiku is relying as much on Ennosuke as on Ganjirō to make the new Shōchiku-za's first season a success. Ennosuke is on the marquee for three months in 1997, two in *Kaguya* and one as the director of the modern play *The Dowager Empress (Seitagō)* about the famous "Dragon Lady" of the last dynasty in Imperial China, a play which has already had two successful runs in Tokyo.

Between his two most recent Super Kabuki plays, Ennosuke did his first revival of a full-length traditional play in over a decade. In October 1996, to celebrate the thirtieth anniversary of the founding of the National Theater, Ennosuke returned to that theater for the first time in nineteen years to direct and star in *The Four Guardian Kings' Maple-Patterned Edo-Style Makeup (Shitennō Momiji no Edo Guma)* by Tsuruya Namboku. Ennosuke has hired many graduates of the National Theater Training School into his company, including Ichikawa Emiya, his leading onnagata, so this production was also a celebration of the school and the talents of its progeny. Ennosuke had long wanted to do a revival of an Edo kaomise play,[41] and *The Four Guardian Kings* was a masterpiece of the genre, replete with special effects and stunts. He used what he had learned in producing and directing Super Kabuki to create a truly memorable kabuki performance, characterized by "speed, spectacle, and story." Breaking with kabuki production practice, which limits rehearsal to about a week at the end of every month, Ennosuke took a full month to rehearse *The Four Guardian Kings*, and the play was marked, from opening night, by high production values that were an eye-opener for kabuki fans.[42]

At the age of fifty-six, Ennosuke has accomplished more in kabuki than most actors could in several lifetimes, but then again he is a man of seemingly boundless creativity who is passionately devoted to his work in the theater. He and his team are planning at least two more Super Kabuki plays, one based on the Chinese epic *The Romance of the Three Kingdoms*, and another on the life of Japan's greatest classical poet, Kakinomoto Hitomaro.[43] Ennosuke is also contemplating even more radical experiments. He has indicated that he might like to try using Western music for the same purpose that Japanese music is now used in kabuki, to provide rhythm and timing (*ma*) for the action of the play. Western and Japanese forms of dress could be deformed and fused in a future Super Kabuki if the story of a play warranted it. No matter what innovations Ennosuke tries, he remains firm in his commitment to entertaining a mass audience.[44] He believes that kabuki, and his kabuki in particular, can be enjoyed not only by ordinary Japanese, but by people around the world, and he considers touring and teaching abroad to be important elements of his work. Europeans rightly regard Ennosuke as one of the great performance innovators of the contemporary world, on a par with Peter Brook and Maurice Béjart.

Ennosuke sees his Eighteen Great Plays and his Super Kabuki as a long-term contribution to kabuki. He is not worried about the cen-

sure of traditionalists. Early shin-kabuki plays received the same criticism, but the best of these works were performed repeatedly and
have now become part of the kabuki repertory. Ennosuke is confident
that the same will happen to his best plays.[45] Ennosuke's son did not
become a kabuki actor, so Ennosuke is counting on his most talented disciples to carry his plays and his style into the next generation. Ennosuke is pinning most of his hopes on young disciples
Ichikawa Ukon, Ichikawa Monnosuke, and his nephew Kamejirō.
Ennosuke has used Ukon as his assistant director and has given him
opportunity to play several leading roles, including that of Yamato
Takeru one day a week during that play's 1995 run. The young members of Ennosuke's troupe regularly perform together at the Asakusa
Kōkaidō theater in traditional and experimental kabuki plays.
Nevertheless, it remains to be seen to what degree Ennosuke's
revivals and Super Kabuki are dependent upon his own immense
skills as an actor and a dancer, and on his unique stage presence.
Ennosuke says that two generations from now, plays of his that have
been able to stand the test of time will become the property of all
kabuki,[46] but for the rest of this century and well into the next, theater fans in Japan and around the world can rely on Ennosuke to
continue to provide the most dazzling dramatic spectacles on the
planet.

Bandō Tamasaburō: A Thoroughly Contemporary Onnagata Superstar

Ennosuke's spectacular approach to kabuki draws huge crowds to
his revivals and to Super Kabuki shows, but there is one kabuki actor
who has even greater box office appeal: the strikingly beautiful forty-
seven-year-old onnagata superstar, Bandō Tamasaburō (Figure 35).
Critics and fans recognize that he is an onnagata unlike any other in
kabuki today. Kabuki is just one of many fields of endeavor for Tamasaburō. He plays Shakespeare's great women's roles, dances with
Western ballet companies, takes leading roles in experimental drama
directed by foreign masters, and directs and acts in films. His appear-

Fig. 35 Bandō Tamasaburō as Kiyohime in the kabuki dance drama *Musume Dōjōji*. Photo courtesy of Bandō Tamasaburō V.

ances in films and in a plethora of visual images such as posters and collectors' edition books of photography have brought Tamasaburō a degree of fame among the general public that no other modern onnagata, not even Ganjirō in his youth, has ever enjoyed. Although many of Tamasaburō's fans attend kabuki only when he is to perform, Tamasaburō, like Ennosuke, has brought many new, young patrons to kabuki. Tamasaburō has also brought kabuki fans to his Shakespeare plays and other experimental Western dramas; they are drawn by his appeal as an actor and as a man who dares to test dangerous artistic waters, and by the intriguing creative potential of fusing theatrical traditions that usually remain discrete.

Tamasaburō was born after World War II and he is a member of the forward-looking, postwar generation of artists. The legacy of

Edo-period onnagata means little to him. Tamasaburō is inspired by living memory and visual imagery, not by history books and hoary tradition. The onnagata he himself saw onstage as a child, his teachers, and the actors whom his parents and teachers described to him in detail are the "old masters" who have influenced him. Play texts also move Tamasaburō and catalyze his creative thinking. The Edo-period onnagata whom he most admires is Iwai Hanshirō V, who took the leading roles in Tsuruya Namboku's works, playing beautiful and dangerous women with contradictory personalities.[47]

Despite Tamasaburō's lack of interest in kabuki's first great onnagata, he has much in common with Ayame. Although no onnagata today wear women's clothes in public, Tamasaburō believes, as Ayame did, that carefully controlled deportment offstage is important to his success as an actor. He feels that he must play the the role of "Tamasaburō the actor" whenever he is in public, as part of his physical and spiritual training. Tamasaburō told me he relaxes only in the privacy of his own apartment, but was quick to add that this situation is not burdensome to him: "Self-control is quintessentially human behavior, and if one cannot exercise it in public one will not be a great actor."[48]

Like Ayame, Tamasaburō's greatest appeal onstage is the "flower of verisimilitude." No other actor convinces audiences that he really is a woman in quite the way that Tamasaburō does. At 5'10" Tamasaburō is tall and slender, as Ayame was reputed to be. Like Ayame in the Genroku period, Tamasaburō is wonderful to watch, even from as close as the front row of the auditorium. In the words of kabuki critic Mizuochi Kiyoshi, "All other onnagata are men playing women, so there is something grotesque about the result. Even beautifully made-up, there is something unsightly about them that is pitiful or cruel. But Tamasaburō never lets you feel his physical reality as a man."[49] Mizuochi is convinced that this is an innate, unique attribute of Tamasaburō's, and writes that even offstage, in his street clothes, Tamasaburō "exudes an ethereal, otherwordly beauty" and "has no physical, corporeal feel to him."[50] I believe that when Tamasaburō conveys this impression offstage it is not a result of innate physical qualities but testimony to the brilliance of his enactment of his chosen public persona.

Tamasaburō attracts hordes of women fans to his performances, just as Ayame did three centuries ago. The nature of his appeal to women is complex, and critics, women fans, and Tamasaburō himself all explain it in different ways. Certainly Tamasaburō takes on the personae of women characters so convincingly that women spectators find that they are easily able to empathize with them; his acting requires little suspension of disbelief.[51] But this does not explain why his appeal surpasses that of the actresses who play alongside him in conventional dramas and film. Surely the basis of this appeal is the fascination and uncanniness of a seemingly real gender transformation. He exudes an aura of mystery and unapproachability. Women fans may well feel that with training and effort they could do what actresses do onstage, but Tamasaburō is clearly in a world apart.[52] The feminine beauty that Tamasaburō projects—marked by purity, cleanness and stylishness—appeals to contemporary young women,[53] as does the romantic, headstrong nature of so many of the women he plays. It is my own opinion that women feel an affinity for Tamasaburō because they feel gratified and flattered that a man has taken such pains to understand and take into his own soul the feelings of women. Women are also intrigued—but not threatened—by the idea of "learning" what it means to be a beautiful woman from a man.

Tamasaburō was born an outsider to the world of kabuki, the seventh child of a restaurateur. He began taking *buyo* dance lessons as a little child, ostensibly to strengthen his weak legs. He excelled at dance. At age four or five, he saw master onnagata Nakamura Utaemon VI (born 1917) perform, and from then on dreamed of becoming an onnagata himself. Mizuochi writes that all other onnagata think of their art as uniquely challenging, and as young men had to overcome embarrassment about playing women's roles, but Tamasaburō reputedly never had these feelings. For as long as he can remember, he yearned to be an onnagata.[54]

Tamasaburō's talent was recognized early, and he was given children's roles in kabuki plays. In 1964 Morita Kan'ya XV adopted the promising teenager as his son. As the successor to the Morita line of former Edo theater proprietors, Kan'ya was an actor of respected lineage, and this adoption opened up the world of kabuki to his new son. Shortly afterward, the young man became the fifth Bandō Tamasaburō, taking a minor acting name that dated back to the mid-1800s. With his adoption Tamasaburō had acquired the requisite family stature necessary to attempt to build a career as a kabuki actor. It would take talent, hard work, and the ability to impress audiences and senior actors if he were to rise to the top of his profession.

One of the first to notice Tamasaburō was the brilliant, mercurial writer Mishima Yukio (1924–1970). Mishima's patronage set a pattern that would continue throughout Tamasaburō's career. Again and again, great artists from outside the world of kabuki have been captivated by Tamasaburō's artistry and beauty, and have worked with him in creative endeavors that have enriched his career as a performer. In the 1960s Mishima was a regular fan and supporter of Utaemon; he wrote plays and dance dramas intended to showcase the great onnagata's skill and the beauty, and even wrote a short story about him.[55] Mishima was similarly impressed by the lithesome beauty and grace of the young Tamasaburō: "With a body like the fine edge of a dragonfly's wing, undulating gracefully on the stage, he overflows with a lyrical beauty accompanied by a sense of danger."[56]

After Mishima watched Tamasaburō perform superbly in the role of a young woman who was brutally murdered, Mishima wrote a long drama for Tamasaburō, featuring a princess who takes delight in the exquisitely beautiful torture of the man whom she believes has murdered her husband.[57] Tamasaburō would continue, throughout his career, to excel as women who either suffer painfully at the hands of men, or destroy men. Among his finest kabuki roles is Sakurahime, one of the most challenging woman's parts in the repertory. Sakurahime begins as a naive and vulnerable princess, but is forced by circumstance to undergo transformations into, first, a tough, worldly prostitute, and then a cold-blooded samurai wife. She is chaste and depraved, evil and virtuous, and filled with carnal desire and maternal love. As played by Tamasaburō, she retains her essential beauty and purity no matter what her changes of fortune, and this romantic approach to a sordid story is one reason for Tamasaburo's popularity in this and similar roles.[58]

As a young onnagata in the 1960s and 1970s Tamasaburō was able to work with the leading male role actors of the day, men twenty to forty years his senior. Tamasaburō credits actors like Onoe Shōroku II with turning him into a mature actor, but Shōroku and other senior tachiyaku urged Tamasaburō to develop his own style.[59] Thanks to the support of older actors, and to popular young actors' shows like the Ebi-Tama Combination that paired Tamasaburō with Ebizō (now Danjūrō), Tamasaburō was able to play many of the great onnagata roles and do most of the important dance dramas at a relatively early age.

Tamasaburō's first regular work off the kabuki stage was in shimpa, a heterogeneous form of theater halfway between kabuki and Western-style "realistic" drama. Shimpa used onnagata for all its women's roles during the 1890s, but since World War II actresses have played most women's parts. From the outset, Tamasaburō was at home onstage among actresses. He was strongly attracted to the plays of Izumi Kyōka (1873–1939), shimpa's most prolific playwright. Kyōka's tragic, romantic heroines and ghost- and spirit-women are difficult to play because their personalities and experiences are so far removed from ordinary life, but they seem substantial and sympathetic when played by Tamasaburō. Tamasaburō's love for Kyōka would later lead him into film as an actor and director. His dual role, as a beautiful provincial wife and goddess of the pond in the 1979 movie *Demon Pond (Yasha ga Ike)* attracted accolades in Japan and abroad (Figure 36).

As a child and as a young man Tamasaburō received strict, traditional training in buyo dance and the other arts of kabuki, but his

Fig. 36 Bandō Tamasaburō
as the wife in *Demon Pond*
(Yasha ga Ike). Directed by
Shinoda Masahiro, adapted
from a play by Izumi Kyōka.
Photo courtesy of Bandō
Tamasaburō V.

love of many forms of music and his unbridled imagination have led
him down artistic paths that no onnagata has ever traveled before.
His career and his artistic style are fascinating fusions of tradition
and innovation. One reason for Tamasaburō's accessibility to general audiences in Japan is his ability to see kabuki with the eyes of a
foreign artist like Béjart who regards kabuki as neither archaic nor
feudal, but as a fascinatingly modern art form that integrates music,
text, and dance. For most Japanese dancers, buyo and ballet are
worlds apart, but for Tamasaburō, as for Béjart, "dance is dance." To
dance means simply to be moved by and move to any kind of
music.[60] Tamasaburō is confident of his artistry as a dancer in any
form and in nearly any woman's costume: Japanese, Western, or
Chinese. He has danced in Peking opera, and has danced solo in live
collaborations with cellist Yo Yo Ma; he was also the last person to
partner Béjart's leading male ballet dancer, Jorge Donn. Tamasaburō
hopes someday to experiment in Balinese dance.[61]

     In the postwar period many kabuki actors have appeared in film,
on television, and in musicals and straight drama, but they have almost always been specialists in the male roles. For traditional onnagata, dancing in a balletic style or wearing dresses to enact foreign
women in classical or modern plays would be all but inconceivable. Onnagata rely on traditional Japanese costumes and a vocabulary of con-

ventionalized feminine movements and vocal styles in order to "become" traditional women on the kabuki stage. After spending years to acquire these tools, the thought of casting them aside and going onstage to portray a woman without them would surely terrify most onnagata. Tamasaburō admits to being frightened each time he begins a new experimental project. He relies on frequent rehearsals in costume to help him grow into less familiar roles, and he is confident that with a good text he can grasp the emotions of women from other parts of the world, and eventually merge his soul with theirs. He says he derives great satisfaction from overcoming his initial fear and achieving a measure of success in experimental Western plays.[62] This constant willingness to push beyond his own limits certainly adds to Tamasaburō's popularity. Today's mainstream audiences and mass media share in common with their counterparts in the Genroku period a tendency to lose interest in even the greatest actors unless they continually challenge themselves. The challenges that Tamasaburō chooses for himself are apparent to everyone in Japan, and not just to kabuki connoisseurs familiar with the traditional progression that Tamasaburō has also made to more and more difficult kabuki roles.

Mizuochi has written that although Tamasaburō is blessed with talent, good looks, and good fortune, "his one source of dissatisfaction is that his fans see only his physical beauty and overlook his skill and artistry as an actor."[63] Tamasaburō shrugs off the comment about beauty, but says he knows that the public does not realize how much physical effort he puts into his work. He is sometimes criticized for "not giving his all," but for Tamasaburō making performances look relaxed and natural is a point of pride, and he often exhausts himself in the effort to make what he does onstage look easy.[64]

Western artists and directors have not been so dazzled by the glare of Tamasaburō's beauty that they are blinded to his artistry. Andre Wajda, the renowned Polish director, says of Tamasaburō:

Tamasaburō is truly remarkable. Most actors imitate actual, normal people, but Tamasaburō creates entirely new people with the remarkable appeal of something almost impossible. His level of imagination is far beyond that of actresses. I was excited when I watched him. I wanted to create a role that only Tamasaburō could play.[65]

Ten years after Wajda first saw Tamasaburō onstage, Tamasaburō played both the male and female lovers in a play created especially for him and directed by Wajda. In *Nastasha*, adapted from Dostoevsky's *The Idiot*, Tamasaburō again showed Japan what a virtuoso actor he was, crafting not only two characters, but three— Prince Myshkin, Nastasha, and the Nastasha of Myshkin's imagination.[66]

What are the secrets behind Tamasaburō's skill as an actor? His methods of preparation and expression, like his career itself, are a fusion of kabuki tradition and Western theory and practice. In rehearsal he carefully calculates the timing of gestures and dialog, but tries to merge his soul with that of a character by using his imagination and by working in costume during practice.[67] We have seen that, as early as the Genroku period, actors recognized the importance of allowing costuming to affect an actor's emotions. Tamasaburō evaluates his performance in later rehearsals using videotapes and on that basis makes final adjustments before opening day.[68] Tamasaburō is quite traditional when he describes "stage presence" as "the unity of form and feeling onstage,"[69] but whereas most kabuki actors emphasize the importance of correct form and assume that form will create feeling onstage, Tamasaburō believes that his feelings must be prepared every day before he goes onto the stage. For this reason, Tamasaburō breaks with the usual custom of kabuki actors and will not allow visitors into the dressing room before performances for interviews or other business.

Certain aspects of traditional Japanese culture excite Tamasaburō. He believes strongly in the affective powers of nature imagery

and the changing of the seasons. He loves the beauty of traditional
kimono and textile design, and has himself become a symbol of traditional feminine beauty in form and fashion. He is also an active con-
servator of provincial kabuki stages. A decade ago he discovered the
Yachiyo-za in the town of Yamaga in Kyushu, a fine Meiji-period
kabuki theater that had fallen on hard times after World War II. He
has performed seven shows there since, ranging in duration from
five to ten days. The income generated by these shows enabled the
Yachiyo-za management to restore the theater to its former condition, and brought prosperity and recognition to a charming but previously obscure provincial town. Tamasaburō has also performed at
several other provincial kabuki theaters, and is a pillar of the
National Association of Provincial Kabuki Theaters. He is a traditionalist in his preference for small, older theaters over large, modern, multipurpose performance halls. "New halls are often built to
showcase interesting architectural design," he says, "but the old theaters were built for kabuki plays and dance. The physical and psychological distance is just right for establishing a rapport with
audiences."[70] Tamasaburō is so serious about the quality of his performance venues and the stages on which he works that in 1995 he
had his own portable stage custom-made that he can use indoors or
outdoors in performances anywhere in Japan.

Gorgeous visual images of Tamasaburō and his international
stage activities dominate Japanese perceptions of his career, but
Tamasaburō is an enthusiastic and talented film director as well. Ki
Kirin, a leading actress in his hit film *The Dream Woman (Yume no
Onna)* told an interviewer that working with Tamasaburō "was easy
and enjoyable, like being a puppet in the hands of a master puppeteer."[71] She surrendered her ego to his vision and design and
enjoyed his influence on even her tiniest gestures.[72] Tamasaburō is a
total film director, even planning the costumes and sets himself, creating his own holistic vision of the worlds depicted in his films,
reflecting his own fusions of fantasy and reality. In 1995 Tamasaburō directed and starred in *The Tale of the Castle Keep (Tenshū*

Monogatari), yet another film adapted from the work of Izumi Kyōka. Tamasaburō's leading role was as a beautiful woman ghost, and the ghost's younger sister was played by one of Japan's most attractive young actresses, testimony to Tamasaburō's continuing confidence in verisimilitude as a beautiful woman.

The mid-1990s have seen Tamasaburō working at a furious pace, often performing in several different cities in the same month, dividing his time almost equally among work in kabuki drama, classical buyō dance, shimpa, and film or experimental work in drama or dance. Thanks to his mobile stage and his interest in preserving old kabuki theaters, he has performed at more Japanese cities and prefectures in recent years than any other kabuki actor.

The major new development in Tamasaburō's career has been the rapprochement with Nakamura Utaemon (who is eighty years old as of this writing). Utaemon had been Tamasaburō's idol and inspiration in his youth, but the two actors had a serious falling-out in the mid-1980s, and were unable to work together. Today Utaemon alone holds the knowledge and mastery of several major onnagata roles—no younger actor can perform them without his instruction and direction. The thaw in the icy relationship between the two enabled Tamasaburō to challenge new, heavyweight onnagata roles between 1995 and 1997. In January and March 1997, under Utaemon's direction, Tamasaburō played the two most important courtesan roles in the kabuki repertory: Akoya, who must play three instruments—koto, shamisen, and *kokyū*—in virtuosic fashion while concealing information during a police interrogation; and Yatsuhashi, a woman so beguiling that a single smile spells obsession and death for her beholder. He did a fine job in both these important debuts. Tamasaburō's kabuki appearances are increasing now as the decade comes to a close, and Shōchiku and fans of kabuki know that if he so chooses, Tamasaburō will stand unchallenged as kabuki's first diva of the new century.

Will there be a successor to the Tamasaburō legacy—a younger onnagata who shares his remarkable combination of beauty, ambition, and artistic curiosity? Today the answer seems to be no. Tamasaburō is unmarried and has no children, but he has professional disciples and is the master teacher at his own academy of modern drama and dance. Most kabuki actors, including Danjūrō, Ganjirō, and Ennosuke, devote years to training disciples, usually their sons, to inherit and carry on their artistic legacies. Tamasaburō differs from them in his lack of confidence that a close disciple can become a true artistic successor. He believes that training a successor leads merely to a smaller-scale copy of the original.[73] Tamasaburō feels that the inheritor of his artistic legacy may well be an outsider, possibly even a stranger he has yet to meet. For Tamasaburō the most important requisite is to be deeply moved by watching a great actor (for instance, on video or in film, not necessarily at live performances), and to yearn and strive to follow in his path.[74] He considers desire to be more essential than master-to-disciple training.

For many kabuki onnagata of the past, the years of their forties and fifties were a time of crisis. Tamasaburō's verisimilitude and beauty as a woman onstage are undiminished, with only the faintest murmurs arising recently to suggest that he may be on the verge of losing his remarkable status as the only onnagata who does not require an audience to suspend its disbelief.[75] The next fifteen years will present Tamasaburō with new and unprecedented challenges, but he clearly has the skill, the imagination, and the will to continue to amaze Japanese and international audiences. Although today he has no peer and no identifiable successor, he has set a precedent for onnagata of the future to enrich performance of all types with the excitement of the gender transformation that is so much a part of the magic of kabuki.

Actors, Biography, and the Future of Kabuki

Kabuki has always been an actors' theater—in the age of Okuni, in the Genroku period, and even today. Actors are at the very center of this art form, completely overshadowing playwrights, directors, and producers. The emergence of brilliant and innovative young actors rivets public attention in Japan now as it did in the Genroku period. The Shōchiku corporation, which controls or supports almost every theatrical project that involves kabuki actors, encourages charismatic and imaginative experimenters like Ennosuke and Tamasaburō because they bring prosperity to the corporation as well as to kabuki.

In Japan kabuki has two audiences. One is composed of dedicated connoisseurs and aficionados who regularly attend traditional kabuki performances. Another, which is larger and part of Japan's mass entertainment audience, attends only what are perceived as remarkable or especially exciting performances, including Ennosuke's Super Kabuki and shows of all kinds by Tamasaburō. In the last decade the former audience has grown, supporting more standard kabuki performances than at any other time in the postwar era. Great actors who have branched out into film, television, and other forms of drama are one reason for this growth. Their charisma and skill have impressed members of the mass entertainment audience, many of whom have followed these actors back to kabuki and become, over time, kabuki aficionados. Ennosuke and Tamasaburō have been leaders in this, but so too have Matsumoto Koshirō, who has won acclaim in *The Man of La Mancha, The King and I*, and other musicals, and Nakamura Kichiemon and Nakamura Kankurō, who work in film and television.

To Japanese, great kabuki actors seem larger than life. Fans are fascinated with their personalities, their life stories, and the secrets of their artistic success. Members of the connoisseur audience are voracious readers of actor biographies. In the United States it is the great film stars who have captured the imaginations of the mass entertainment audience, and more biographies are written of movie stars than any other performers; in Japan it is kabuki actor biographies that are the most numerous.

It is clear that the future of kabuki rests on the talent and charisma of its leading actors. On this, the four contemporary kabuki stars introduced above and the management of Shōchiku are in agreement. Today, as was true in the Edo period, the art cannot be sustained by even the best playwrights and producers. Given this situation, actor biography takes on a significance greater than its entertainment value because biography lends insights into the secrets of the greatness and fame that future actors must achieve if kabuki is to thrive in the twenty-first century.

The biographies of the Genroku pioneers and of today's top actors provide hints about the requisites of greatness. Most of the best actors were (or are) strong-willed individuals who overcame serious hardships in order to succeed on the kabuki stage. Many were born as outsiders to the world of kabuki. In the present day, outsider status is even more of a hardship than it was in the Genroku period. At first glance, Tamasaburō's rise to stardom seems smooth and effortless, but he had to win the respect and support of teachers and senior colleagues through his skill, dedication, and demeanor, while most of his peers received support and respect as a matter of course because of their fathers' status. That Tamasaburō had to fight to receive what came automatically to others certainly gave him the confidence to pursue an artistically innovative, and sometimes dangerous, career later in life.

The tension between the activities of insider actors and outsider actors in kabuki, and the activities of kabuki actors in other forms of performance, will strongly influence the development of the art in the next century. The Shōchiku corporation is in a delicate situation. It supports the actors' hierarchy and artistic status quo in traditional kabuki because these uphold the foundations of the art, yet it also promotes and assists innovators like Ennosuke and Tamasaburō who are essential to kabuki's future popularity and financial success. The insider-outsider issue is central to a problem that all leading contemporary actors address: how to build on their own achievements and innovations for the benefit of future generations. Danjūrō is training his son with the connoisseur audience as his focus of attention. This is because of the highly traditional expectations placed on any actor with the Danjūrō name. Ganjirō has trained his two sons

personally, but with a family acting heritage shorter and more heterogeneous than Danjūrō's, Ganjirō can allow his sons more freedom in developing their career paths. Ennosuke is seeking to solidify
his Super Kabuki, which incorporates elements of modern drama
and modern dance, as part of the permanent kabuki repertory. He is
relying on his nephews and on at least one outsider as possible successors. The outsider is Ichikawa Ukon, who left home at age eleven
to enter the troupe of the actor he adored. Ukon, in turn, has taken
under his wing a young man who at age three saw Ukon perform in
Yamato Takeru and has yearned to follow in Ukon's footsteps ever
since.[76] The Ennosuke troupe seems to subscribe to Tamasaburō's
theory that desire can be as important as bloodlines in choosing
one's artistic successors. Since Ukon has become one of Ennosuke's
top disciples the two have worked closely and intensively together.
Ukon's career somewhat resembles Tamasaburō's: Tamasaburō too
was an outsider who became the most intimate disciple of an established actor. But Morita Kan'ya, unlike Ennosuke, was not a daring
innovator, and this forced Tamasaburō to forge his own artistic path
when he was a young actor. Ukon still believes that Ennosuke is
moving so fast as a kabuki innovator that no one will be able to overtake him in the near future.[77]

One of the most important lessons to be learned from the biographies of the Genroku pioneers is that competition breeds excellence.
When he was murdered Danjūrō I was at the peak of his career and
was striving to become an all-around tachiyaku so that he could best
Shichisaburō even in wagoto roles. Ayame was arguably at his very
best during the years of competition with Tatsunosuke, and Tōjūrō
relished theatrical competition, even giving free advice on acting
and production to his rival Hanzaemon so that Kyoto kabuki would
be more competitive, inspiring everyone to do better onstage. The
message for future kabuki is clear. If there are not several superstars
in kabuki, competing for audience acclaim with clearly different acting styles, the rank-and-file actors and the theater in general are
unlikely to perform to peak potential. Without internal competition

kabuki will surely lose to competition from other forms of entertainment.

Danjūrō I, Tōjūrō, and Ayame were passionately in love with theater and felt driven to innovate and grow as artists through the very end of their careers. They were highly competitive and they recognized that failure to grow would open the way for younger rivals to supplant them at the top of the yearly actor ratings and salary charts. Using daring artistic experiments and dangerous roles as their weapons, Danjūrō I, Tōjūrō, and Ayame brilliantly fought off their young challengers until each old master was physically unable any longer to compete. Kabuki has a few actors of that stature now, but it will need more if it is to thrive in the coming century.

NOTES

1: SETTING THE STAGE: THE KABUKI THEATER IN 1680

1. Suwa Haruo, *Genroku Kabuki no Kenkyū* (Tokyo: Kazama Shoin, 1967), pp. 2–7 includes descriptions of the earliest kabuki performances. Sideshow acts included animal tricks, a dancer balancing a long pole on his nose, juggling, acrobatics and martial arts displays, presentations of exotic European clothing, and so on. Several programs for women's kabuki survive. One women's kabuki program, given on page 7, reads as follows (note that this program does not mention sideshow acts and comic skits, although they were probably performed between some of the listed numbers): 1) Opening dance, 2) Okuni dance, 3) Narihira dance, 4) Okuni and Nagoya love scene, 5) Kabuki dance, 5) Furo-agari scene, 6) Closing song, 7) Finale.

2. The serious, austere nō drama and the slapstick, often satiric kyōgen farces that were performed between nō plays, date back to the late 1300s. In the medieval era, most Japanese would have attended nō and kyōgen, but in the early 1600s the central government banned all but five nō troupes and all but three kyōgen troupes and designated the two art forms as the official theater of the ruling samurai class. Commoners were only allowed to attend occasional benefit performances. Many of the performers from the nō and kyōgen troupes that had been abolished joined the kabuki theater.

3. See Gary P. Leupp, *Male Colors : The Construction of Homosexuality in Tokugawa Japan* (Berkeley, California: University of California Press, 1994), pp. 27–57 for information on pre–Tokugawa-era homosexual practices among samurai and priests.

4. Asai Ryōi, *Edo Meishoki,* in Donald Shively, "The Social Environment of Tokugawa Kabuki," Brandon, Malm, & Shively, *Studies in Kabuki : Its Acting, Music, and Historical Context* (Honolulu: The University Press of Hawaii, 1978), p. 10.

5. Ihara Saikaku, *The Great Mirror of Male Love,* trans. by Paul Gordon Schalow (Stanford, California: Stanford University Press, 1990), p. 307.

6. Matsushima Han'ya retired from the stage at age twenty in 1686. While working as an actor he studied *haikai* poetry with Saikaku. Ibid, p. 342.

7. Ibid., pp. 254–255.

8. This figure is estimated roughly, on the basis of actors' salaries as compared with the known costs of certain commodities in the Genroku period.

9. Ibid. p. 266, for one example.

10. Leupp, pp. 95–101.

11. Yoshikawa Yoshio, "Genroku no Onnagata," *Engeki-shi Kenkyū*, Engekishi Gakkai ed. (Tokyo: Daiichi Shobō, 1932), p. 182.

12. Ihara Toshirō, *Kabuki Nenpyō* vol. I (Tokyo: Iwanami Shoten, 1956), p. 93. Later versions of *The Outlaw's Revenge* were in three acts, but Ihara believes that the 1664 version was a two-act play.

13. Ibid., p. 94.

14. Ibid., p. 95.

15. See C. J. Dunn, *The Early Japanese Puppet Drama* (London: Luzac & Co., Ltd., 1966), pp. 88–89.

16. Ihara, Ibid., p. 74.

2: ICHIKAWA DANJŪRŌ I: THE WILD GOD OF KABUKI

1. In an informal survey I conducted in the fall of 1994 among adult Japanese residents of Portland, Oregon, every respondent was able to identify the name "Ichikawa Danjūrō" as that of a kabuki actor.

2. Ihara Seiseien, *Ichikawa Danjūrō no Daidai* (Tokyo: Ichikawa Sōkezō, 1917), p. 1.

3. Ibid., p. 2.

4. Ichikawa Danjūrō, *Ganmon*, in Ihara Toshirō, "Gansō Danjūrō no Zangeroku," *Danjūrō no Shibai* (Tokyo: Waseda Daigaku Shuppan-bu, 1934), p. 148.

5. Carmen Blacker, *The Catalpa Bow: A Study of Shamanistic Practice in Japan* (London: George Allen and Unwin, 1975), p. 175.

6. Ihara, *Ichikawa Danjūrō no Daidai*, p. 3.

7. Ibid., p. 4.

8. Suwa Haruo, *Genroku Kabuki no Kenkyū* (Tokyo: Kasama Shoin, 1977), p. 365.

9. Ibid.

10. Ihara, *Ichikawa Danjūrō no Daidai*, p. 12.

11. Suwa, *Genroku Kabuki no Kenkyū*, p. 365.

12. This was the *kami suki*, or "hair combing," in which the courtesan Tora tenderly dressed the hair of her lover Jūrō's hair before he left for his final battle.

13. "*Yarō Yakusha Fūryū Kagami* (1688)," *Kabuki Hyōbanki Shūsei* vol. 1 (Tokyo: Iwanami Shoten, 1972), pp. 277–278.

14. Suwa, *Genroku Kabuki no Kenkyū*, p. 367.

15. Ichikawa, *Ganmon*, pp. 113–114.

16. Mary Douglas, *Natural Symbols; Explorations in Cosmology* (London: Barrie & Rockliff the Cresset Press, 1970), pp. 126, 144.

17. Hattori Yukio, *Edo Kabuki-ron* (Tokyo: Hōsei Daigaku Shuppan-kyoku, 1980), p. 304.

18. "*Yakusha Ōkagami* (1692)," *Kabuki Hyōbanki Shūsei* vol. 1 (Tokyo: Iwanami Shoten, 1972), p. 325.

19. Ichikawa, *Ganmon*, p. 113.

20. Ibid., p. 117.

21. "*Yakusha Ōkagami*," p. 325.

22. Ibid.

23. The rating system for actors was adapted from the terms used to predict varying levels of good or bad fortune that are listed on divination slips (*omikuji*) that worshippers purchase when visiting temples and shrines. In 1692, the highest rating for an actor was "high high" (*jō jō*). "Middle" (*chū*) was the lowest rank. For several decades, "high high good fortune" (*jō jō kichi*) was the highest rank possible. Later, great actors, especially Ayame, inspired the insertion of additional superlatives, such as "extreme" (*goku*) and "incomparable" (*murui*).

24. *Yakusha Ōkagami*," p. 325.

25. Ichikawa, *Ganmon*, p. 137.

26. "*Kokon Shibai Iro-kurabe Hyakunin Isshu (1693)*," *Kabuki Hyōbanki Shūsei* vol. 1 (Tokyo: Iwanami Shoten, 1972), p. 477.

27. Ibid.

28. Ibid.

29. Ichikawa, *Ganmon*, p. 122.

30. Ibid., p. 123.

31. Ibid., p. 127.

32. Ibid., p. 126.

33. Ibid., p. 128.

34. Ibid.

35. Ibid., p. 129.

36. Suwa, p. 372.

37. Ihara Toshirō, *Kabuki Nenpyō* vol. 2 (Tokyo: Iwanami Shoten, 1966) pp. 189–190, provides all the details of the opening day excitement for Danjūrō's *The Power and the Glory of the Genji Warrior*. Two hyōbanki, *Yakusha Ōkagami* (1695 edition), and *Mikuni Yakusha Butai Kagami* (1698) confirm that this play was a tremendous success. *Kabuki Hyōbanki Shūsei* vol. 2 (Tokyo: Iwanami Shoten, 1972), pp. 29, 119.

38. Ibid.

39. Dunn and Torigoe, *The Actors' Analects* (Tokyo: The University of Tokyo Press, 1969), pp. 17–18.

40. Suwa, in his "Shodai Ichikawa Danjūrō Nenpyō," does not note in which month this play was performed. Ihara, in *Kabuki Nenpyō* vol. 1, p. 191, writes that it was put on in the third month.

41. Ihara Toshirō, *Kabuki Nenpyō* vol. 1, p. 191.

42. Ibid., p. 194, for source of plot summary.

43. Ichikawa, *Ganmon*, p. 149.

44. Ibid.

45. Ichikawa Danjūrō in Ihara Toshirō, *Kabuki Nenpyō* vol. 1, p. 190.

46. Ihara, *Kabuki Nenpyō* vol. 1, p. 194, and "*Yakusha Dankōzuku* (1700)," *Kabuki Hyōbanki Shūsei* vol. 2 (Tokyo: Iwanami Shoten, 1972), p. 420.

47. Excerpted from *Kabuki Kotohajime* in Ihara, *Kabuki Nenpyō* vol. 1, p. 195.

48. "*Yakusha Ōkagami* (1695 edition)," *Kabuki Hyōbanki Shūsei* vol. 2 (Tokyo: Iwanami Shoten, 1972), p. 29.

49. Ibid., p. 30.

50. "*Yakusha Ikazuchi* (1694)," *Kabuki Hyōbanki Shūsei* vol. 1 (Tokyo: Iwanami Shoten, 1972), p. 593.

51. Ibid.

52. Ichikawa, *Ganmon*, p. 138.

53. Ibid.

54. Ibid., p.139.

55. Ibid., pp. 139–141.

56. Ibid., p. 141.

57. Ibid., pp. 141–142.

58. Ibid., p. 135.

59. Ibid., p. 137.

60. Ibid.

61. Ibid., p. 147.

62. Ibid.

63. Ibid., p. 143.

64. Ibid. It is impossible to determine just what his "old illness" was.

65. Ibid.

66. Ibid., pp. 131–133.

67. Ibid., p. 131.

68. Ibid., p. 133.

69. Ibid., p. 125.

70. Ibid., p. 148.

71. Ibid., p. 138.

72. Ibid., p. 149.

73. Ibid., p. 133.

74. Ibid., p. 150.

75. The earliest extant kabuki book published in the city of Edo is *Wankyu Ukiyo Jūkai,* which dates from 1686, but none survive from the decade between 1687 and 1696. Numerous illustrated kabuki books survive that were published in Edo from 1697 on.

76. In the nō play *Chōbuku Soga* by Miyamasu, the Hakone Temple abbot prays for Fudō to intervene to help Soga Gorō, and in the second act of the play the *shite* plays Fudō. This nō play is the only work prior to *Tsuwamono Kongen Soga* in which Fudō comes to the aid of Gorō on the occasion of his first meeting with his father's murderer.

77. Akashi Seizaburō and Ichikawa Danjūrō, *"Tsuwamono Kongen Soga,"* in Hattori Yukio ed., *Kotobuki Kongen Soga,* Kokuritsu Gekijō Jōen Shiryō-shū no. 46 (Tokyo: Kokuritsu Gekijō Chōsa Yoseibu Geinō Chōsashitsu, 1970), p.90.

78. Ihara Toshirō, *Kabuki Nenpyō* vol. 1, p. 206. After the play closed, Danjūrō contributed to Shinshōji a holy mirror, a curtain, and 500 *mon* in cash. The records are not clear about what became of the money and gifts offered by spectators to the onstage Fudō during the run.

79. Ibid., p. 207. Audience members often shout out actors' yago during particularly striking moments in a performance.

80. Ibid.

81. These actions are quoted from two different hyōbanki: *Yakusha Dankōzuku* (1700) vol. 2, p. 420, *Yakusha Mangokubune* (1701), vol. 3, p. 145. In *Kabuki Nenpyō* vols. 2, 3.

82. In Japanese, "Black Fan K'uai" is *Hankai Kuro*. Fan K'uai was a general who fought for the first Han emperor.

83. Akashi and Ichikawa, p. 90.

84. "*Mikuni Yakusha Butai Kagami* (1698)," *Kabuki Nenpyō* vol. 2, p. 119.

85. The word *shosa* is used twice, and *odori* and *michiyuki* once each.

86. "*Mikuni Yakusha Butai Kagami,*" p. 119.

87. Ihara Toshirō, *Kabuki Nenpyō* vol. 1, p. 207.

88. The print is by Torii Kiyomasu (dates uncertain) and probably dates from between 1697 and 1700.

89. Early illustrators of e-iri kyōgen-bon did not sign their names to their work. Howard Perry Link believes that Torii Kiyonobu (1664–1729) and Torii Kiyomasu collaborated on the illustrations of *Tsuwamono Kongen Soga*, with the aragoto figures likely done by Kiyomasu. *The Theatrical Prints of the Torii Masters: A Selection of 17th and 18th Century Ukiyo-e Prints* (Honolulu: Honolulu Academy of Arts, Riccar Museum, 1977), p. 24.

90. *Kokon Yakusha Rongo Sakigake* excerpted in C. Andrew Gerstle, "Flowers of Edo: Eighteenth-Century *Kabuki* and its Patrons," *Asian Theatre Journal* vol. 4, no. 1 (Spring 1987), p. 56.

91. See Laurence Kominz, "Ichikawa Danjūrō V and Kabuki's Golden Age," in Donald Jenkins, *The Floating World Revisited* (Portland, OR.: Portland Art Museum, 1993), pp. 63–83.

92. "*Yakusha Nichō Jamisen*" (1702), *Kabuki Hyōbanki Shūsei* vol. 3 (Tokyo: Iwanami Shoten, 1972), pp. 221–222.

93. *Yakusha Mangoku Fune,*" p. 145.

94. Takano Tatsuyuki and Kuroki Kanzō ed., *Genroku Kabuki Kessaku-shū* (Tokyo: Waseda Daigaku Shuppan-bu, 1925), p. 124.

95. "*Yakusha Gozen Kabuki*" (1703), excerpted in Suwa, p. 396.

96. "*Yakusha Nichō Jamisen,*" p. 222.

97. This includes the 1696 play in which Danjūrō intended to play Fudō but could not, due to an illness.

98. Danjūrō rewrote portions of his plays for publishers, cut some dialogue, and did not include song lyrics, which were the responsibility of musicians, not playwrights.

99. Suwa, p. 116.

100. Suwa, pp. 129–136 shows that Danjūrō's plays had certain seasonal characteristics, but these are nascent at best and far less definitive than the seasonal characteristics apparent in Kansai plays at the time. Clear seasonal requirements in Edo kabuki begin a few years after Danjūrō's death, and by the mid-1700s they dominated the imaginations of playwrights, producers, and actors.

101. Kenneth Yasuda, *Masterworks of the Nō Theatre* (Bloomington & Indianapolis: Indiana University Press, 1989), p. 1.

102. Ichikawa Danjūrō, *Naritasan Funjin Fudō* in *Genroku Kabuki Kessaku-shū*, pp. 568–657. The six nō plays are: *Sōshi Arai Komachi, Ikkaku Sennin, Kayoi Komachi, Tenko, Sumidagawa,* and *Sekidera Komachi.*

103. Perhaps Danjūrō's finest evocation of a pleasure district scene is in *Kagemasa Kaminari Mondo,* Act Three, in *Genroku Kabuki Kessaku-shū,* pp. 217–225.

104. Asahi Jūzan, *Naritasan to Ichikawa Danjūrō Narabi ni Geinōjin no Shinkō* (Narita: Narita-shi Bunka Zaidan, 1968), pp. 4–5.

105. "*Yakusha Nigiri Kobushi* (1696)," *Kabuki Hyōbanki Shūsei* vol. 2 (Tokyo: Iwanami Shoten, 1972), p. 73.

106. Ibid.

107. One of the earliest examples is the 1703 play *Keisei Asama Soga,* which starred Nakamura Shichisaburō. Its playwright is unknown. For a summary of this play, see Laurence Kominz, *Avatars of Vengeance: Japanese Drama and the Soga Literary Tradition* (Ann Arbor: University of Michigan Press, 1995), pp. 175–177. The Japanese text is available in *Genroku Kabuki Kessaku-shū,* pp. 537–568.

108. Douglas, p. 128.

109. Asahi, p. 15.

110. Ibid., p. 14.

111. Miyata Noboru, "Kinsei no Hayarigami" *Nihonjin no Kōdō to Shisō* vol. 17 (Tokyo: Hyōronsha, 1975), p. 127.

112. Ichikawa, *Ganmon,* p. 146.

113. "*Yakusha Dankōzuku,*" p. 420, and *Yakusha Nichō Jamisen,* p. 221. First-aid scenes were one of Tōjūrō's fortes.

114. "*Yakusha Mangokubune,*" p. 146.

115. Ibid.

116. "*Yakusha Gozen Kabuki,*" p. 394.

117. "*Yakusha Mai Ōgi,*" *Kabuki Hyōbanki Shūsei* vol. 3 (Tokyo: Iwanami Shoten, 1972), pp. 508–509.

118. "*Yakusha Gozen Kabuki,*" p. 393.

119. Ichikawa, *Ganmon,* p. 146.

120. Ihara Seiseien, p. 6. The original account is from a 1705 record entitled *Hōei Tadanobu Monogatari.*

121. Ibid. The original account is in *Mushashino Zokudan.*

122. One possible motive is that Hanroku owed a large sum of money to Danjūrō and Danjūrō had been pressing him to return it. Ibid.

123. Ejima Kiseki (attr.), "*Daijin Mitsu Sakazuki* (1704)," *Kabuki Hyōbanki Shūsei* vol. 3 (Tokyo: Iwanami Shoten, 1972), p. 576. This hyōbanki, many of whose blocks were carved before the murder, rated both Danjūrō and Shichisaburō as jō-jō-kichi, but Shichisaburō was placed above Danjūrō. The other 1704 hyōbanki, *Yakusha Mai Ōgi*, was written before Danjūrō's death and rated him above Shichisaburō. It came out two months after Danjūrō was killed.

124. Ejima (attr.), ibid., p. 577.

125. For a detailed account of Danjūrō II's development of the Sukeroku role, see Barbara E. Thornbury, *Sukeroku's Double Identity: The Dramatic Structure of Kabuki* (Ann Arbor: Michigan Papers in Japanese Studies No. 6, 1982), pp. 55–74. A translation of the text of the enduring version of Sukeroku, *Sukeroku Yukari no Edo Zakura*, is available in James Brandon, *Kabuki Five Classic Plays* (Cambridge, MA: Harvard University Press, 1975), pp. 55–92.

126. For an analysis and translation of *Ya no Ne*, see Laurence Kominz, *Avatars of Vengeance: Japanese Drama and the Soga Literary Tradition*, pp. 194–217.

127. For a biography of Danjūrō V, see Laurence Kominz, "Ichikawa Danjūrō V and Kabuki's Golden Age," in Donald Jenkins ed., *The Floating World Revisited* (Portland, OR: The Portland Art Museum, 1993), pp. 63, 71–82.

3: SAKATA TŌJŪRŌ: KABUKI'S FIRST TRUE ACTOR

1. Tsuchiya Keiichirō, *Genroku Haiyū Den* (Tokyo: Iwanami Shoten, 1991), p. 13.

2. Ibid., pp. 12–13.

3. Ibid., p. 14.

4. Ihara Toshirō, *Nihon Engeki-shi* (Tokyo: Waseda Daigaku Shuppan-bu, 1906), p. 171.

5. Kaneko Kichizaemon, "Dust in the Ears," in *The Actors' Analects*, Dunn and Torigoe tr. (Tokyo: The University of Tokyo Press, 1969), pp. 74–75.

6. Ibid., p. 75.

7. Dunn and Torigoe, *The Actors' Analects* (Tokyo: The University of Tokyo Press, 1969), p. 190.

8. Kaneko, ibid., p. 240.

9. Ejima Kiseki, *Kankatsu Yakusha Katagi*, excerpted in Ihara, *Nihon Engeki-shi*, p. 209.

10. *Beku Sakazuki* (1675) in Torigoe Bunzō, *Genroku Kabuki Kō* (Tokyo: Yagi Shoten, 1991), p. 306.

11. An "older brother" was not the sort of male image that the wakashu had made popular.

12. Ihara Toshirō, *Kabuki Nenpyō* vol. 1 (Tokyo: Iwanami Shoten, 1966), p. 126.

13. Ibid., p. 127.

14. Kaneko, "Dust in the Ears," p. 102.

15. Mizuochi Kiyoshi, *Kamigata Kabuki* (Tokyo: Tokyo Shoseki, 1991), p. 31.

16. Ibid., pp. 32–33.

17. "Shin Taketoki Monogatari" quoted in Ihara, *Kabuki Nenpyō* vol. 1, p. 162.

18. *Yarō Tachiyaku Butai Kagami* (1687) in *Kabuki Hyōbanki Shūsei* vol. 1 (Tokyo: Iwanami Shoten, 1972), p. 247. See Note 23, Chapter Two, for an explanation of the abbreviated actor rating system.

19. Ibid.

20. Ibid.

21. Ibid.

22. Ibid.

23. Ihara, *Kabuki Nenpyō* vol. 1, pp. 169–173.

24. *Yakusha Ōkagami* (1692) in *Kabuki Hyōbanki Shūsei* vol. 1 (Tokyo: Iwanami Shoten, 1972), p. 318.

25. Azuma Sanpachi, "The Kengai Collection," in Dunn and Torigoe, *The Actors' Analects* (Tokyo: The University of Tokyo Press, 1969), p. 126. Azuma wrote that he was recording the words of actor Somekawa Jūrobei (d. 1708 or 1711).

26. *Yakusha Ōkagami,* p. 317.

27. Ibid.

28. *Yakusha Ōkagami Gassai* (1692) in *Kabuki Hyōbanki Shūsei* vol. 1 (Tokyo: Iwanami Shoten, 1972), p. 417.

29. Ibid., p. 416.

30. Ibid., p. 417.

31. Ibid., p. 416.

32. Tsuchiya, *Genroku Haiyū Den,* p. 103.

33. Chikamatsu has sometimes been given credit for a Yūgiri-Izaemon play written in about 1685, but today scholars doubt that this play was really by Chikamatsu. The first kabuki play certain to have been written by Chikamastu was *Butsumo Mayasan Kaichō* in 1693.

34. Chikamatsu Monzaemon, *Butsumo Mayasan Kaichō,* in *Chikamatsu Zenshū* vol. 15 (Tokyo: Iwanami Shoten, 1989), p. 30.

35. Laurence Kominz, *Avatars of Vengeance: Japanese Drama and the Soga Literary Tradition* (Ann Arbor: University of Michigan Press, 1995), pp. 124–128.

36. A plot summary of the play is available in Chikamatsu Monzaemon, *Soga Tayū Zome*, in Takano Tatsuyuki ed., *Chikamatsu Kabuki Kyōgen-shū* (Tokyo: Roku-gōkan, 1927), pp. 500–506, and an English plot summary appears in Kominz, *Avatars of Vengeance*, pp. 126–128.

37. See Kominz, *Avatars of Vengeance*, pp. 108–109.

38. Kaneko's elegaic writing in "Dust in the Ears" is evidence of his esteem for Tōjūrō. Chikamatsu never worked on a regular basis for any kabuki producer other than Tōjūrō. For his part, Tōjūrō once reputedly said that good plays were harder to come by than money.

39. Suwa Haruo, "Kaneko Ikkō Nikki ni Miru Chikamatsu to Kaneko Kichizaemon no Kankei," *Kabuki Kenkyū to Hihyō* vol. 11, 1993, p. 43.

40. Imao Tetsuya, "Ikkō Nikki o Yomu," *Kabuki Kenkyū to Hihyō* vol. 11, 1993, p. 33, and Kaneko, "Dust in the Ears, pp. 98–100.

41. Kaneko, "Dust in the Ears," p. 72.

42. Ibid., p. 263.

43. Ibid., p. 72.

44. For a translation of part of the latter scene, see pages 143–145.

45. Tsuchiya, *Genroku Haiyū Den*, p. 105.

46. *Sangoku Yakusha Butai Kagami* (1698) in ibid., p. 108.

47. Ibid., p. 104.

48. Ibid., p. 113.

49. *Yakusha Ōkagami*, p. 317.

50. Ejima Kiseki, *Yakusha Kuchijamisen Hentō Yakusha Shitatsuzumi* (1699) in *Kabuki Hyōbanki Shūsei* vol. 2 (Tokyo: Iwanami Shoten, 1972), p. 303. *Nori* is paper-thin, edible seaweed.

51. Ejima Kiseki, *Yakusha Nichō Shamisen* (1702) in Tsuchiya, *Genroku Haiyū Den*, p. 101.

52. Kaneko, "Dust in the Ears," p. 71.

53. Good examples of Tōjūrō's teaching style can be found in Tamiya Shirogorō's "Sequel to Dust in the Ears," in Dunn and Torigoe, *The Actors' Analects* (Tokyo: The University of Tokyo Press, 1969), pp. 120–121, and Somekawa, "The Kengai Collection," pp. 126–127. In the latter he gave instruction to Hanzaemon, and the episode is translated on page 132.

54. Kaneko, "Dust in the Ears," p. 96.

55. Ibid., pp. 76, 79.

56. Fukuoka Yagoshirō, "The Words of Ayame," in Dunn and Torigoe, *The Actors' Analects* (Tokyo: The University of Tokyo Press, 1969), p. 57.

57. Azuma, "The Kengai Collection," pp. 126–127.

58. Kaneko, "Dust in the Ears," p. 242.

59. Dunn and Torigoe, *The Actors' Analects,* pp. 17–18.

60. Chikamatsu Monzaemon, *Hyakuya Komachi & Yūgiri Shichinenki* in *Genroku Kabuki Kessaku-shū* (Ge), (Tokyo: Waseda Daigaku Shuppan-bu, 1925), pp. 1–34. *Yūgiri Shichinenki* is a discrete play. One-act plays unrelated to the main play were often performed at the end of a kabuki show. These plays were called *kiri kyōgen.*

61. Suwa Haruo, "Kaneko Ikkō Nikki ni Miru Chikamatsu to Kaneko Kichizaemon no Kankei," p. 39.

62. See C. Andrew Gerstle, *Circles of Fantasy Convention in the Plays of Chikamatsu* (Cambridge: Harvard University Press), 1986, pp. 71–80, and Kominz, *Avatars of Vengeance,* pp. 112–119, for analysis of Chikamatsu's first puppet play, *Yotsugi Soga,* and Kominz, pp. 129–130, for a comparison of *Yotsugi Soga* and *Daimyō Nagusami Soga.*

63. Chikamatsu Monzaemon, *Daimyō Nagusami Soga* in *Chikamatsu Zenshū* vol. 16 (Tokyo: Iwanami Shoten, 1989), pp. 280–303.

64. Ihara, *Kabuki Nenpyō* vol. 1, p. 207.

65. Ibid., p. 208.

66. Suwa Haruo, "*Keisei Hotoke no Hara* Sakuhin Shōkai," in *Chikamatsu Monzaemon,* Suwa Haruo ed. (Tokyo: Shūeisha, 1989), p. 119.

67. Azuma, "The Kengai Collection," p. 133.

68. Tsuchiya, *Genroku Haiyū Den,* p. 67. There are just three documented meetings between the two men.

69. Ibid., pp. 69–74. The summary of Tōjūrō's advice to Hanzaemon and Shichisaburō in this paragraph derives from this source.

70. Ibid. p. 74. The puppet play was *Nandaimon Aki no Higan.*

71. Azuma, "The Kengai Collection," pp. 217–218; 134.

72. Ibid., pp. 133–134.

73. Imao, "Ikkō Nikki o Miru," pp. 24–30.

74. Suwa Haruo, "Kaneko Ikkō Nikki ni Miru Chikamatsu to Kaneko Kichizaemon no Kankei," p. 38.

75. Ihara's *Kabuki Nenpyō* shows that Arashi-za in Osaka opened their *Keisei Hotoke no Hara* the same month that this play opened at the Mandayū-za in Kyoto. Chikamatsu and Kaneko—who had sent scripts to Osaka theaters in the past—may

well have written the script for the Arashi-za. Otherwise, if the Arashi-za opening date in *Kabuki Nenpyō* is accurate the company would have had just a week to ten days to have a playwright complete the script and also have the actors finish rehearsing. This would have been a fast job, even in Genroku Kabuki.

76. "Genroku Jūyonnen Jissoku Dai Ezu," a map in the collection *Keichō Shōwa Kyoto Chizu Shūsei 1611 (Keichō Jūrokunen)–1940 (Shōwa Jūgonen)*, Ōtsuka ed. (Tokyo: Kashiwa Shobō, 1994).

77. Suwa Haruo, "*Keisei Hotoke no Hara* Sakuhin Shōkai," p. 119.

78. I have omitted a section of the dialogue which includes damaged and illegible characters, and also a monolog during which Bunzō reels off puns on various kinds of cuisine while rebuking Imagawa for her supposed infidelity.

79. Chikamatsu Monzaemon, *Keisei Hotoke no Hara* in *Chikamatsu Zenshū* vol. 15 (Tokyo: Iwanami Shoten, 1989), pp. 284–285.

80. *Yakusha Dankō Zuku* (1700) in *Kabuki Hyōbanki Shūsei* vol. 2 (Tokyo: Iwanami Shoten, 1972), p. 19.

81. *Yakusha Itchō Tsuzumi* (1702) in *Kabuki Hyōbanki Shūsei* vol. 3 (Tokyo: Iwanami Shoten, 1972), p. 304.

82. Torigoe, *Genroku Kabuki Kō*, p. 318. Torigoe notes during the course of his chapter on Tōjūrō that the term *i-kyōgen* was used first for Tōjūrō and was never used to describe the acting of Hanzaemon. It was used to describe the work of Tōjūrō's successors and others who consciously imitated Tōjūrō's style.

83. *Yakusha Dankō Zuku*, p. 384, and Ejima, *Yakusha Kuchijamisen Hentō Yakusha Shitatsuzumi*, p. 303.

84. *Yakusha Itchō Tsuzumi*, p. 304.

85. *Yakusha Itchō Tsuzumi* in Tsuchiya, *Genroku Haiyū Den*, p. 30. The authorship of this hyōbanki is unknown.

86. This one-sentence crystallization of a rich and complex critical term is based on my own study of Zeami's writings.

87. *Yakusha Kuchijamisen Hentō Yakusha Shitatsuzumi*, p. 303.

88. *Yakusha Itchō Tsuzumi*, p. 302.

89. Kaneko, "Dust in the Ears," p. 268.

90. Ibid., p. 265.

91. *Yarō Seki Sumō* in *Kabuki Hyōbanki Shūsei* vol. 1 (Tokyo: Iwanami Shoten, 1972), p. 549.

92. Kaneko, "Dust in the Ears," p. 86.

93. Azuma, "The Kengai Collection," p. 129.

94. Kaneko, "Dust in the Ears," p. 96.

95. Azuma, "The Kengai Collection," pp. 136–137.

96. Ihara, *Nihon Engekishi,* p. 208.

97. Azuma, "The Kengai Collection," p. 130.

98. Kikuchi Kan's play has been translated into English in *Tōjūrō's Love and Four Other Plays by Kikuchi Kan,* Glenn Shaw tr. (Tokyo: Hokuseido Press, 1925).

99. Kaneko, "Dust in the Ears," pp. 80–81. The date of the play is unknown.

100. Ibid., p. 83.

101. Ejima Kiseki, *Yakusha Mannen Goyomi* (1700) in *Kabuki Hyōbanki Shūsei* vol. 2 (Tokyo: Iwanami Shoten, 1972), p. 485.

102. I believe that Japanese theater historians have been overly scholarly in their attempts to explain why Tōjūrō was so popular among women theatergoers. In his chapter on Tōjūrō, Tsuuchi establishes theories of how women enjoyed Tōjūrō's acting because he "destroyed the real from the inside," or because his acting "was the real expanded beyond limitation." (p. 26.) Other scholars have written that the almost cosmic transformativity of the yatsushi character was the source of Tōjūrō's appeal. None of these theories is convincing to me.

103. This scene took place in the play *Keisei Gusei no Fune,* the Mandayū-za's second play in 1700. The character Tōjūrō played was named Hakozaki no Samon.

104. Tōjūrō did monkey trainer impersonations in several Yūgiri plays and in *Keisei Saga no Hara,* 1701.

105. Ejima Kiseki, *Yakusha Yatsushi Ukejō* (1701), in *Kabuki Hyōbanki Shūsei* vol. 3 (Tokyo: Iwanami Shoten, 1972), p. 21.

106. *Yakusha Hyōban Irojamisen* (1703), in *Kabuki Hyōbanki Shūsei* vol. 3 (Tokyo: Iwanami Shoten, 1972), p. 340.

107. Ibid.

108. Azuma, "The Kengai Collection," pp. 131–132.

109. Ihara Seiseien, *Ichikawa Danjūrō no Daidai,* p. 109.

110. Ibid.

111. In postwar Japan, women viewers sustained the remarkable run of over forty-five feature films showing the unhappy love affairs of a warm-hearted peddler named Tora-san. He has a sister in Tokyo, and her family loves Tora very much and in every movie she tries to help Tora find the right woman so that he can settle down and enjoy the pleasures of family life. But nothing ever goes right for Tora-san, and he ends every film alone again. Tora is invariably fun-loving and nonchalant on the surface, but deep inside he is a lonely man because he has no wife and children. Women who are wives and do have children find his story sad, and their hearts go out to Tora-san.

   Women audiences also form the main support for the great contemporary kabuki onnagata such as Tamasaburō (see pages 250–261) as well as the top actresses of the Takarazuka all-women's musical theatre. It is clear that the ambiguous sexuality of these stars constitutes an important part of their appeal.

112. *Yakusha Hyōban Irojamisen,* p. 340.

113. Azuma, "The Kengai Collection," pp. 123–124.

114. Ibid., p. 125.

115. Ibid., p. 134.

116. Ibid.

117. Ejima Kiseki, *Kankatsu Yakusha Katagi* in Ihara, *Nihon Engeki-shi,* p. 210.

118. Ibid., p. 209.

119. Azuma, "The Kengai Collection," p. 132.

120. Examples of such behavior are described in Kaneko, "Dust in the Ears," pp. 92–93 and 96.

121. *Yakusha Dankō Zuku,* p. 386.

122. Ibid., p. 385.

123. Fukuoka, "The Words of Ayame," pp. 64–65.

124. Kaneko, "Dust in the Ears," p. 91, describes how Tōjūrō prepared for a stuttering role in the play *Muramatsu.* No such play exists in surviving records of Tōjūrō's career and scholars speculate that the stuttering role was for the fourth act of *Imayō Nō Kyōgen,* which was based on a well-known kyōgen play called *Domori,* in which a stuttering husband quarrels with his wife.

125. Ibid.

126. Azuma, "The Kengai Collection," p. 128.

127. In an incident described by Kaneko in "Dust in the Ears," pp. 99–100, Tōjūrō was unable to evaluate or understand a play written by Chikamatsu and Kaneko until he put on his costume. He then recognized the quality of the play. After this experience Tōjūrō advocated holding dress rehearsals earlier than had been the custom in kabuki.

128. From *Kabuki Kotohajime,* excerpted in Ihara, *Nihon Engeki-shi,* p. 198. Ihara believes that there are "nonsensical aspects" to the story, but that it is a good demonstration of Tōjūrō's dedication to his craft.

129. Shintarō is a retainer in Min'ya's family. His sister went to serve Min'ya's fiancee, Princess Katsu.

130. Chikamatsu Monzaemon, *Keisei Mibu Dainenbutsu,* in *Genroku Kabuki Kessaku-shū,* pp. 520–521.

131. Ibid., p. 524.

132. Ibid.

133. *Yakusha Itchō Tsuzumi,* pp. 302–303.

134. *Yakusha Mai Ōgi* (1704), in *Kabuki Hyōbanki Shūsei* vol. 3 (Tokyo: Iwanami Shoten, 1972), pp. 469–470.

135. Ibid., p. 470.

136. Ejima Kiseki, *Yakusha Sanzesō* (1705), in *Kabuki Hyōbanki Shūsei* vol. 4 (Tokyo: Iwanami Shoten, 1972), p. 39.

137. Ibid., p. 40.

138. Ibid., p. 39.

139. *Yakusha Otoshibumi* (1708) in Takano Tatsuyuki, "Meiyū no Rōkū Sakata Tōjūrō no Bannen," *Engekishi Kenkyū* (Tokyo: Daichi Shobō, 1932), pp. 9–10.

140. *Yakusha Shōgi Daizen Kōmoku* (1708), in *Kabuki Hyōbanki Shusei* vol. 4 (Tokyo: Iwanami Shoten, 1972), p. 253.

141. Kaneko, "Dust in the Ears," pp. 96–97.

142. Ibid., p. 14.

143. Tsuda, p. 61.

144. Takano, p. 17.

145. Ihara, *Kabuki Nenpyō* vol. 1, p. 377.

146. Takano, p. 17.

147. Torigoe, pp. 321–322.

148. Ibid., p. 317.

149. *Shinpan Utazaimon/Kuruwa Bunsho* Kokuritsu Gekijō Shiryō-shū no. 160 (Tokyo: Kokuritsu Gekijō Chōsa Kyōseibu Geinō Chōsa-shitsu, 1979), pp. 97–120.

4: YOSHIZAWA AYAME: THE PATRON SAINT OF THE ONNAGATA PRO-FESSION

1. Akiba Yoshimi, "Onnagata-gei no Sōritsusha," *Meiyū Yoshizawa Ayame no Tsuioku* (Wakayama-ken: Nakamura Kōminkan, 1958), p. 22.

2. Tomimoto Shigekiyo, "Seichi Kōshō no Isshaku," *Meiyū Yoshizawa Ayame no Tsuioku* (Wakayama-ken: Nakamura Kōminkan, 1958), pp. 56–65.

3. Fukuoka Yagoshirō, "Ayame Gusa" (*The Words of Ayame*) in *The Actors' Analects,* Dunn and Torigoe tr., ed. (Tokyo: The University of Tokyo Press, 1969), pp. 58–59.

4. Audience members shout actors' "house names" (*yago*) as a form of applause during kabuki performances. Today yago are inherited, but in the Genroku period

actors chose their own. Danjūrō chose "Narita-ya" for his yago, in honor of the city where his patron temple was located.

5. *Yakusha Ōkagami* (1692) in Tsuchiya Keiichirō, *Genroku Haiyū Den* (Tokyo: Iwanami Shoten, 1991), p. 39.

6. Ibid., p. 41.

7. When Ayame returned in triumph to Edo in 1713 almost everyone, including the cognoscenti, believed it was his first trip to the city. The one hyōbanki to comment on Ayame's early work in Edo was *Yakusha Iro Keizu* (1714), published by Hachimonjiya, the publishing house with the longest history of publishing hyōbanki. The reference is in *Yakusha Irokeizu, Kabuki Hyōbanki Shūsei* vol. 6 (Tokyo: Iwanami Shoten, 1972), p. 422.

8. *Yakusha Ōkagami Gassai* (1692) in *Kabuki Hyōbanki Shūsei* vol. I, (Tokyo: Iwanami Shoten, 1972), p. 401.

9. Ibid.

10. "Kinsei Kōto Chakubun-shū" in Ihara Toshirō, *Nihon Engeki-shi* (Tokyo: Waseda Daigaku Shuppan-bu, 1906), p. 217. Nothing more than this single sentence is recorded about the priest who was obsessed with love for Ayame.

11. *Yarō Seki Sumō* (1693) in *Kabuki Hyōbanki Shūsei* vol. 1, (Tokyo: Iwanami Shoten, 1972), p. 401. One very specific criticism was that "his fear of thunder was unconvincing" (p. 401).

12. Tsuchiya, p. 38. In *The Tale of Genji*, Genji's wife's pet cat had featured prominently in a love affair in which she betrayed Genji, and the Chikamatsu-Tatsunosuke version was a parody of the original work.

13. *Butai Ōkagami* (1695) in *Kabuki Hyōbanki Shūsei* vol. 2, (Tokyo: Iwanami Shoten, 1972), p. 349.

14. Ibid.

15. Ibid.

16. *Yakusha Iro Keizu*, p. 422. *Kabuki Jinmei Jiten* states that Ayame appeared in the Yamamura-za kaomise under the name Yoshizawa Kikunojō (p. 674).

17. Tsuchiya, p. 55.

18. The plot summary for *Keisei Asama Dake* is based on a text in *Genroku Kabuki Kessaku-shū* vol. 2 (Tokyo: Waseda Daigaku Shuppan-bu, 1925), pp. 393–453.

19. Ejima Kiseki, *Yakusha Kuchi Jamisen* (1699) in *Kabuki Hyōbanki Shūsei* vol. 2, (Tokyo: Iwanami Shoten, 1972), p. 313.

20. *Yakusha Mai Ōgi* (1704) in *Kabuki Hyōbanki Shūsei* vol. 3 (Tokyo: Iwanami Shoten, 1972), p. 548.

21. Tsuchiya, pp. 44–46.

22. Ibid., p. 45, and Ejima, p. 313.

23. Tsuchiya, pp. 49–50.

24. Ejima, p. 313. Other flowers used to symbolize Ayame included the lotus (*hasu*) and the rose mallow (*fuyō*). Tsuchiya, p. 44.

25. *Yakusha Gozen Kabuki* (1703) in *Kabuki Hyōbanki Shūsei* vol. 3 (Tokyo: Iwanami Shoten, 1972), p. 452.

26. Fukuoka, p. 56.

27. Ihara Toshirō, *Kabuki Nenpyō* vol. 1 (Tokyo: Iwanami Shoten, 1966), p. 315, and *Yakusha Mai Ōgi*, p. 549.

28. *Yakusha Dankō Zuku* (1700) in *Kabuki Hyōbanki Shūsei* vol. 2 (Tokyo: Iwanami Shoten, 1972), p. 402.

29. *Yakusha Itchō Tsuzumi* (1702) in *Kabuki Hyōbanki Shūsei* vol. 3 (Tokyo: Iwanami Shoten, 1972), p. 316.

30. *Yakusha Dankō Zuku*, p. 402 and *Yakusha Yatsushi Ukejō* (1701) in *Kabuki Hyōbanki Shūsei* vol. 3 (Tokyo: Iwanami Shoten, 1972), p. 38.

31. *Yakusha Mai Ōgi*, p. 548.

32. The first quote is from Ejima, p. 313, and is attributed to a spectator who dislikes Ayame. The second opinion is stated by an Ayame fan in Ejima, p. 314, and is reiterated in *Yakusha Itchō Tsuzumi*, p. 316.

33. Fukuoka, p. 56.

34. *Yakusha Gozen Kabuki*, p. 452.

35. Ibid.

36. *Yakusha Mai Ōgi*, p. 548.

37. Ejima Kiseki, *Yakusha Mannen Goyomi* (1700) in *Kabuki Hyōbanki Shūsei* vol. 2 (Tokyo: Iwanami Shoten, 1972), p. 502.

38. Tsuchiya, pp. 49–52.

39. Fukuoka, p. 53.

40. Ibid., p. 56.

41. Ibid., p. 66.

42. Ibid., p. 62.

43. Ejima Kiseki, *Yakusha Hyōban Irojamisen* (1703) in *Kabuki Hyōbanki Shūsei* vol. 3 (Tokyo: Iwanami Shoten, 1972), p. 349.

44. Fukuoka, p. 50. Onnagata wore scarves or caps to conceal their masculine, shaven pates.

45. Ibid., p. 61.

46. Ibid., p. 54.

47. Ibid., pp. 57–58, 60.

48. Ibid., p. 58. The object of court kickball *(kemari)* is to pass the ball from player to player without letting it fall to the ground.

49. "Mikuni Butai Kagami" (1698) in Ihara Toshirō, ibid., p. 316; and Yoshikawa Yoshio, "Genroku no Onnagata" in *Engeki-shi Kenkyū*, Engeki-shi Gakkai ed. (Tokyo: Daiichi Shobō, 1932), p.215.

50. Fukuoka, p. 64.

51. Dunn and Torigoe, p. 188.

52. Tsuchiya, p. 58.

53. Fukuoka, pp. 62–63.

54. Ibid., p. 62.

55. *Yakusha Sanzesō* (1703) in *Kabuki Hyōbanki Shūsei* vol. 3 (Tokyo: Iwanami Shoten, 1972), p. 103.

56. Ihara, *Kinsei Engeki-shi,* p. 324, and Ejima Kiseki, *Yakusha Daifukuchō* (1711) in *Kabuki Hyōbanki Shūsei* vol. 5 (Tokyo: Iwanami Shoten, 1972), p. 515.

57. Ihara, ibid.

58. Ibid.

59. Takahashi Hiroko, "Shosei Yoshizawa Ayame ni Okeru Tachiyaku Gei," *Engeki Gahō,* no. 27, 1986, p. 37.

60. Ejima, *Yakusha Daifukuchō,* p. 516.

61. Ibid.

62. Yoshikawa Yoshio, "Genroku no Onnagata," *Engeki-shi Kenkyū* (Tokyo: Daiichi Shobō, 1932), p. 196.

63. Tsuchiya, p. 142. Zenkōji, in the central mountains of Japan (in Nagano City), was one of the most popular temples in Japan in the Edo period, and kaichō in Edo were always jammed with worshippers and revelers.

64. Ejima Kiseki, *Yakusha Mekikikō* (1714) in Takahashi, p. 34.

65. Tsuchiya, p. 143.

66. *Yakusha Iro Keizu,* p. 423.

67. Ejima Kiseki, *Yakusha Mekikikō* (1714) in *Kabuki Hyōbanki Shūsei* vol. 6 (Tokyo: Iwanami Shoten, 1972), p.304.

68. Takahashi, p. 37.

69. Ejima Kiseki, *Yakusha Hangonkō* (1715) in Takahashi, p. 37.

70. Donald Shively, "The Social Environment of Kabuki," in *Studies in Kabuki: Its Acting, Music, and Historical Context* (Honolulu: University of Hawaii Press,

1978), p. 29. Shively's essay contains a detailed account of the Ejima-Ikushima incident on pp. 29–36, including a list of the government restrictions on kabuki that were promulgated following the investigation.

71. Ibid., p. 35.

72. Ejima Kiseki, *Yakusha Hangonkō* (1715) in *Kabuki Hyōbanki Shūsei* vol. 6 (Tokyo: Iwanami Shoten, 1972), p. 590.

73. Ibid.

74. *Yakusha Iro Keizu,* p. 423.

75. Ejima Kiseki, *Yakusha Kake Sugoroku* (1717) in Takahashi, p. 43.

76. Ihara, p. 326.

77. Ibid.

78. Ejima Kiseki, *Yakusha Uwasa Buro* (1721) in *Kabuki Hyōbanki Shūsei* vol. 8 (Tokyo: Iwanami Shoten, 1972), p. 141.

79. Takahashi, p. 33.

80. Ibid., p. 34.

81. Ejima Kiseki, *Yakusha Uwasa Buro,* pp. 140–141.

82. Takahashi, p. 31.

83. *Yakusha Gei Shina Sadame* (1722) in ibid.

84. Ibid., p. 32.

85. Ejima Kiseki, *Yakusha Tatsugoyomi Gei Shina Sadame* (1724) in *Kabuki Hyōbanki Shūsei* vol. 8 (Tokyo: Iwanami Shoten, 1972), p. 509.

86. Ibid.

87. Ibid.

88. *Yakusha Mitsu Domoe* (1724) in Takahashi, p. 32.

89. *Yakusha Sode Kotatsu* (1727) in *Kabuki Hyōbanki Shūsei* vol. 9 (Tokyo: Iwanami Shoten, 1972), p. 303.

90. *Yakusha Iro Kamiko* (1728) in *Kabuki Hyōbanki Shūsei* vol. 9 (Tokyo: Iwanami Shoten, 1972), p. 486.

91. *Yakusha Wakazaki Sake* in Akiba, p. 26.

92. Tsuda Rui, *Edo no Yakusha-tachi* (Tokyo: Perikansha, 1987), p. 87.

93. Ibid., p. 88.

94. *Onnagata Hiden* in ibid., p. 90.

95. Tsuda, p. 120.

96. Ibid., p. 118.

5: FOUR LEADING ACTORS IN KABUKI TODAY

1. Ichikawa Danjūrō XII in an interview with Suzuki Haruhiko in Kanamori Kazuku, ed. *Ichikawa Danjūrō* (Tokyo: Shōchiku, Inc., 1984), p. 106.

2. Author's interview with Ichikawa Danjūrō XII, 17 December 1994.

3. Uno Nobuo, "Umai Yakusha Yori," in Kanamori Kazuku, ed. *Ichikawa Danjūrō* (Tokyo: Shōchiku, Inc., 1984), p. 19.

4. Ichikawa Danjūrō XII in an interview with Suzuki Haruhiko in Kanamori Kazuku, ed. *Ichikawa Danjūrō* (Tokyo: Shōchiku, Inc., 1984), p. 105.

5. Author's interview with Ichikawa Danjūrō XII, 6 January 1997.

6. The interview is in Kanamori Kazuku, ed. *Ichikawa Danjūrō* (Tokyo: Shōchiku, Inc., 1984), and Danjūrō's thoughts on the timing and the import of his shūmei that appear in this paragraph are taken from pages 104–106.

7. Author's interviews with Ichikawa Danjūrō XII, 17 December 1994 and 6 January 1997.

8. Author's interview with Ichikawa Danjūrō XII, 17 December 1994.

9. Author's interviews with Ichikawa Danjūrō XII, 17 December 1994 and 6 January 1997.

10. Mizuochi Kiyoshi, *Heisei Kabuki Haiyū Ron* (Tokyo: Engeki Shuppansha, 1993), p. 104.

11. Ibid., p. 106.

12. Ibid.

13. Takechi Tetsuji in conversation with Ganjirō III in *Kamigata to Onnagata to Chikamatsu Nakamura Senjaku Shashin-shū* (Osaka: Kōyō Shobō, 1984), p. 75.

14. Mizuochi, p. 108.

15. Ibid., p. 110. *Taishū engeki* includes dancing, short romantic dramas and samurai heroics.

16. Ibid.

17. Author's interview with Nakamura Ganjirō III, 7 January 1997.

18. Author's interview with Nakamura Ganjirō III, 21 December 1994.

19. Author's interview with Nakamura Ganjirō III, 21 December 1994.

20. Author's interview with Nakamura Ganjirō III, 21 December 1994.

21. Author's interview with Nakamura Ganjirō III, 21 December 1994.

22. Author's interview with Nakamura Ganjirō III, 7 January 1997.

23. Author's interview with Nakamura Ganjirō III, 7 January 1997.

24. Author's interview with Ichikawa Ennosuke, 16 December 1994.

25. Faith Bach, "Breaking the Kabuki Actors' Barriers, 1868–1900," *Asian Theatre Journal,* Fall 1995, p. 211.

26. Ibid.

27. Ichikawa Ennosuke, *Shura Butai* (Tokyo: PHP Bunkō, 1994), p. 41.

28. Ibid., pp. 96–99.

29. Ibid., p. 95.

30. Ibid., pp. 192, 194.

31. Ibid., p. 193.

32. Ibid., p. 123.

33. Ibid., pp. 149–151.

34. Ibid., pp. 161–163.

35. Ibid., pp. 169–170.

36. Ichikawa Ennosuke III, "Amakakeru Yamato Takeru," *Johakyū,* December, 1986, p. 130.

37. Ibid., p. 129.

38. Author's interview with Ichikawa Ennosuke, 16 December 1994.

39. Ennosuke in interview with Umehara Takeshi and Fujita Yō, 27 February 1997 in *Ōkuninushi Supaa Kabuki* (gala program), published by Shinbashi Enbujō Publicity Department, 6 April 1997, p. 65.

40. It was published in 1997 by Bungei Shunju under the title *Ōkuninushi.*

41. Author's interview with Ichikawa Ennosuke, 11 January 1997.

42. Author's interview with kabuki expert Mark Oshima, 5 January 1997.

43. Author's interview with Ichikawa Ennosuke, 11 January 1997.

44. Author's interview with Ichikawa Ennosuke, 16 December 1994.

45. Author's interview with Ichikawa Ennosuke, 16 December 1994.

46. Author's interview with Ichikawa Ennosuke, 16 December 1994.

47. Author's interview with Bandō Tamasaburō, 30 March 1995.

48. Author's interview with Bandō Tamasaburō, 30 March 1995.

49. Mizouchi Kiyoshi, *Heisei Kabuki Haiyū Ron* (Tokyo: Engeki Shuppansha, 1993), p. 167.

50. Ibid. For Shimomura Mitsuko the freshness of Tamasaburō's ideas and convictions and his direct manner of expressing them were absolutely remarkable and made her wonder if "he were not from outer space." "Tamasaburō Sankō," *Engeki Kai* vol. 49, no. 2, February, 1991, p. 48.

51. Author's interview with Bandō Tamasaburō, 30 March 1995. Tamasaburō was initially hesitant to speculate on the nature of his appeal to women theatergoers, but when pressed he suggested this as a possible cause.

52. The previous two sentences are based on conversations with various women who admire Tamasaburō as an actor.

53. Mizuochi, ibid., p. 168.

54. Ibid., p. 166.

55. The short story is entitled "Onnagata" and it appears in English translation in the anthology *Death in Midsummer and Other Stories by Mishima Yukio* (New York: New Directions, 1966), pp. 139–161.

56. Tsuda Rui, "Tamasaburō Hyakka Ensaikuropedia," *Engeki Kai* vol. 49, no. 2, February, 1991, p. 44.

57. The young woman who was brutally murdered was Hototogisu in *Soga Moyō Gosho no Gorozō* (December, 1967) and the princess was Princess Shiranui in Mishima's *Chinzetsu Yumiharizuki*(November, 1969).

58. Mizuochi, ibid., p. 172.

59. Oda Kōji interview with Bandō Tamasaburō published in *Sankei Shimbun,* 7 January 1995.

60. Author's interview with Bandō Tamasaburō, 30 March 1995.

61. Interview with Bandō Tamasaburō in NHK documentary *"Hana:" Bandō Tamasaburō no Sekai,* Part II, broadcast 2 January 1993.

62. Author's interview with Bandō Tamasaburō, 30 March 1995.

63. Mizuochi, ibid., p. 173.

64. Author's interview with Bandō Tamasaburō, 30 March 1995.

65. Andre Wajda, in a videotaped statement, broadcast by NHK, 2 January 1993 in Part 3 of a documentary entitled *"Hana:" Bandō Tamasaburō no Sekai.*

66. Mizuochi, ibid., p. 170.

67. Author's interview with Bandō Tamasaburō, 30 March 1995. For his timing, or *ma,* in acting Tamasaburō uses a system he calls "reception, assimilation, response" in which he assimilates sensory input (including other actors' speeches) and reacts to it, first physically and then, if necessary, a moment later verbally.

68. Yorimitsu Takaaki , "Intabyū V. 14," *Engeki Kai* vol. 49, no. 2, February, 1991, p. 35.

69. Oda, interview with Bandō Tamasaburō published in *Sankei Shimbun,* 10 January 1995.

70. "Bandō Tamasaburō to Zenkoku no Shibai Koya," in performance program entitled *Bandō Tamasaburō Buyō Kōen,* October 1–11, 1994, published by Bandō Tamasaburō Yachiyo-za Kōen Jikkō Iinkai.

71. Ki Kirin in interview in NHK documentary *"Hana:" Bandō Tamasaburō no Sekai,* Part II, broadcast 2 January 1993.

72. Ibid.

73. Author's interview with Bandō Tamasaburō, 30 March 1995.

74. Author's interview with Bandō Tamasaburō, 30 March 1995.

75. "Sankagetsu Funtō Kōen de mo Kageri no Mieta 'Tamasaburō Ninki,'" *Shūkan Shinchō,* March 16, 1995, p. 32: a theater review signed "SS." The author quotes another reviewer who said he had a seat close to the stage at the Nissay Gekijō and was surprised that he could easily tell that Tamasaburō was a man.

76. Saitō Akemi, "Supottoraito Ichikawa Ukon," *Shūkan Bunshun,* 12 January 1995, p. 108.

77. Ibid.

BIBLIOGRAPHY

English-language Sources and Other Works on Kabuki

Bach, Faith. "Breaking the *Kabuki* Actors' Barriers, 1868–1900." *Asian Theatre Journal* 12.2 (1995).

Bach, Faith. "New Directions in *Kabuki*." *Asian Theatre Journal* 6.1 (1989).

Blacker, Carmen. *The Catalpa Bow: A Study of Shamanistic Practice in Japan.* London: George Allen and Unwin, 1975.

Bowers, Faubion. *Japanese Theatre.* London: Peter Owen, Ltd., 1954.

Brandon, James, ed. *Chushingura: Studies in Kabuki and the Puppet Theater.* Honolulu: The University of Hawaii Press, 1982.

Brandon, James. *Kabuki: Five Classic Plays.* Cambridge, MA: Harvard University Press, 1975

Brandon, Malm, and Shively. *Studies in Kabuki: Its Acting, Music, and Historical Context.* Honolulu: The University of Hawaii Press, 1978.

Cavaye, Roland. *Kabuki: A Pocket Guide.* Rutland, VT: Tuttle, 1993.

Clark and Ueda, with Jenkins. *The Actors' Image: Print Makers of the Katsukawa School.* Chicago: The Art Institute of Chicago, 1994.

Douglas, Mary. *Natural Symbols: Explorations in Cosmology.* London: Barrie & Rockliff The Cresset Press, 1970.

Dunn, C. J. *The Early Japanese Puppet Drama.* London: Luzac & Co., Ltd. 1966.

Dunn and Torigoe. *The Actors' Analects.* Tokyo: The University of Tokyo Press, 1969 (includes original Japanese text for all entries).

Ernst, Earle. *The Kabuki Theatre.* New York: Grove Press, 1956.

Ernst, Earle ed. *Three Japanese Plays from the Traditional Theatre.* New York: Grove Press, 1959.

Gerstle, C. Andrew. *Circles of Fantasy: Convention in the Plays of Chikamatsu.* Cambridge, MA: Harvard University Press, 1986.

Gerstle, C. Andrew. "Flowers of Edo: Kabuki and its Patrons." in *Eighteenth Century Japan: Culture and Society,* edited by C. Andrew Gerstle. Sydney: Allen & Unwin, 1990.

Gunji Masakatsu. *Kabuki.* Tokyo: Kodansha International, 1970.

Gunji Masakatsu. *The Kabuki Guide.* Translated by Christopher Holmes. Tokyo: Kodansha International, 1987.

Halford, Aubrey S. and Halford, Giovanna M. *The Kabuki Guide.* Tokyo: Tuttle, 1961.

Hibbett, Howard. *The Floating World in Japanese Fiction.* New York: Oxford University Press, 1959.

Ihara Saikaku. *The Great Mirror of Male Love.* Translated by Paul Gordon Schalow. Stanford, California: Stanford University Press, 1990.

Inoura Yoshinobu and Kawatake Toshio. *The Traditional Theater of Japan.* New York and Tokyo: Weatherhill and the Japan Foundation, 1981.

Izzard, Sebastian. *Kunisada's World.* New York: Japan Society, Inc., 1993.

Kanjincho and the Zen Substitute. Translated by James Brandon, with Miwa Tamako. New York: Samuel French, 1966.

Kawatake Mokuami. *The Love of Izayoi and Seishin.* Translated by Frank T. Motofuji. Rutland, VT: Tuttle, 1966.

Keene, Donald. *World Within Walls: Japanese Literature of the Pre-modern Era, 1600-1867.* New York: Holt, Reinhart and Winston, 1976.

Keyes and Mizushima. *The Theatrical World of Osaka Prints.* Philadelphia: Philadelphia Museum of Art, 1973.

Kikuchi Kan. *Tojuro's Love and Four other Plays.* Translated by Glenn Shaw. Tokyo: Hokuseido Press, 1925.

Kominz, Laurence. *Avatars of Vengeance: Japanese Drama and the Soga Literary Tradition.* Ann Arbor: Center for Japanese Studies, The University of Michigan, 1995.

Kominz, Laurence. "Ichikawa Danjuro V and *Kabuki's* Golden Age." In *The Floating World Revisited,* edited by Donald Jenkins. Portland, OR: Portland Art Museum, 1993.

Kominz, Laurence. "Origins of *Kabuki* Acting in Medieval Japanese Drama." *Asian Theatre Journal* 5.2, (1988).

Leiter, Samuel L. *The Art of Kabuki: Famous Plays in Performance.* Berkeley: The University of California Press, 1979.

Leiter, Samuel L. *Kabuki Encyclopedia: An English-Language Adaptation of Kabuki Jite.* Westport, CT: Greenwood Press, 1979.

Leiter, Samuel L. "*Keren:* Spectacle and Trickery in Kabuki Acting." Theatre Journal 28.2, (1976).

Leiter, Samuel L. "The Depiction of Violence on the *Kabuki* Stage" *Theatre Journal* 21, (1969).

Leiter, Samuel L. "Kumagai Battle Camp: Form and Tradition in *Kabuki* Acting." *Asian Theatre Journal* 8.1, (1991).

Leupp, Gary P. *Male Colors: The Construction of Homosexuality in Tokugawa Japan.* Berkeley, California: University of California Press, 1994.

Link, Howard Perry. *The Theatrical Prints of the Torii Masters: A Selection of 17th and 18th Century Ukiyo-e Prints.* Honolulu: Honolulu Academy of Arts, Riccar Museum, 1977.

Link, Howard A., with Suzuki and Keyes. *Primitive Ukiyo-e.* Honolulu: The University of Hawaii Press, 1980.

Malm, William P. *Japanese Music and Musical Instruments.* Rutland, VT: Tuttle, 1959.

Malm, William P. *Nagauta: The Heart of Kabuki Music.* Rutland, VT: Tuttle, 1963.

Nakamura Matazo. *Kabuki Backstage, Onstage: An Actors' Life.* Translated by Mark Oshima. Tokyo: Kodansha International, 1990.

Raz, Jacob. *Audience and Actors: A Study of their Interaction in Traditional Japanese Theatre.* Leiden: E. J. Brill, 1983.

Scott, Adolphe Clarence. *The Kabuki Theatre of Japan.* London: George Allen and Unwin, 1956.

Shively, Donald. "*Bakufu* versus *Kabuki.*" In *Studies in the Institutional History of Early Modern Japan,* edited by John W. Hall and Marius B. Jansen. Princeton: Princeton University Press, 1968.

Six Kabuki Plays. Translated by Donald Richie and Miyoko Watanabe. Tokyo: The Hokuseido Press, 1963.

Thornbury, Barbara E. *Sukeroku's Double Identity: The Dramatic Structure of Kabuki.* Ann Arbor: Michigan Papers in Japanese Studies No. 6, 1982.

Yasuda, Kenneth. *Masterworks of the No Theatre.* Bloomington & Indianapolis: Indiana University Press, 1989.

Japanese-language Sources

Akashi Seizaburō and Ichikawa Danjūrō I. "Tsuwamono Kongen Soga." In *Kotobuki Kongen Soga,* Kokuritsu Gekijō Jōen Shiryō-shū No. 46, edited by Hattori Yukio. Tokyo: Kokuritsu Gekijō Chōsa Yoseibu Geinō Chōsa-shitsu, 1970.

Akiba Yoshimi. "Onnagata-gei no Sōritsusha." In *Meiyū Yoshizawa Ayame no Tsuioku.* Wakayama: Nakamura Kominkan, 1958.

Asahi Juzan. *Narita-san to Ichikawa Danjūrō Narabi ni Geinōjin no Shinkō.* Narita: Narita-shi Bunka Zaidan, 1968.

Chikamatsu Monzaemon. "Butsumo Maya-san Kaichō." In *Chikamatsu Zenshū vol. 15*. Tokyo: Iwanami Shoten, 1989.

Chikamatsu Monzaemon. "Daimyō Nagusami Soga." In *Chikamatsu Zenshū vol. 16*. Tokyo: Iwanami Shoten, 1989.

Chikamatsu Monzaemon. "Hyakuya Komachi & Yūgiri Shichinenki." In *Genroku Kabuki Kessaku-shū ge*, edited by Takano Tatsuyuki and Kuroki Kanzo. Tokyo: Waseda Daigaku Shuppan-bu, 1925.

Chikamatsu Monzaemon. *Keisei Hotoke no Hara*. In *Chikamatsu Zenshū vol. 15*. Tokyo: Iwanami Shoten, 1989.

Chikamatsu Monzaemon. *Keisei Mibu Dainenbutsu*. In *Genroku Kabuki Kessaku-shu ge*, edited by Takano Tatsuyuki and Kuroki Kanzo. Tokyo: Waseda Daigaku Shuppan-bu, 1925.

Chikamatsu Monzaemon. "Soga Tayu Zome." In *Chikamatsu Kabuki Kyōgen-shū*, edited by Takano Tatsuyuki. Tokyo: Rokugōkan, 1927.

Gunji Masakatsu. *Kabuki no Hassō*. Tokyo: Kobundō, 1959.

Gunji Masakatsu. *Kabuki Ronsō*. Kyoto: Shinbungaku Shuppan, 1979.

Gunji Masakatsu. *Kabuki Yōshiki to Denjū*. Tokyo: Gakugei Shorin, 1969.

Hattori Yukio. *Edo Kabuki Ron*. Tokyo: Hōsei Daigaku Shuppan-kyoku, 1980.

Hattori Yukio. *Ichikawa Danjūrō: Nihon o Tsukutta Hitobito No. 20*. Tokyo: Heibonsha, 1978.

Hiruma Hisashi. *Edo no Kaichō*. Tokyo: Yoshikawa Kōbunkan, 1980.

Ichikawa Danjūrō I. *Ganmon*. In Ihara Toshirō "Gansō Danjūrō no Zangeroku," *Danjūrō no Shibai*. Tokyo: Waseda Daigaku Shuppan-bu, 1934.

Ichikawa Danjūrō I. "Narita-san Funjin Fudō." In *Genroku Kabuki Kessakū-shū jō*, edited by Takano Tatsuyuki and Kuroki Kanzo. Tokyo: Waseda Daigaku Shuppan-bu, 1925.

Ichikawa Ennosuke. *Shura Butai*. Tokyo: PHP Bunkō, 1994.

Ichikawa Ennosuke. "Amakakeru Yamato Takeru." In *Johakyū*, December, 1986.

Ihara Seiseien (Toshirō). *Ichikawa Danjūrō no Daidai*. Tokyo: Ichikawa Sokezo, 1917.

Ihara Toshirō. *Danjūrō no Shibai*. Tokyo: Waseda Daigaku Shuppan-bu, 1934.

Ihara Toshirō. *Kabuki Nenpyō vols. I, II*. Tokyo: Iwanami Shoten, 1956.

Ihara Toshirō. *Nihon Engeki-shi*. Tokyo: Waseda Daigaku Shuppan-bu, 1906.

Imao Tetsuya. "Ikko Nikki o Yomu." In *Kabuki Kenkyū to Hihyō* 11 (1993).

Kabuki Hyōbanki Shūsei vols. 1–9. Tokyo: Iwanami Shoten, 1972.

Kamigata to Onnagata to Chikamatsu: Nakamura Senjaku Shashin-shū. Osaka: Kōyō Shobō, 1984.

Kanamori Kazuku, ed. *Ichikawa Danjūrō.* Tokyo: Shōchiku, Inc., 1984.

Miyata Noboru. *Kinsei no Hayarigami: Nihonjin no Kōdō to Shisō vol. 17.* Tokyo: Hyōronsha, 1975.

Mizuochi Kiyoshi. *Heisei Kabuki Haiyū Ron.* Tokyo: Engeki Shuppansha, 1993.

Mizuochi Kiyoshi. *Kamigata Kabuki.* Tokyo: Tokyo Shoseki, 1991.

Suwa Haruo, ed. *Chikamatsu Monzaemon.* Tokyo: Shūeisha, 1989.

Suwa Haruo. *Genroku Kabuki no Kenkyū.* Tokyo: Kasama Shoin, 1967.

Suwa Haruo. "Kaneko Ikko Nikki ni Miru Chikamatsu to Kaneko Kichizaemon no Kankei." In *Kabuki Kenkyū to Hihyō* 11 (1993).

Takahashi Hiroko. "Shosei Yoshizawa Ayame ni Okeru Tachiyaku-gei," *Engei Gahō* 27 (1986).

Takano Tatsuyuki. "Meiyū no Roku Sakata Tōjūrō no Bannen." In *Engeki-shi Kenkyū,* edited by *Engeki-shi* Gakkai. Tokyo: Daiichi Shobō, 1932.

Takano Tatsuyuki and Kuroki Kanzō, ed. *Genroku Kabuki Kessaku-shū.* Tokyo: Waseda Daigaku Shuppan-bu, 1925.

Tomimoto Shigekiyo. "Seichi Kosho no Isshaku." In *Meiyū Yoshizawa Ayame no Tsuioku.* Wakayama: Nakamura Kominkan, 1958.

Torigoe Bunzō. Genroku Kabuki Kō. Tokyo: Yagi Shoten, 1991.

Tsuchiya Keiichirō. *Genroku Haiyū Den.* Tokyo: Iwanami Shoten, 1991.

Tsuda Rui. *Edo no Yakushatachi.* Tokyo: Perikansha, 1987.

Tsuda Rui. "Tamasaburō Hyakka Ensaikoropedia." In *Engeki Kai* 49.2 (1991).

Uno Nobuo. "Umai Yakusha Yori." In *Ichikawa Danjūrō,* edited by Kanamori Kazuku. Tokyo: Shōchiku Inc., 1984.

Yoshikawa Yoshio. "Genroku no Onnagata." In *Engeki-shi Kenkyū,* edited by Engekishi Gakkai. Tokyo: Daiichi Shobō, 1932.

INDEX